Shaping Entrepreneurial Marketing, Volume 1

EMERALD STUDIES IN SUSTAINABLE BUSINESS DEVELOPMENT

Series Editor: Payal Kumar, Indian School of Hospitality, India

The *Emerald Studies in Sustainable Business Development* series covers cutting-edge, interdisciplinary perspectives on sustainable development in the Global North and the Global South, with a focus on environmental and social dimensions relevant for today's businesses and for the people that work in them. This seven-volume book series covers critical contemporary issues from sustainability and innovation to gender and environment, to global supply chain and the dark side of ESF and sustainable development.

Forthcoming Volumes:

Dark Side of ESG and Sustainable Development: Inequality, Market Failure and Global North-South Divisions
Edited by Payal Kumar and Anirudh Agrawal

Inclusive Green Finance in South Asia
Edited by Narayanage Jayantha Dewasiri and Payal Kumar

Rethinking Gender Mainstreaming
Edited by Sangita Dutta Gupta and Manjula Menon

Marketing Intelligence: Understanding Customers in the Era of Digitalization
Edited by Mudita Sinha, Arbinda Bhandari, Samant Shant Priya and Sajal Kabiraj

Discursive foundations of responsibility, sustainability and innovation
Edited by Andre Martinuzzi and Svetlana Ivanova

Sustainability and ESG: Business as a Force for Good
Edited by Chris Laszlo

Big Science for Sustainable Development: Pathways Towards Wellbeing on a Healthy Planet
Edited by Shantha Liyanage, Marilena Streit-Bianchi, Payal Kumar and Faiz Shah

Shaping Entrepreneurial Marketing, Volume 1: A South Asian Perspective

EDITED BY

NARAYANAGE JAYANTHA DEWASIRI
Sabaragamuwa University of Sri Lanka, Sri Lanka

PAYAL KUMAR
Indian School of Hospitality, India

NIRMA SADAMALI JAYAWARDENA
University of Bradford, UK

AND

MANANAGE SHANIKA HANSINI RATHNASIRI
Sabaragamuwa University of Sri Lanka, Sri Lanka

emerald
PUBLISHING

United Kingdom – North America – Japan – India – Malaysia – China

Emerald Publishing Limited
Emerald Publishing, Floor 5, Northspring, 21-23 Wellington Street, Leeds LS1 4DL

First edition 2025

Printed and bound by CPI Group (UK) Ltd, Croydon, CR0 4YY

British Library Cataloguing in Publication Data
A catalogue record for this book is available from the British Library

ISBN: 978-1-83708-853-9 (Print)
ISBN: 978-1-83708-852-2 (Online)
ISBN: 978-1-83708-854-6 (Epub)

INVESTOR IN PEOPLE

Contents

List of Figures and Tables

Figures

Tables

About the Editors

Dr Narayanage Jayantha Dewasiri is a Professor in Finance attached to the Department of Accountancy and Finance, Sabaragamuwa University of Sri Lanka. He is also the president of the Sri Lanka Institute of Marketing. He holds a Doctor of Philosophy from the University of Colombo, an MSc in Applied Finance, a Postgraduate Diploma from the University of Sri Jayewardenepura and a BA (Hons) in Business from Glyndwr University, UK. Further, he is a member of the Sri Lanka Institute of Marketing and Chartered Institute of Marketing, a fellow member of the Chartered Management Institute and a Certified Management Accountant. After serving 17 years in the industry, he joined academia and is a pioneer in applying triangulation research approaches in management. He is currently serving as the Co-Editor-in-Chief of the *South Asian Journal of Marketing*, published by Emerald Publishing; Senior Associate Editor of the *FIIB Business Review*, published by SAGE Publishing; an academic editor of *PLOS One*, a Q1 journal indexed by the Web of Science.

Prof (Dr) Payal Kumar is the Principal Academic Advisor at ISH, India; the South Asian ambassador for the A*cademy of Management Discoveries Journal*; and the Emerald Publisher Brand Ambassador. As an institutional builder, Payal has made several strides for start-up universities, enhancing academic excellence, international ties and student experience. As a researcher, her accolades include the best symposium for the MED division, the Academy of Management Conference, Seattle, USA, 2022, and the Andre Delbecq & Lee Robbins MSR (AOM) Scholarship. Payal is an Associate Editor for *JMSR* and a senior reviewer for journals such as *JOB*. She has published 15 books and several papers so far. She is also a reputed L & D trainer, having curated and conducted highly acclaimed management development workshops for executives from the Hero Group, HP, Omax, Rana, Schneider Electric, Yum Brands, Leela Hotels and Broadridge Consulting. Weaving her 25 years of corporate experience with academic knowledge suits her to deliver meaningful training interventions.

Dr Nirma Sadamali Jayawardena is an Assistant Professor at the University of Bradford, UK. She completed her Graduate Diploma of Business Research and PhD in Marketing from Griffith University, Australia. Further, she completed her BSc in Business Management (first-class honours) from NSBM Green University, Sri Lanka, and her MBA in International Business from the University of Colombo, Sri Lanka. Her research interests include consumer psychology, social cognition, digital video advertising and experimental research. She has published her research in leading journals such as *Industrial Marketing Management, Journal of Business Research, Technological Forecasting and Social Change, Journal of Global Information Management, Journal of Strategic Marketing, Asia Pacific Journal of Marketing and Logistics, Production Planning and Control, Young Consumers, International Journal of Educational Management* and *Journal of Electronic Commerce in Organizations.*

Ms Mananage Shanika Hansini Rathnasiri is a Senior Lecturer at the Department of Marketing Management, Faculty of Management Studies, Sabaragamuwa University of Sri Lanka. She obtained her BSc (Special) in Marketing Management from the Department of Marketing Management, Faculty of Management Studies, Sabaragamuwa University of Sri Lanka. Then, she obtained an MSc in Business and Organization Psychology from Coventry University, United Kingdom, and an MBA from the Postgraduate Institute of Management (PIM), University of Sri Jayewardenepura. Her research interests are consumer behaviour, sustainability, services marketing, tourism marketing, entrepreneurial marketing, retail marketing and consumer psychology. She serves as an Associate Editor cum Editorial Assistant of the *South Asian Journal of Marketing*, published by Emerald Publishing. Furthermore, she contributes as an Editor to the *Sri Lankan Marketer Magazine*, published by the Sri Lanka Institute of Marketing (SLIM).

About the Contributors

Wanninayake Mudiyanselage Chandrarathne Bandara Wanninayake is the Dean of the Faculty of Commerce and Management Studies at the University of Kelaniya and a Marketing Professor at the Department of Marketing Management, University of Kelaniya. He has also served as the Head of the Department of Marketing Management. In addition, he was the former Director of the Staff Development Center at the University of Kelaniya and a research consultant for several major corporations. He is a veteran researcher, corporate consultant and exceptional scholar. His professional expertise is utilized in various capacities at the university and in the industry.

Batuwan Thudawa Kankanamge Chathuranga is a Lecturer at the Department of Marketing Management, Faculty of Management Studies and Commerce, University of Sri Jayewardenepura. He has a marketing management (Special) degree from the University of Sri Jayewardenepura and is currently studying for his Master's degree at the University of Colombo. His research contributions have been published in local and international conferences and journals, and he has engaged in several industry-related research projects.

Vilasini De Silva is a Senior Lecturer (Grade I) of the Department of Marketing Management, Faculty of Management Studies, Sabaragamuwa University of Sri Lanka. She is the Head of the Department of Marketing Management at the Faculty of Management Studies, Sabaragamuwa University of Sri Lanka.

Thilini Chathurika Gamage is a Professor of Marketing attached to the Department of Marketing Management, Sabaragamuwa University of Sri Lanka. Her research works were published in top-tier management and marketing journals, including *Tourism Management* (A*), *Journal of Retailing and Consumer Services* (A), *Journal of Product & Brand Management* (A), *Journal of Strategic Marketing* (A) and *International Journal of Hospitality Management* (A*), among other outlets. She is an editor/guest editor for leading management journals, including *Service Industries Journal*, *Annals of Leisure Research*, *Middle East Journal of Management*, *Iranian Journal of Management* and *South Asian Journal of Marketing*.

Narmada Gunawardhana is an HR professional at MILC Group Pty Ltd in Victoria, Australia. She holds a degree in HRM from the University of Colombo and is pursuing an MBA at PIM in Sri Lanka. With over 10 years of experience in both Sri Lanka and Australia, she has worked in banking, health, hospitality, retail and packaging sectors. She is a Professional Member of the Australian HR Institute (AHRI) and a scholarship recipient from the Indian Institute of Technology, India. Additionally, she contributed as a writer for the *Ferntree Gully* local newspaper in Victoria, Australia.

Keragala Rallage Hemendra Lal Gunasekara is a Senior Lecturer in Supply Chain Management at the Department of Tourism Management, Sabaragamuwa University of Sri Lanka, and the Head of the Department of Tourism Management, Faculty of Management Studies, Sabaragamuwa University of Sri Lanka.

Sonali Diyamanthi Jayasooriya is now pursuing her doctoral studies at the Department of Commerce, Faculty of Commerce and Management Studies, University of Kelaniya. She has an MBA in IT from the University of Moratuwa, a BSc (General) from the University of Rajarata and a BSc (IT) from the Sri Lanka Institute of Information Technology (SLIIT). She is a Director of a BOI-registered solid tyre manufacturing company in Sri Lanka. She oversees the company's international marketing, managerial and administrative activities. She is also a member of Plastic and Rubber Institute of Sri Lanka (PRISL).

Agostheenu Paris Kankanamalage Jinendri Prasadika (first-class honours from the Department of Industrial Management at the University of Kelaniya, Sri Lanka, in 2022). She earned her BSc (Honors) in Management and Information Technology, specializing in Operations and Supply Chain Management. She is currently an Assistant Lecturer at the Department of Information Systems Engineering and Informatics, Faculty of Computing, University of Sri Jayewardenepura.

Konalingam Kajenthiran is a young, passionate and research-focused academic at the Department of Marketing, Faculty of Management Studies, and Commerce, University of Jaffna, Sri Lanka. His research focuses on corporate social responsibility (CSR), retail service quality (RSQ), consumer behaviour and technology adoption. Kajenthiran's research has been published in journals like the *Social Responsibility Journal*, *Society and Business Review*, *Services Marketing Quarterly*, *Journal of Business Studies* and conference proceedings, including the *Australian and New Zealand Marketing Academy Conference (ANZMAC)*.

Kumudu Kushlani Kapiyangoda is a Senior Lecturer in the Department of Management and Organization Studies, Faculty of Management and Finance of the University of Colombo, Sri Lanka. She holds a Bachelor of Business Administration (Accounting) Special Degree from the University of Colombo. She also has an MBA from the University of Colombo with a gold medal for Financial Reporting and Management Controls. She is a CIMA passed finalist. She is currently reading for her PhD at the University of Colombo.

Mahadevan Karunanithy is based at the Department of Marketing, Faculty of Management Studies and Commerce, University of Jaffna, Sri Lanka. He received his PhD in Marketing in 2022. Karunanithy's research has been published in the *Journal of Business Studies*, the *International Journal of Accounting and Business Finance* and the *Australian and New Zealand Marketing Academy Conference (ANZMAC)*. He is a fellow member of the Institute of Management

Sri Lanka, a life member of the Association of Accounting Technicians (Sri Lanka), a member of the Institute of Professional Financial Managers, UK, and an associate member of the United Kingdom Association of Professionals.

Arun Kaushal has 17 years of teaching experience and another 2 years in industry. He works as an Associate Professor at Mittal School of Business, Lovely Professional University, Punjab. He has published various papers in journals indexed with Scopus, Web of Science and ABDC rankings and presented multiple papers at national and international conferences nationwide. He has also attended various faculty development programmes and workshops on supply chain management, operations management, strategic management, etc.

Pawan Kumar is working as a Professor in the Department of Marketing at Mittal School of Business, Lovely Professional University, Punjab, India. He has 17 years of experience in academic research in business. His areas of research interest include entrepreneurship, marketing, e-commerce, consumer behaviour, marketing research, etc. He is active in PhD research supervision and has a good number of publications in Q1 and Q2 journals to his credit in various research papers published in indexed journals, namely The *TQM Journal* from Emerald, *Visions: Journal of Business Perspectives* from Sage, *International Journal of Business and Globalization*, *International Journal of Business Information Systems*, etc.

Vidana Gamage Pavani Lakshika is a Senior Lecturer in the Department of Marketing Management at the University of Sri Jayewardenepura. Her research interests lie in sustainability, technology adoption and consumer decision-making. As an early career researcher, Ms Lakshika is passionate about exploring innovative approaches in marketing and is committed to enhancing the field with her insightful findings.

Abiththa Godage Vishva Maithri has over 5 years of experience in the Information Technology industry in Sri Lanka and overseas. He is studying for his Master of Business Administration in Information Technology at the Department of Computer Science and Engineering at the University of Moratuwa, Sri Lanka. With a solid academic foundation related to computer science, Vishva combines theoretical expertise with practical insights gained from his professional experience in IT.

Udgam Mishra is an accomplished academic and Assistant Professor at Tribhuvan University, Nepal, specializing in consumer behaviour. With over a decade of experience in academia and administration, he has significantly contributed to management education and research. His areas of interest include consumer behaviour, purchase intention, perceived service quality and the role of trust in organic food consumption. Udgam has published papers in international journals and book series, focusing on themes like mobile commerce, renewable energy and the impact of consumer beliefs on purchasing behaviour.

Renusha Mithulan is a Senior Lecturer with a demonstrated 7+ years of working in the education industry in Sri Lanka. She is attached to the Department of Human Resource Management, Faculty of Management Studies and Commerce,

University of Jaffna, Sri Lanka. She has extensive experience lecturing at undergraduate and diploma levels across many different subject specializations in management. Further, she has published her work in international conferences and peer-reviewed journals. As an early career researcher, she is passionate about publishing her research works in reputed journals.

Xuan-Hoa Nghiem received his PhD in Economics from the School of Economics, Finance and Marketing, College of Business, RMIT University, Melbourne, Australia, and an MSc in Banking and Finance from Chinese Culture University, Taiwan. He is the team leader in Economics Group, Faculty of Economics and Management, International School, Vietnam National University, Hanoi, Vietnam. His research interests include macroeconomics, technology and growth, monetary policy, international finance, corporate finance, energy economics and environmental economics. He has published in reputed journals such as *Technological Forecasting and Social Change*, *Renewable Energy*, *Economic Analysis and Policy* and others.

Sivananthan Nishanthi is a Senior Software Engineer with over 7 years of extensive experience in architecture, design and web and mobile application development in Singapore and Sri Lanka. She holds an MBA in Information Technology from the University of Moratuwa, Sri Lanka, complemented by a BSc in Computer Science and Technology from Uva Wellassa University, Sri Lanka. With a solid academic foundation in business administration and computer science, Nishanthi combines theoretical expertise with practical insights from her professional experience in IT.

Dona Hiruni Hansinie Niwunhella is a Lecturer in the Department of Industrial Management, University of Kelaniya, Sri Lanka. She received her BSc (honours) in Management and Information Technology from the University of Kelaniya, Sri Lanka, specializing in Business Systems Engineering. She received the 'Best Graduating Student in 2018' award from the Department of Industrial Management, Faculty of Science. Furthermore, she received the Fulbright scholarship in 2021 and is currently reading for her PhD in Industrial Engineering at the North Carolina State University, USA.

Ashutosh Pandey earned his doctorate in Marketing from ABV-Indian Institute of Information Technology and Management, Gwalior. He holds a UGC-NET Management qualification and has worked in industry and academics for over 10 years. His research has appeared in many prestigious journals, including *Environment, Development, and Sustainability*, the *Journal of Quality Assurance in Hospitality & Tourism* and the *International Journal of Tourism Cities*. He has worked as a Visiting Professor at IMT Ghaziabad, the Indian Institute of Foreign Trade (IIFT) in New Delhi and the Indian Institute of Travel and Tourism Management in Gwalior.

Sivarajah Rajumesh is a Senior Lecturer at the Department of Marketing, University of Jaffna, Sri Lanka. He holds a PhD in Marketing and an MBA, BBA and PGD. His research interests lie in marketing, focusing on sustainability, the application of artificial intelligence in marketing, consumer behaviour, industry 5.0, green marketing, service quality and branding. He is passionate about advancing the marketing field through rigorous research and teaching, and his contributions have earned him a reputation as a leading scholar.

Rathnayake Mudiyanselage Nilmini Malkanthi Rathnayake is a PhD candidate at Tasmanian School of Business and Economics, University of Tasmania and she completed MPhil in Business and Economics from University of Sri Jayewardenepura. She was a Lecturer at the Business School, Sri Lanka Institute of Information Technology. Her research interests include Work-life balance, Decent and Digital work, Sustainable Development, and Higher Education. Nilmini serves as a reviewer for several reputed journals and has published in international journals including *PLOS ONE*, *Education and Information Technologies*, *Quality and Quantity*, *Environmental Science and Pollution Research*, *Journal of Asia Business Studies* and *Heliyon*.

Ajit Kumar Sarangi, a distinguished HR professional at a leading multinational corporation, has 14 years of experience as an HR leader. He excels in his field while pursuing a PhD at Lovely Professional University. His expertise extends to reviewing for Sage Publications, published and presented in several Scopus-indexed journals, showcasing his commitment to advancing HR practices. Recognized as HR Young Leader of the Year, he has garnered numerous accolades for his leadership and contributions to the industry.

Rubee Singh is an Assistant Professor of Human Resources at the Institute of Business Management, GLA University, India. She is a post-doctoral researcher (D. Lit) at Kumaun University, Nainital, India. She holds a PhD in Management from Noida International University, India, and an MBA in HR from Dr A.P.J. Abdul Kalam Technical University, India. She has published 20 academic books and more than 75+ research papers in SCI, ABDC-A, Scopus- and UGC-indexed journals. She has been honoured with many prestigious awards, which include the Best Researchers Award of the Year 2022 by GLA University, Child Ambassador Award of The Year 2022, Iconic Faculty Award 2019, International Young Researchers Award-2021, Young Scientist Award 2020 and Nari Ratan Award 2023.

Wathudura Sanduni Dumalka Somawardana is a Group HR Manager of Araliya Hotels Nuwara Eliya Sri Lanka and she completed her MBA from University of Colombo. Further, she has completed professional qualification in Human Resource Management in Chartered Institute of Personnel Management, Chartered Qualification from Chartered Institute of Personnel and Development, MSc in Human Resource Management and Development from Salford University, Chartered Marketing Qualification from Chartered Institute Marketing. Also, she has completed Executive MSc in Finance from Asia e University. Moreover, she is doing research in different sectors in Sri Lanka and numerous publications in various journals in the way that filling the gap in knowledge and practical atmosphere.

Ranitha Sachinthana Weerarathna is a Senior Lecturer in Human Resource Management attached to SLIIT Business School, Sri Lanka Institute of Information Technology, Malabe, Sri Lanka. He completed Bachelor of Business Management (Human Resource) special degree from University of Kelaniya with second upper class and he holds MBA from University of Sunderland and Master in Labour Relations and Human Resources Management from University of Colombo. He published in several international journals including *PLOS ONE*, *Quality and Quantity*, *Heliyon* and *Journal of Innovation and Entrepreneurship*.

Hewa Waduge Mano Chathurangi Weligodapola is working as an Assistant Professor at SLIIT Business School, Sri Lanka Institute of Information Technology, Malabe, Sri Lanka, and she has 17 years of experience in academic field. She completed Bachelor of Commerce (Hons) in International Business, University of Sri Jayewardenepura and she holds Master of Economics from University of Colombo and completed her PhD from Sheffield Hallam University, United Kingdom. Her teaching and research interests include Entrepreneurship and Innovation, International Business, Economics, Small Business Management and Human Resource Management.

Annista Nishanthy Wijayanayake is a Lecturer in the Department of Information Systems and Business Analytics at Deakin University, Australia. She holds a Doctor of Engineering and a Master of Industrial Engineering from the Tokyo Institute of Technology, Japan. Prior to joining Deakin University, she served as a Lecturer at the University of Melbourne and as a Professor in Operations Research and Supply Chain Analytics at the University of Kelaniya, Sri Lanka. Her research interests span a wide range of areas, including optimization, decision science, predictive analytics, mathematical modelling, management science, supply chain analytics, supply chain risk management, logistics, and transportation.

Mohit Yadav is an Associate Professor of HRM at Jindal Global Business School (JGBS). He has a rich blend of work experience in academia and industry. Prof Mohit holds a PhD from the Department of Management Studies, Indian Institute of Technology Roorkee (IIT Roorkee), and has completed a Master of Human Resource and Organizational Development (MHROD) from the prestigious Delhi School of Economics, University of Delhi. He also holds a B.Com. (Hons.) degree from the University of Delhi and a UGC-JRF scholarship.

Kaushalya Yatigammana is a Professor in Digital Learning in the Department of Commerce and Financial Management, Faculty of Commerce and Management Studies, and also serves as the current coordinator of the Doctor of Business Administration (DBA) programme at the University of Kelaniya. Her primary expertise is in digital learning. She has previously held the position of Director at the University of Kelaniya's National E-Learning Resource Centre. She is the Chairperson of the Board of Study in Digital Learning at the University's Faculty of Graduate Studies. She has authored numerous research articles and book chapters and edited volumes on e-learning.

Foreword

It is an honour to write the foreword for *Shaping Entrepreneurship Marketing, Volume 1: A South Asian Perspective*. This book explores an area of marketing that is increasingly critical in today's fast-changing world: entrepreneurial marketing, specifically in the unique context of South Asia. As someone deeply familiar with this field – my esteemed co-authors for *Marketing 6.0*, Philip Kotler and Hermawan Kartajaya, also wrote the *Entrepreneurial Marketing* book – I can attest to the increasingly intertwined nature of entrepreneurship and marketing. Both entrepreneurs and marketeers need a balanced perspective combining creativity, innovation, entrepreneurship and leadership (CIEL) with productivity, improvement, professionalism and management (PIPM).

Entrepreneurs are innovators, extracting value in otherwise untapped markets, which requires a marketing-oriented mind. This notion is especially true in South Asia, where the entrepreneurial ecosystem has great sociocultural diversity and economic complexities. The book brilliantly captures the role of marketing in empowering entrepreneurs to identify everyday customer challenges, make way for opportunities and scale their businesses.

Disruptions of the global economy are underway; technology and sustainability are the two main drivers. I have extensively written about these themes in *Marketing 3.0*, *Marketing 4.0*, *Marketing 5.0* and *Marketing 6.0*. South Asian entrepreneurs increasingly use digital platforms to grow their businesses, accelerated by the COVID-19 pandemic. The book contains insightful stories of these entrepreneurs, serving as practical examples to show how other entrepreneurs adapt to this new reality.

Sustainability is equally important. Since Marketing 3.0, we have argued that the future of marketing is about balancing profitability with social and environmental impact. In this book, the chapters show how South Asian entrepreneurs combine business goals with impact by integrating sustainability into their marketing strategies. This makes them more appealing to the market while contributing to sustainable development goals.

The book excites me because it can inspire current and future entrepreneurs. Exploring how South Asian entrepreneurs navigate a complex and evolving environment, the book benefits academics, practitioners and policymakers alike. With this focus on community-based enterprises, social entrepreneurship, digital transformation and sustainable marketing, the book also provides a comprehensive view of the entrepreneurial scene in the region.

Finally, I am particularly pleased to know that the authors of this book are preparing a second volume, which will explore the future directions of social entrepreneurship and sustainable development in entrepreneurial marketing. This next volume will enrich our understanding of how entrepreneurs can help drive positive change through innovative but responsible business practices.

In conclusion, *Shaping Entrepreneurship Marketing, Volume 1: A South Asian Perspective* is a timely and valuable contribution to entrepreneurial marketing. This book represents the entrepreneurial spirit of South Asia and reflects its global relevance. The aim is for readers to open their minds to its chapters and discover what lessons it contains for application in other countries and industries.

Iwan Setiawan
Co-Author, *Marketing 6.0: The Future is Immersive*

Chapter 1

Introduction to Entrepreneurship Marketing in South Asia: Editors' Perspective

Narayanage Jayantha Dewasiri[a], *Payal Kumar*[b], *Nirma Sadamali Jayawardena*[c] *and Mananage Shanika Hansini Rathnasiri*[a]

[a]Sabaragamuwa University of Sri Lanka, Sri Lanka
[b]Indian School of Hospitality, India
[c]University of Bradford, UK

Abstract

This chapter examines the contextuality characterizing entrepreneurial marketing in adopting specific marketing techniques to overcome South Asian cultural, economic and technological barriers. The South Asian region, with its unique and diverse culture and rapidly progressing start-up environment, offers challenges and benefits for aspiring start-ups. The roles of entrepreneurship marketing are highlighted in this chapter as a tool central to creating sustainable businesses in environments of resource scarcity and competition. A discussion of the synergies of 'conventional' and emerging forms of marketing explores how a company uses technology and social media to increase the breadth of its market and communicate with its consumers. In this chapter, the authors use cases and research findings to emphasize promoting sustainable and socially responsible entrepreneurship marketing in South Asia. Finally, this chapter offers valuable information for academicians, especially scholars, who are inclined to comprehend the research agenda and opportunities and threats of South Asian entrepreneurship marketing within the context of entrepreneurship in emerging economies.

Shaping Entrepreneurial Marketing, Volume 1, 1–11

doi:10.1108/978-1-83708-852-220251001

Keywords: Entrepreneurship marketing; South Asia; digital marketing; consumer behaviour; sustainability

Introduction

The South Asian region has recently witnessed a change in the state of new ventures due to increased economic growth rates, technology and new business start-ups (Hemmert et al., 2022). Entrepreneurship is one of the main drivers of economic growth for modernizing countries like India, Sri Lanka, Bangladesh and Pakistan, which consider globalization and regional identities (Arif et al., 2022). At the same time, entrepreneurship marketing, a comprehensive plan to advertise and support enterprises, has emerged as critically important for many industries (Ouragini & Lakhal, 2024).

This book, *Shaping Entrepreneurship Marketing, Volume 1: A South Asian Perspective*, presents a current analysis of how marketing is being transformed in South Asia and what a future marketing landscape in the region may look like. The goal is to establish a more complex analysis of how IT entrepreneurs manage uncertainties, capture opportunities and market their products to establish and grow sustainable business ventures.

Why South Asia?

South Asia, where more than 1.8 billion people live, is promising and problematic. Due to its immense cultural diversity, an increasing middle-income populace and a young population, the region presents excellent potential for business growth. South Asia has made impressive advancements in attaining economic growth considerably higher than the average global rate. At the same time, it experiences significant challenges like insufficient infrastructure, regulatory issues and issues of socio-economic inclusion that sometimes make the entrepreneurial journey challenging.

When it comes to the challenges that they encounter in their businesses, South Asian entrepreneurs are quick to adapt but are even more creative when it comes to their market approach. Given the sociocultural nature of the region's environment, it is apparent that the current ideas of entrepreneurship marketing have essential gaps that the development of new approaches should address (Bussolo et al., 2024). This book's objective, therefore, is to bring to the forefront the various tactics that different entrepreneurs employ, focusing on the fact that the environment keeps changing.

The Importance of Entrepreneurship Marketing

As a concept, entrepreneurship marketing is considered a unique practical and tactical approach to marketing that differs in several ways from the classical marketing methods (Guerola-Navarro et al., 2024). Significant resource shortage and extensive partnering are characteristic of switching costs and resource dependency in this context. Entrepreneurs work on several key constraints, including large advertising budgets, large staff and entrenched positions, as opposed to firms that have access to significant resources, including, most importantly, limited resources. This discrepancy alone requires enhanced marketing strategies and creativity on the part of the entrepreneur.

As with any part of the globe, several opportunities and risks arise from undertaking business in the South Asian region, such as new trends in marketing strategies. Due to financial limitations in directing themselves to the targeted audiences, entrepreneurs must also employ pedestrian strategies such as guerrilla, social media and grassroots marketing. What is clear, though, is that these are not options but necessities most of the time to sustain and grow. Business people can create meaningful value at low costs using these innovative approaches. This book shall explore the creative measures most people use to overcome challenges and ensure they work hard to realize their dreams and become successful entrepreneurs.

In addition, entrepreneurship marketing plays a crucial role in positioning and creating a customer base (Guerola-Navarro et al., 2024). The modern world is full of many competitors, and every single company tries to gain the attention of consumers, which is possible to achieve in the long term only if it is unique. South Asian entrepreneurs know the necessity of creating relevant and emotionally appealing value propositions and stories. These factors will be elaborated in this book to show how the marketing strategies employed by these entrepreneurs in developing brand narratives influence customers' choice of products, brand loyalty and repeat patronage.

Similarly, it is essential to note the applicability of storytelling as a critical marketing strategy in attracting entrepreneurs' attention. If marketing messages are sent frequently, inputs such as experiences, struggles or victories can keep the audience emotionally invested. These narratives are a means of applying personalities to brands, and since this brings interest and attractiveness, consumers will find it exciting. The emerging theme in marketing strategy is authenticity, which is also advantageous in building trust – the basis of customer relations. This book will show how narrative and relationship management are both seminal to South Asian entrepreneurship and, hence, the foundation of sustainable competitive advantage in this dynamic environment.

Finally, this book's analysis of entrepreneurship marketing will serve as an enlightening reference to the different approaches adopted by South Asian entrepreneurship. We believe people will be inspired to use entrepreneurship marketing in their business through resourceful and strategic thinking. This exploration will highlight the importance of entrepreneurship marketing in driving economic growth and showcase its vital role in shaping the future of business in the region.

The Role of Culture in Entrepreneurship Marketing

Various cultural factors play a vital role in the marketing strategies implemented in South Asia (Hussain et al., 2024). It is revealed that business people in the region establish new businesses in connection with familial and community-based business practices. Everybody, for instance, extends their business by using trust, connections, and local and international networks. That is why cultural marketing is possible in this region, considering the strong influence of traditional culture and the growth of a more modern, progressive culture. For example, culturally sensitive marketing initiatives are more effective than generic ones because culture determines behaviour.

The cultural dimension is both a threat and a potential for South Asian entrepreneurs in their business environment. Many innovative solutions make local cultural references but, at the same time, are applicable globally. As indicated in this section, this book will provide case examples showing how these two forces influence entrepreneurship marketing strategies. Besides, attitudes are often culturally determined and may impact buying behaviour – the tendency to stick to a specific brand. Analyzing such narratives helps the entrepreneur modify their set market stimuli to align with their existing belief systems, thus enhancing their viability.

Navigating Technology and Innovation

It is essential to understand that the change we are witnessing is the emergence of technology across various industries, including those in South Asia (Tanabe, 2022). Mobile phone usage has become rampant, and internet usage in rural areas has increased, making the entrepreneurship marketing opportunities available to the outside world more fluid. Technology and e-business are steadily changing the way that companies interact with buyers.

The COVID-19 pandemic further propelled this shift, forcing many business owners into the new world of digital marketing and to receive new tools for connecting with their target market. The tools companies use could be as small as WhatsApp for marketing and as big as the latest Artificial Intelligence (AI) mechanisms, embodying technology as a tool for entrepreneurship marketing in South Asia.

However, digital inequality persists, evident in the rural environment and among the deprived population. A significant number of business people lack the appropriate marketing technologies. This book will look at how entrepreneurs in this region adapt to minimize this chasm and seize new technologies to advance their marketing.

Nevertheless, using advanced technologies such as AI and data analytics influences many marketing tactics. Marketing automation has gradually become a phenomenon within the business environment by expounding customer trends and improving return on investment. This book argues that with the help of technology, South Asian entrepreneurs can compete at the global level and target local South Asian consumers.

Sustainability and Social Responsibility in Entrepreneurship Marketing

The global economy has, in the recent past, shifted to sustainability and corporate social responsibility (CSR). It has become evident that climate change and social inequality have been persistent for some time. South Asian entrepreneurs have realized that sustainability cannot be neglected in their marketing messages. This also corresponds with a global change in the concept and can be a means to pay more attention to consumers who are geared towards ecological and social problems. Consumers of the present generation are likelier to buy from companies that have embraced sustainable practices in their business operations, their buying decisions being perceived as a way of influencing change.

This book shows how South Asian entrepreneurs make marketing sustainable to stand out in a world of competition. Moreover, as these entrepreneurs clearly state that their businesses are sustainable, they can create powerful brands that appeal to clients willing to buy from sustainability-minded companies. With campaigns such as going green, socially responsible sourcing and clear statements on how they do business, young South Asian entrepreneurs are now targeting a genus of clients who value sustainability, affordability and quality of the products and services they obtain.

Furthermore, sustainability is not just a fashion; it is evidence of a change in people's attitudes and perceptions. With more attention being paid to climate change, environmental pollution and inequality issues, the companies that promote sustainable practices will have an advantage. Customer behaviours show a shift towards socially responsible consumption, which means that sustainability has to be integrated into the fundamental marketing concepts that young entrepreneurs use. The book will examine how marketing strategies automatically ensure sustainable development in South Asian businesses.

The role of social responsibility as an aspect of entrepreneurship marketing cannot be overemphasized. South Asian entrepreneurs use their marketing covers to support social causes like education, health and other communal causes. Through philanthropy or supporting causes and engaging with the community, entrepreneurs may strengthen the bonds with consumers who are now calling on companies to go out and be the change that is needed in society. In this book, the reader will learn how incorporating social responsibility into the marketing agenda benefits a company's image and garners customers with an appreciation of CSR.

Consequently, this book's examination of sustainability and social responsibility in entrepreneurship marketing is intended to offer insights into how South Asian entrepreneurs manage these problems. By demonstrating the radical strategies used by South Asian entrepreneurs to effect positive change, we wish to encourage new entrepreneurs to embrace sustainable marketing as a core value. This study will seek to demonstrate not only the feasibility of sustainable practices but also the possibility of forging an economic future for a region or a continent in terms of affirmative change.

Structure of the Book

The chapters of this book have been arranged to give readers an understanding of entrepreneurship marketing from a theoretical and applied perspective. Every chapter focuses on definite topics: digital marketing management, cultural factors in marketing, innovation management and the impact of socio-economic factors on entrepreneurial performance. Cross-country examples from several South Asian countries will provide practical opportunities to learn about the strategies and actions taken by different business people across the region.

Chapter Overview

Every chapter of this book deals with one particular segment of entrepreneurship marketing and its configuration within the South Asian region. The following section outlines each chapter's contribution and indicates how it helped expand the existing literature on the topic.

Entrepreneurship marketing in community-based enterprises in Nepal.
This chapter comprehensively analyses entrepreneurship marketing within community-based enterprises in Nepal. The chapter concludes by stressing the role of applying entrepreneurship marketing to enhance the internationalization of community-based enterprises (CBEs) and provides a set of actionable suggestions for Nepalese entrepreneurs and policymakers.

Overview of managing digital agility among South Asian family business firms during the ongoing economic crisis.
This chapter examines how family business firms in South Asia handle digital agility during economic crises. Drawing from semi-structured interviews of family business owners in four South Asian countries, it outlines the antecedents of digital agility, such as resource orchestration, workforce transformation, technology orientation and digital risk strategy. It suggests a conceptual model to address digital agility in family businesses and offers practical recommendations regarding digital transformation during a crisis.

Antecedents of knowledge-hiding behaviour amongst Sri Lankan entrepreneurial undergraduates: An empirical study.
This empirical research focuses on the antecedents that lead to knowledge-hiding behaviour (KHB) among Sri Lankan entrepreneurial undergraduates. The study indicates that distrust, mutual reciprocity and psychological ownership significantly impact KHB. This chapter helps advance the existing literature by providing information to educational institutions on measures and actions to inhibit knowledge hiding and encourage knowledge sharing among learners to enhance the collaborative learning process.

Quest for student engagement and loyalty from a private higher education perspective.
This chapter analyses the interaction between service quality and student loyalty in private universities. The author examines the impact of service quality on student loyalty in a study conducted on 346 university students and confirms a positive impact on student loyalty, which is mediated by student satisfaction and engagement. The findings can help higher education marketers and administrators develop

policies to enhance service quality and engagement plans to retain students, which is essential for small and medium higher education institutions.

The moderating effects of transformational leadership behaviour and firm performance of SMEs in Sri Lanka.
This chapter examines how transformational leadership (TL) impacts the association between entrepreneurial orientation (EO) and the performance of small and medium enterprises (SMEs) in Sri Lanka. It reveals that TL and EO are significant drivers of SME performance, offering critical insights for SME owner–managers seeking to enhance organizational outcomes. The chapter validates the resource-based view (RBV) theory and contributes to the literature on SME management and leadership in developing South Asian economies.

Business continuity strategies during COVID-19 pandemic: A case from a small and medium enterprise (SME).
This research aims to identify measures adopted by a leading software development firm in the context of COVID-19 in Sri Lanka. Employing a qualitative research epistemology and case study research design, interviews constituted data collection tools. To explain the strategies concerning business continuity, the research follows Castillo's (2005) theoretical framework. Significant activities include developing a crisis response team, risk mapping and using crisis experiences as knowledge assets. ISO incorporation enables suitable responses and chances from software development to apply cost control and especially fine-tune human resources. The results presented have practical implications for managers interested in developing continuity plans in times of crisis.

Factors affecting the performance of the pickers in 3PL warehouses in Sri Lanka: A systematic review of literature.
This chapter examines factors affecting pickers' productivity in 3PL warehouses in Sri Lanka. Since warehousing is the most outsourced function in the supply chain, this research uses a systematic narrative review to present synthesized literature on 3PL (third-party logistics) providers, order-picking processes and employee performance. The parameters have been broadly divided into employee factors and order-picking factors. This exploration highlights aspects of motivation, leadership and financial incentives that significantly impact the performance of employees; however, routing and storage assignments have consequences on order picking. All these insights are essential to 3PL warehouse managers seeking to improve picker and warehouse efficiencies.

Do human resource management practices ensure employee happiness? Unveiling the moderating effect of work–life balance.
This chapter examines the connection between human resource management (HRM) practices for engaging working people and their overall well-being or job satisfaction, with work–interference balance as a mediating factor in the travel trade sector in Sri Lanka. A quantitative research methodology was adopted, with data from 379 participants using structured questionnaires. The results confirm a positive correlation between HRM practices and employee happiness, with work–life

balance as a moderator. This research fills an existing gap in the literature by presenting the analyzed data and providing suggestions on improving employee well-being.

Implications of job hopping on employees: A case study from the Sri Lankan software development industry.
This research examines the consequence of job hopping by employees in Sri Lanka's software development sector and whether job hopping fulfils employee expectations. The study used a qualitative method following the Tonnquist model; the findings show a mismatch between expectations and job roles among job hoppers. Studies indicate that job-hopping increases pay but may lead to inconveniences related to job security, benefits and organizational relations. Also noted in the study are the implications of the findings, which offer insights for employees and human resource managers on tailoring retention approaches and career actions.

The causes and effects of work–life conflict in copreneurial couples in South Asia.
This paper analyses work–life conflict often observed among South Asian copreneurial couples, such as long working days, cultural restrictions and division of labour. Through qualitative research that involved interviews with focus groups including entrepreneurs, psychologists and sociologists, it was found that rigorous gender roles and poorly defined work–life balance affect well-being and business success. This research suggests further measures to eliminate such difficulties, including flexible working arrangements, mental well-being services and work–life conflict management among copreneurial couples in South Asia.

Employee branding and SME growth in India: Towards a US$5 trillion economy.
This study focuses on the relationship between employee branding (EBR) and SME development in India, thereby contributing towards the growth of the Indian economy in its bid to attain a 5-trillion-dollar economy. Based on a qualitative method of inquiry, the study gathered data from SME leaders and human resource professionals via purposefully designed open-ended questions. Preliminary outcomes reflect the importance of EBR in SMEs' development, organizational culture, and staff maintenance. The findings outline the significance of EBR in improving organizational and SME performance and supporting leaders and policymakers in creating prospects for sustainable economic development.

How can social media support improve the sustainability practices of Sri Lankan small and medium enterprises (SMEs)?
This chapter examines the factors influencing the adoption and use of social media for sustainability purposes by SMEs in Sri Lanka through a systematic literature review. Based on an analysis of 40 articles from several identified databases, the study outlines seven spheres of social media support for sustainability across supply chain management, sustainability communication and brand building. The study fills the existing gap in the literature on social media and sustainability in a way that benefits SMEs, academics and policymakers by offering practical and valuable suggestions on how to use social media to enhance sustainable practices.

Factors affecting the green purchase behaviour for SMEs in Sri Lanka. Surveying 510 SMEs in Sri Lanka, this paper examines the various determinants of green purchasing behaviour. From the analysis of the responses to emailed questionnaires, it was concluded that regulation has a highly significant effect along with environmental awareness and competition on green purchasing. Other factors revealed by the research include perceptions of product quality and customer pressure. The findings from this study can inform policymakers and practitioners to embrace SMEs' awareness of the environment to effect improvements towards achieving sustainable development goals.

Sustaining employee engagement during the COVID-19 pandemic and beyond. This chapter aims to analyze the factors that affected employee engagement during the COVID-19 pandemic and economic crisis in Sri Lanka. Exploring the proper function of HR departments in the adjustment of portfolios of employee management, this paper used structured interviews with executives from a selected bank as the research method. The study indicates that HR managers engaged employees through 'other activities' such as decentralization, flexibility and communication. The findings provide practical implications for understanding the relationship between employee health and organizational performance during health challenges, as well as the flexibility of organizations in the constantly changing work environment.

Conclusion

In conclusion, this book, *Shaping Entrepreneurship Marketing, Volume 1: A South Asian Perspective*, presents an appropriate and timely discussion of entrepreneurship marketing within a part of the global community characterized by a diverse populace and fluid economic environment. As highlighted in this chapter, the socio-economic environment of the South Asia region is complex in ways that offer both risks and potential, which further impact entrepreneurial marketing. Thus, this book concentrates on these attributes and is a productive addition to the literature on entrepreneurship and innovation.

This book, the first of its kind, concentrates solely on South Asia to offer a multidisciplinary theoretical and practical approach. We hope that by featuring true accounts of entrepreneurial marketing in this area, a greater appreciation for the role of entrepreneurial marketing in creating the foundations of lasting businesses and future research can be sparked. Through the application and discussion of entrepreneurship marketing, theories that include sustainability, social responsibility and relationship development take a broader view of the world's current dynamic business environment.

So, as readers progress through the following chapters, we encourage them to learn from the stories of these South Asian entrepreneurs and their strategies for surviving and thriving in a constantly changing world of business. These genuine and diverse narratives show that business success is possible even in harsh conditions. The cases illustrated in this book not only provide international audiences with insights into how business owners from South Asia are marketing different products and services but also inspire other budding entrepreneurs across the globe.

In addition, it is hoped that the findings derived from this collection will help to fill the gap in the critical application of theory and facilitate the interaction between practitioners, policymakers and scholars with the entrepreneurial society in South Asia. Through the interaction of academicians and practitioners, there is a real possibility of identifying the local factors and trends that affect entrepreneurship marketing. A more coherent strategy can, in turn, be created with better business outcomes, positively contributing to regional development simultaneously.

Ultimately, this book plays a significant role in analyzing the concept of entrepreneurship marketing in the context of South Asian countries. It also sharpens the impact of cultural and social contexts and economic imperatives on marketing and entrepreneurs' capacities for offering solutions. We sincerely hope this work drives further scholarship and comforts all forward-thinking entrepreneurs and marketers, giving them the tools to confront the unpredictable future in fresh, exciting and effective ways.

Future Directions

As entrepreneurship marketing expands, several critical areas show tremendous potential for future research and practice – especially in South Asia. Such an area is the symbiosis of social entrepreneurship and marketing, highlighted by Agrawal and Kumar (2018). South Asia is an area of social and economic concerns wherein social entrepreneurship presents a business model for a successful change. Analyzing marketing strategies and their use by social entrepreneurs is a promising area of study that can demonstrate how these ventures may solve different social problems (poverty, education, healthcare). This viewpoint and the specifics of the marketing environment allow these entrepreneurs to develop new, long-lasting, pro-business, and socially oriented forms of enterprise that will significantly interest scholars and practitioners alike.

Sustainability concerns are another dimension of entrepreneurial marketing requiring further scholarly interrogation and exploration. Since the topic touches on environmental degradation and climate change, which are well-understood societal issues, businesses are expected to implement practices to address them. More research should be done on how sustainability can be incorporated into the marketing mix and how it can be utilized to compete gainfully in the market. This involves exploring the role of green marketing, the effects of an institutional environment and the changes in end-user preferences towards going green.

Therefore, it is crucial to understand how digital transformation, mainly social media and e-commerce, can be used sustainably and responsibly as entrepreneurship marketing unfolds. These technologies offer new opportunities for business people to respond to customers, open the figurative space for dialogue and prove their environmental responsibility. Future research should analyze how these digital platforms build customer trust and brand equity.

Since entrepreneurship marketing is a fast-growing and fast-changing field of study, the editors of this book are assembling a second edition that deals with these future directions in greater detail. The next volume will provide multicultural insights into contemporary developments, issues and prospects of entrepreneurship marketing, particularly emphasizing social entrepreneurship, sustainable development and technology. The next volume of this series offers hope and vision to researchers, practitioners and policymakers on how it is possible for entrepreneurship marketing to extend optimal practices in sustainable business in South Asia and beyond.

Acknowledgements

We want to express our sincere gratitude to the authors, reviewers and copyeditors for their invaluable contributions to this edited book. The reviewers' insightful feedback was instrumental in refining the book to its current form. We also extend our heartfelt appreciation to the Team ICMR at the Sabaragamuwa University of Sri Lanka for their unwavering support throughout the process.

References

Agrawal, A., & Kumar, P. (Eds.). (2018). *Social entrepreneurship and sustainable business models: The case of India*. Springer.

Arif, A., Sadiq, M., Shabbir, M. S., Yahya, G., Zamir, A., & Bares Lopez, L. (2022). The role of globalisation in financial development, trade openness, and sustainable environmental-economic growth: Evidence from selected South Asian economies. *Journal of Sustainable Finance & Investment*, *12*(4), 1027–1044.

Bussolo, M., Ezebuihe, J. A., Muñoz Boudet, A. M., Poupakis, S., Rahman, T., & Sarma, N. (2024). Social norms and gender disparities focusing on female labour force participation in South Asia. *The World Bank Research Observer*, *39*(1), 124–158.

Castillo, C. (2005). Disaster preparedness and business continuity planning at Boeing: An integrated model. *Journal of Facilities Management*, *3*(1), 8–26.

Guerola-Navarro, V., Gil-Gomez, H., Oltra-Badenes, R., & Soto-Acosta, P. (2024). Customer relationship management and its impact on entrepreneurial marketing: A literature review. *International Entrepreneurship and Management Journal*, *20*(2), 507–547.

Hemmert, M., Cross, A. R., Cheng, Y., Kim, J. J., Kotosaka, M., Waldenberger, F., & Zheng, L. J. (2022). New venture entrepreneurship and context in East Asia: A systematic literature review. *Asian Business & Management*, *21*(5), 831–865.

Hussain, K., Imran, M., & Abid, S. K. (2024). Women entrepreneurship and sustainable innovation in South Asian economies: A SWOT analysis. *Journal of Asian Development Studies*, *13*(3), 649–662.

Ouragini, I., & Lakhal, L. (2024). The impact of entrepreneurial marketing on the firm performance. *Journal of the Knowledge Economy*, *15*(2), 6003–6025.

Tanabe, A. (2022). The South Asian path of development: A historical and anthropological perspective. In K. Mino & T. Yagi (Eds.), *The cultural basis of economic growth in India* (pp. 1–27). Springer Nature.

Chapter 2

Entrepreneurship Marketing in Community-Based Enterprises in Nepal

Udgam Mishra[a], *Mananage Shanika Hansini Rathnasiri*[b] *and Rubee Singh*[c]

[a]Tribhuvan University, Nepal
[b]Sabaragamuwa University of Sri Lanka, Sri Lanka
[c]GLA University, India

Abstract

This chapter delves into entrepreneurship marketing (EM) within the context of community-based enterprises (CBEs) in Nepal. It unfolds in two primary dimensions: firstly, it provides a comprehensive overview of the current landscape of CBEs in Nepal and globally; secondly, it scrutinizes the diverse motivations driving EM within CBEs during their internationalization journey. The authors employ a research methodology combining a narrative literature review with subsequent content analysis for this exploration. This study seeks to provide insight into the five crucial aspects of marketing for community-based firms in entrepreneurship. The authors' contribution lies in bridging these two models to facilitate the application of EM principles within CBEs in Nepal, ultimately enabling their successful internationalization. The authors offer practical recommendations for entrepreneurs and governmental stakeholders while suggesting future research directions for scholars in this domain. The study has implications for both CBEs and the government. CBEs should utilize all five elements to implement EM. The government should support and enable such firms appropriately. In addition, community-based firms should apply the knowledge gained by leveraging their network positions.

Keywords: Community-based enterprises; entrepreneurship marketing; entrepreneurial orientation; entrepreneurial network; internationalization; Nepal

Shaping Entrepreneurial Marketing, Volume 1, 13–27

Published under exclusive licence by Emerald Publishing Limited
doi:10.1108/978-1-83708-852-220251002

Introduction

This chapter explores the intricate relationship between marketing and Nepal's burgeoning wave of community-based entrepreneurship. Scholars have diligently examined the nexus between marketing and entrepreneurship (Hultman & Hills, 2011; Ngo et al., 2019), recognizing that effective marketing is a pivotal function for entrepreneurs to successfully launch and nurture their ventures (Hisrich, 1992; Ngo et al., 2019). Entrepreneurship marketing (EM) denotes the transformative process of abandoning archaic marketing practices and favouring innovative strategies and actions (Sadiku-Dushi et al., 2019). EM is a tactical approach that seizes opportunities, often taking calculated risks. The field of EM has expanded to include aspects such as creativity, networking, strategy and its influence on education and development (Collinson & Shaw, 2001), and it is essential to note that marketing and entrepreneurship, despite their synergies, remain distinct disciplines. Presently, community-based entrepreneurship is considered a viable remedy to restore the economic state of a community in the face of an economic crisis. Furthermore, it can serve as a business opportunity that can create additional jobs, alleviate poverty, decrease urbanization and enhance the quality of life within the community (Suryani et al., 2022).

The concept of community-based enterprise (CBE) was introduced to business and management studies more than 15 years ago by Ana Maria Peredo and James Chrisman in 2006. A CBE is a collaborative endeavour in which a community assumes the roles of an entrepreneur and an enterprise to accomplish a shared objective (Georgiou, 2022). It entails substantial participation of community members who jointly possess, manage and collaborate in the firm's operations. However, contemporary scholars have predominantly concentrated on specific industries, as seen in the research of Ngo et al. (2019) and Hertel et al. (2019), without offering a comprehensive exploration across diverse sectors. Moreover, empirical evidence in the field of EM remains relatively scarce. Extensive research has been conducted on tourism in small communities in developing countries. However, there is a lack of studies examining the methods for enhancing and fortifying tourism in Nepalese villages. This has drawn attention to Nepal's community-based entrepreneurship concept (Pradhan et al., 2022). Hence, our study examines CBEs within Nepal and globally while also probing into the multifaceted motivations necessitating the integration of EM within these enterprises. The chapter unfolds in two key dimensions: firstly, it provides a comprehensive review of existing literature on EM, encompassing global and Nepalese contexts, followed by an exploration of the history of community-based entrepreneurship, the associated challenges in Nepal, and a subsequent deep dive into the application of EM principles within Nepalese CBE. Our research agenda also encompasses an in-depth analysis of entrepreneurship networking. Ultimately, this chapter concludes by shedding light on the prospects within the EM landscape in CBE and emphasizing the importance of entrepreneurship rooted in local communities within developing economies.

Methodology

This study employs a narrative review process comprising several vital steps. Firstly, we identified the research objectives, which revolve around comprehending EM in CBE, particularly within the context of Nepal. We conducted an extensive systematic literature review, as employed by Dewasiri (2024), Rathnasiri and Gunathilaka (2024) and Dewasiri et al. (2024), using relevant keywords and databases, screening and selecting studies that addressed the relationship between EM and CBE. Data from the literature chosen were extracted, synthesized and comparatively analyzed to identify common themes, gaps and emerging trends. Through this narrative review, we aim to comprehensively understand EM and community-based entrepreneurship, extend existing models and offer new insights. This process informs the subsequent sections of the study, enabling us to contribute valuable knowledge to the field and provide implications and recommendations for entrepreneurs and policymakers in Nepal's CBE.

Literature Review

Entrepreneurship Marketing

EM has become a research domain in various contexts like social enterprises (Asgari-Ghods, 2019; Kishor, 2021; Sadiku-Dushi et al., 2019), tourism and hospitality (Alareeni et al., 2022), education (Ouragini & Lakhal, 2024). EM is crucial in growing businesses, corporations, communities and societal standing (Prihadini, 2021). The intersection and distinctiveness of the relationship between marketing and entrepreneurship have emerged as a subject of investigation by numerous researchers (Whalen et al., 2015). In the 1980s, Murray and Tyebjee investigated the potential correlation between entrepreneurship and marketing. Nwankwo and Kanyangale (2022) proposed the notion of 'entrepreneurial marketing' as a solution to the challenges associated with product promotion and the advancement of modern marketing strategies. Key interface areas are change, opportunity and innovation (Collinson & Shaw, 2001). There have been several studies on the interface of marketing and entrepreneurship, commonality and convergence (Collinson, 2002), and methodological behaviour (McCartan-Quinn & Carson, 2003). Diverse researchers have debated the distinction between experiential marketing and marketing conducted by well-established, more recognized companies. Entrepreneurial marketing is an organizational approach with seven important aspects: proactivity, focus on opportunities, calculated risk-taking, innovativeness, customer intensity, resource leveraging and value creation. This approach enables firms to entrepreneurially implement and strategize modern marketing practices (Alareeni et al., 2022).

Community-Based Entrepreneurship

It is imperative to appreciate the global connectedness of all societies and equally crucial to understand the role of local-level business development activities in alleviating poverty at community standards with new value creation and innovation (Peredo & Chrisman, 2006). Community-based entrepreneurship as a contemporary part of society has received recognition and requires special attention because of its distinct form of entrepreneurship (Pradhan & Samanta, 2022). CBE are organizations that prioritize the development or improvement of community well-being, especially for marginalized populations, rather than focusing on maximizing private profit (Oates et al., 2023).

Community-based entrepreneurship refers to the interdependence of individuals and institutions within a community, where a socially integrated network functions as an entrepreneur with a shared objective (Dana et al., 2008). In the entrepreneurship literature, community-based ventures are called CBEs. CBEs are characterized by a community that functions collectively as an entrepreneur and an enterprise to achieve the common good (Peredo & Chrisman, 2006).

To learn about a global perspective of community-based entrepreneurship, we can take the example of reindeer herding in Northern Europe. In the 12th century, individual reindeer owners collectively cared for the animals using their networks. Because of flexible schedules, owners could look after the reindeer quickly. Northern Europe still practises this system using the latest technologies like snowmobiles, GPS and helicopters. If herding becomes part of the food industry, the essence of community-based, symbiotic entrepreneurship will be undermined (Dana et al., 2008).

CBE in Nepal have a lengthy historical background, with forestry management being the initial recorded instance of CBE. In the early 1980s, Nepal implemented a community forestry programme by granting the village community a lease on the forest land. In the early 1990s, the Leasehold Forestry Programme was established to lease damaged woods from impoverished people. Nepal's Community-based Forest Management (CBFM) system initiated pioneering community and leasehold forestry programs. Nepal adopted the Community-Based Forest Management (CBFM) system when developing the National Forestry Plan in 1976, recognizing the need to involve local communities in the sustainable management and conservation of forest resources (Pandit et al., 2009; Pathak et al., 2017). Nepal is among the first nations to implement the CBFM method (Kanel et al., 2005). Here are other examples of community-based entrepreneurship:

- *Sikre community:* The community at Sikre village, Sindhupalchowk, recognized the importance of natural products and, with joint investments of community groups, started an oil distillation unit and bee-hive briquette enterprise (Subedi & Khanal, 2017).
- *Talkot community:* The communities of Talkot Bajhang started producing allo thread and wool. Gradually, after the aftermarket feasibility and financial analysis, allo yarn was more fruitful. They now produce more allo wool than threads (Subedi, 2006).
- *Shankadevi community:* The forest user group initiated an income-generating idea for conserving their forest. They started vegetable farming, goat

rearing, retail shops and poultry farming, utilizing local resources (ANSAB, 2003).

- *Kavre community:* The locals experienced an inflow of tourists in their locality and realized the importance of community-based tourism. Namo Buddha Resort is the first of its kind in the area to start community-based tourism (Baniya et al., 2018).

Nepal witnessed rapid growth in CBE. Opportunities and challenges are the two facets of a coin. The development of CBE has contributed to halting the wastage of resources and instruments, promoting resource management, incentives and areas for investment for the local community, and access to national and international markets. It alleviates poverty in Nepal (Paudel et al., 2018). Various policies and plans have been continuously implemented to promote local community-based ventures; however, these tactics must be upgraded to suit local contexts fully (Lamsal et al., 2017). Nepal has a tremendous number of resources and acknowledgement of value by local communities, but community-based entrepreneurship has not grasped its height. One of the factors that have constrained the progress of CBE is the technical know-how of the local community (Dangal, 2012). The deficiency of human resources skilled in converting resources into commodities is a paramount reason behind the lack of growth of CBEs. A critical reason for unskilled human resources and lack of technological know-how in Nepal is the education system and the economic standard of rural areas. The topographical pattern of Nepal has fiercely challenged transportation and created regional disparities (Pokharel & Acharya, 2015), hindering the dissemination of CBE products and services. The topographical pattern of Nepal and poor transportation mechanisms do not allow rurally produced commodities to reach the market on time, creating uneven supply and demand. This irregularity in access has led to the emergence of intermediaries, which in turn poses a challenge to the expansion of CBE. Local firms can achieve a 13% boost in income by bypassing intermediaries and selling their products directly in the market (Maraseni et al., 2006) and yet another strategic challenge that CBE face is the improper formulation and execution of policies by the government (Kanal & Kandel, 2004).

If we dive deeper into the drawbacks of CBEs in Nepal, networking is a crucial constraint (Pandit et al., 2009). Locals do not have legal grounds to work together and thus are unauthorized to transact as a formal organization. While some groups have formed and decided to work together and register as cooperatives, not all groups can do so because of various confusing legal formalities. Another drawback of CBE in Nepal is the impractical bans on production and illogical royalty rates and taxes (Subedi, 2006).

Entrepreneurial Marketing in CBE

The existence of enterprises relies on originality, innovativeness and entrepreneurship regardless of their magnitude. Researchers have developed marketing orientation (MO) measures and scales to understand the effectiveness of marketing over a specific time frame. A business culture in which all employees are dedicated to creating super value for customers is a marketing/market orientation; however, only a few organizations have been successful (Narver et al., 1998). Researchers have developed entrepreneurial orientation (EO) along with market orientation.

EO is the fundamental notion in which entrepreneurs formulate strategies to capitalize on existing market opportunities by introducing innovative offerings ahead of competition (Ta'Amnha et al., 2023). Several academics have regarded EO and MO as distinct concepts. However, both EO and MO represent interconnected systems, where mediated EO is directly associated with market orientation (Kwak et al., 2013). Firms choosing one mechanism ultimately have to follow another tool.

EM is the marketing process driven by an entrepreneur's innovative, proactive and risk-accepting nature to acquire and retain customers (Morrish et al., 2010). Entrepreneurial marketing undertakes the challenge of initiating decisions under volatile external environmental forces (Gilmore, 2011) and being proactive to market changes (Morris et al., 2002). EM is more likely to fit the highly uncertain environment and low level of information, while decision-makers have limited marketing competency (De Sá et al., 2016). Empirical findings showed a strong correlation between MO and EO, indicating that marketing should adopt an entrepreneurial approach when dealing with a competitive environment (Murray, 1981).

EM has seven underlying dimensions: value creation, calculated risk-taking, proactiveness, customer intensity, innovativeness, source leverage and opportunity focus (Morris et al., 2002). Subsequently, a four-dimensional model was presented encompassing customer orientation, EO, market orientation and innovation orientation (Jones & Rowley, 2011).

Various empirical studies have shown a significant relationship between entrepreneurial marketing and CBE, for instance, Ngo et al. (2019) and Hertel et al. (2019). CBE operates under unrecognized, fluctuating internal and external surroundings that hinder effortless growth and success. Unlike large-scale organizations that produce essential products and services, obtain profit through customer satisfaction and have solid and resourceful marketing wings, CBE marketing programs are unsystematic and unorganized because of limited acquaintance with marketing do's and don'ts. Entrepreneurial marketing is suitable for the creative and innovative formulation of marketing mix elements that contrast traditional marketing.

A study conducted by Gautam (2016) on Nepalese handicraft enterprises illustrates that autonomy, risk-taking, proactiveness and competitive aggressiveness have significant relationships with business performance. In contrast, innovativeness has no connection with business performance. As we know, Nepal is the least developed country. An immature market, lower purchasing power and resistance to change hamper choice and consumption of new offers. The Nepalese market is filled with imported products, and the new product development process still follows the traditional style (Sharma, 2006). The majority of production houses do not believe in innovative products. The presence of tried and tested imported products has dominated the Nepalese market, and local par-value products are often ignored (Dhungana & Pfefferle, 2017). Entrepreneurial marketing, by nature, is an innovative and creative process that suits impulsive and adolescent markets like Nepal's. Gyanwali and Bunchapattanasakda (2019) reveal a notable correlation between entrepreneurial marketing and the performance of micro, small and medium enterprises. They argue that a lack of entrepreneurial practice plays a noteworthy role in Nepal's slow development of micro, small and medium enterprise (MSME).

Findings

Jones and Rowley's small and medium enterprise (SME) entrepreneurial MO (2011) was established in an environment entirely different from the Nepalese market. The researcher proposes an extension of the model by Jones and Rowley as the chapter studies the CBE marketing behaviour in a distinct sluggish, developing and infant market setting.

This chapter proposes a fifth entrepreneurial dimension, encouragement orientation. Nepal is a multifaceted, evolving market with numerous undiscovered hindrances. CBE cannot implement traditional marketing, unlike large-scale organizations that can adopt traditional marketing. The CBE in Nepal requires effective marketing because the actors in the CBE have low or no knowledge of marketing insights and are directly impacted by the unpredictable external environment. Nepal is blessed with natural resources, and mismanagement is the factor that hinders the establishment of innovative ventures. A fresh dimension called encouragement orientation consists of four elements: local-level promotion, economically strong environment, ease of registration and even infrastructure development. Fig. 2.1 presents the proposed dimensions.

Entrepreneurial Network

Researchers have acknowledged the worth of networks as an integral part of the success of entrepreneurship (Elfring & Hulsink, 2003). The classical entrepreneurship theory explains that when making decisions, entrepreneurs' individualistic and risk-bearing nature overlooks the social environment staking innovation (Chiesi, 2017). Innovative ideas arise when problems are better understood; an entrepreneur should deeply connect with society to read problems profoundly. Network intensity positively impacts SMEs' performance (Das & Goswami, 2019). The aptitude to leverage and grasp networks is one of the prime characteristics of an entrepreneur. The social network provides a pipeline for entrepreneurs to access heterogeneous private information and enables the recognition of opportunities within the market (Stuart & Sorenson, 2005).

A study by Bengt and Anders (1989) reveals that networking is crucial to the success of community enterprises rather than autonomous entrepreneurs. There is no standardized formula for supporting community-based firms. However, one

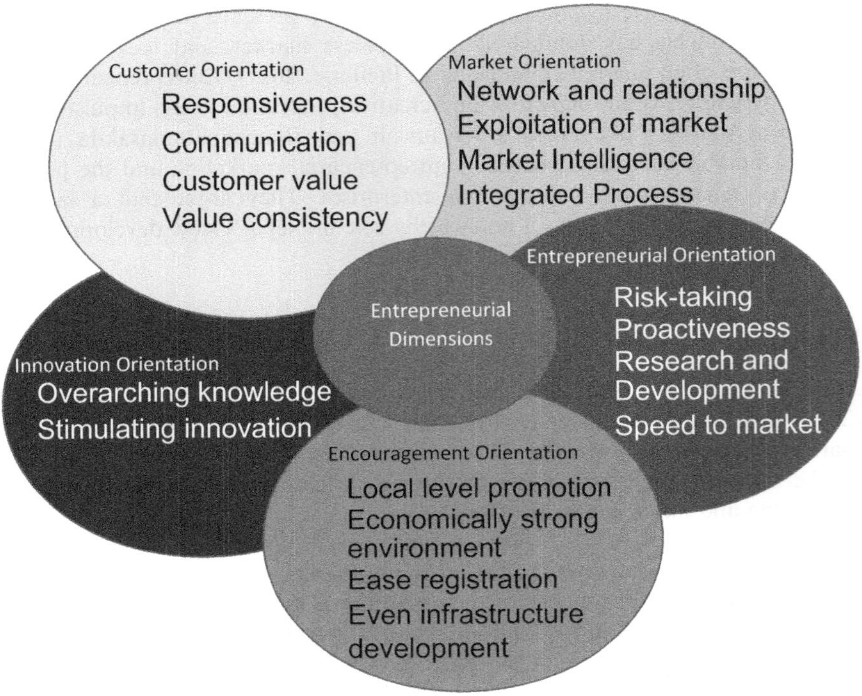

Fig. 2.1. Proposed Five-Dimensional Model. *Source:* Author's own.

practical approach is to create connections with individuals and organizations at various political levels across different geographical regions (Seixas & Davy, 2008). Community entrepreneurs are found to interact and maintain networks with nonmarket agents twice as much as autonomous entrepreneurs (Bengt & Anders, 1989).

From Community to International

No matter how global the venture is, it is started locally; networking is a prime factor in the business expansion of a CBE. Internationalization is when an entity endeavours to a better position in a foreign market (Schweizer et al., 2010). Internationalization is not limited to exporting but includes collaborations, joint ventures and alliances beyond the home country's political boundaries. With the increase in the contribution of CBEs to economic development, several researchers have shown interest in internationalization as an area of study. As in infrastructure and nature, CBEs differ from large-scale ventures and encounter many hindrances and barriers. The constraints that CBEs face are external competitiveness (Pedersen, 2000), international competency (Rahman et al., 2017), cultural differences and exchange rates.

Previous studies have focused on core competencies and opportunities in foreign markets as critical factors for internationalization (Prahalad & Hamel, 1990); international entrepreneurs argued that personal factors and founder human capital influence the choice of internationalization of small firms (Manolova et al., 2002), whereas Johanson and Vahlne (2009) state that increased internationalization depends on business networks. A tight connection between networking and entrepreneurship must exist, and this dominant relationship accelerates business expansion from local to international standards. As the business expands in foreign markets, it can capture more opportunities for joint ventures, acquisitions and mergers that can provide exhaustive knowledge of the local market.

Johanson and Vahlne (2009) proposed a new internationalization model (Fig. 2.2), a reworking of their 1977 model. The revised model focuses on business networks as market structures. It shifts focus from knowledge of opportunities to relationship commitment decisions, learning, creating trust and networking positions.

Unskilled and untrained employees, an inability to gauge the tastes and preferences of the foreign market, cultural differences and a lack of knowledge of the foreign market are some of the parameters that hinder the internationalization of SMEs in Nepal (Niroula, 2018). The internationalization model mentioned above was studied and formulated in Sweden. However, Sweden's economic outlook is more prosperous than Nepal's regarding R&D, production, innovation and

Fig. 2.2 Proposed Model of Internationalization.
Source: Author's own.

networking infrastructure. This model may not be applicable in Nepal in every arena and scope. Fig. 2.2 presents the proposed model of internationalization for Nepal.

Conclusion

This chapter examines EM in Nepal's CBE and the motives for its application in CBE for internationalization. A narrative literature review followed by content analysis was the principal research methodology. The study provides a vital understanding of the five aspects of EM required for CBE as a novel model that extends Jones and Rowley's (2011) model. Then, the study broadens the internationalization model of Johanson and Vahlne (2009) by incorporating the motives for applying EM in CBE in the internationalization process. The study's main contribution is the extension of these two models to apply EM in CBE in Nepal and facilitate their internationalization through the identified motives. These two extended models are not limited to any specific industry or area of CBE. It adds value to the community-based enterprise and EM literature.

Implications to Stakeholders

The study has some implications for CBE and the government. CBE should use all five dimensions to apply EM. The primary constraint of community-based entrepreneurship is the absence of communal orientation in contemporary culture and the inability to apply and adapt a model in other contexts. Engaging in entrepreneurial activities within the community can be a viable solution to address the lack of connectivity between indigenous, informal and formal institutions. Several governmental actions should be implemented to promote a favourable attitude towards entrepreneurship among disadvantaged individuals and encourage them to drive further development.

Converting the community into a business entity can influence knowledge, strategy, business endeavours, creativity, innovative management and comprehension of the idea of a community-based enterprise, involving member participation, providing support and sharing benefits. Therefore, members of CBE and group leaders must prioritize innovative management as a catalyst for CBE. Furthermore, the partnership between the group and the public sector enhances inventive funding, product advancement, service provision and marketing efforts, further reinforcing CBE. The government should, therefore, facilitate such enterprises. Further, CBE should utilize the identified knowledge opportunities through identified network positions.

Limitations and Future Research Directions

Future scholars can extend these two models, investigate their applicability in contexts similar to those of other developing countries and modify them if required. Another possible area of study is whether these two models are industry-specific and whether the motives identified in the internationalization process are market-specific.

Acknowledgements

We want to extend our sincere gratitude to the reviewers and editors of this book. The reviewers' insightful feedback and the editors' dedicated efforts were invaluable in shaping this work. Their attention to detail and commitment to quality have significantly enhanced the book, and we are deeply grateful for their contributions.

References

Alareeni, B., Hamdan, A., Hamdan, R., & Shoaib, H. M. (2022). Marketing and entrepreneurship: Challenges and opportunities. *Journal of Strategic Marketing*, 1–8.

Asia Network for Sustainable Agriculture and Bioresources (ANSAB). (2003). *Forest products-based enterprise development*. Field Manual (In Nepali).

Asgari-Ghods, M. (2019). Entrepreneurial marketing: The missing link in social enterprise studies. *Journal of Global Entrepreneurship Research*, *9*(39). https://doi.org/10.1186/s40497-019-0163-5

Baniya, R., Shrestha, U., & Karn, M. (2018). Local and community well-being through community-based tourism: A study of transformative effect. *Journal of Tourism and Hospitality Education*, *8*, 77–96. https://doi.org/10.3126/jthe.v8i0.20012

Bengt, J., & Anders, N. (1989). Community entrepreneurs: Networking for local development. *Entrepreneurship & Regional Development: An International Journal*, *1*(1), 3–19. http://doi.org/10.1080/08985628900000002

Collinson, E., & Shaw, E. (2001). Entrepreneurial marketing: A historical perspective on development and practice. *Management Decision*, *39*, 761–766. https://doi.org/10.1108/EUM0000000006221

Chiesi, A. M. (2017). Entrepreneurial networks. In R. Alhajj & J. Rokne (Eds.), *Encyclopedia of social network analysis and mining*. Springer. https://doi.org/10.1007/978-1-4614-7163-9_367-1

Collinson, E. (2002). Editorial: The marketing/entrepreneurship interface. *Journal of Marketing Management*, *18*(4), 337–340.

Dana, L. P., Etemad, H., & Wright, W. R. (2008). Toward a paradigm of symbiotic entrepreneurship. *International Journal of Entrepreneurship and Small Business*, *5*(2), 109–126.

Dangal, S. (2012). *A report on a rapid contextual study of five MSFP districts (Kalikot, Dailekh, Jajarkot, Accham, and Bajhang)*. A Report Submitted to Multi-Stakeholder Forestry Program.

Das, M., & Goswami, N. (2019). Effect of entrepreneurial networks on small firm performance in Kamrup, a district of Assam. *Journal of Global Entrepreneurship Research*, *9*(7). https://doi.org/10.1186/s40497-018-0122-6

De Sá, E. S., Farhangmehr, M., & Pinho, J. C. (2016). The context and outcomes of entrepreneurial marketing as a decision-making process under uncertainty. In L. Petruzzellis & R. Winer (Eds.), *Rediscovering the essentiality of marketing. Developments in marketing science: Proceedings of the academy of marketing science*. Springer. https://doi.org/10.1007/978-3-319-29877-1_71

Dewasiri, N. J. (2024). Sustainable strategies for net zero: An Asia Pacific perspective. In R. Singh & D. Crowther (Eds.), *Transition towards a sustainable future. Approaches to global sustainability, markets, and governance*. Springer. https://doi.org/10.1007/978-981-97-5756-5_1

Dewasiri, N. J., Gnanapala, W. K. A. C., Rathnasiri, M. S. H., Yadav, M., Tewari, L. M., & Mishra, U. (2024). The way forward for net zero: Aligning nationally determined contributions (NDCs) and holistic sustainable development in South Asia. In R. Singh & D. Crowther (Eds.), *Transition towards a sustainable future. Approaches to global sustainability, markets, and governance*. Springer. https://doi.org/10.1007/978-981-97-5756-5_5

Dhungana, R., & Pfefferle, A. (2017). Challenging localisation of rural Nepali market: The role of education. *Journal of Education and Research*, *5*, 31–48. https://doi.org/10.3126/jer.v5i0.15729

Elfring, T., & Hulsink, W. (2003). Networks in entrepreneurship: The case of high-technology firms. *Small Business Economics*, *21*, 409–422. https://doi.org/10.1023/A:1026180418357

Gautam, P. R. (2016). Entrepreneurial orientation and business performance of handicraft industry: Study of Nepalese handicraft enterprises. *International Journal of Small Business and Entrepreneurship Research*, *4*, 48–63.

Georgiou, A. (2022). Local communities as cultural entrepreneurs: A methodological reflection on the study of community-based enterprises. In *Cultural entrepreneurship: New societal trends* (pp. 85–93). Springer Nature.

Gilmore, A. (2011). Entrepreneurial and SME marketing. *Journal of Research in Marketing and Entrepreneurship*, *13*(2), 137–145. https://doi.org/10.1108/14715201111176426

Gyanwali, S., & Bunchapattanasakda, C. (2019). Application of entrepreneurial marketing in micro, small and medium enterprises in Dhaulagiri, Nepal. *Open Journal of Business and Management*, *7*, 693–708.

Hertel, C., Bacq, S., & Belz, F. M. (2019). It takes a village to sustain a village: A social identity perspective on successful community-based enterprise creation. *Academy of Management Discoveries*, *5*(4), 438–464.

Hisrich, R. D. (1992). The need for marketing in entrepreneurship. *Journal of Consumer Marketing*, *7*(3), 53–57.

Hultman, C. M., & Hills, G. E. (2011). Influence from entrepreneurship in marketing theory. *Journal of Research in Marketing and Entrepreneurship*, *13*(2), 120–125.

Johanson, J., & Vahlne, J. E. (2009). The Uppsala internationalisation process model revisited: From liability of foreignness to liability of outsider ship. *Journal of International Business Studies*, *40*(9), 1411–1431.

Jones, R., & Rowley, J. (2011). Entrepreneurial marketing in small businesses: A conceptual exploration. *International Small Business Journal*, *29*(1), 25–36. https://doi.org/10.1177/0266242610369743

Kanal, K. R., & Kandel, B. R. (2004). Community forestry in Nepal: Achievements and challenges. *Journal of Forest and Livelihood*, *4*(1).

Kanel, K. R., Poudyal, R. P., & Baral, J. P. (2005). Nepal community forestry. http://www.recoftc.org/site/fileadmin/docs/publications/The_Grey_Zone/2006/CF_Forum/policy_nepal.pdf. Accessed on May 12, 2007.

Kishor, J. (2021). Moderating role of entrepreneurial marketing in enhancing society through social entrepreneurship: An Indian perspective. *International Journal of Business and Globalisation*, *28*(4), 450–467.

Kwak, H., Jaju, A., Puzakova, M., & Rocereto, F. J. (2013). The connubial relationship between market orientation and entrepreneurial orientation. *Journal of Marketing Theory and Practice*, *21*(2), 141–162. https://doi.org/10.2753/MTP1069-6679210202

Lamsal, P., Pant, K., & Bhatta, D. (2017). Forest-based micro and small enterprises in Nepal: Review of status, constraints, scope and approach effectiveness. *International Forestry Review*, *19*, 42–54.

Manolova, T. S., Brush, C. G., Edelman, L. F., & Greene, P. G. (2002). Internationalisation of small firms: Personal factors revisited. *International Small Business Journal*, *20*(1), 9–31. https://doi.org/10.1177/0266242602201003

Maraseni, T. N., Shivakoti, G. P., Cockfield, G., & Apan, A. (2006). Nepalese non-timber forest products: An analysis of equitability of profit distribution across a supply chain to India. *Small Scale Forest Economics, Management and Policy*, *5*(2), 119–206.

McCartan-Quinn, D., & Carson, D. (2003). Issues which impact upon marketing in the small firm. *Small Business Economics*, *21*(2), 201–213.

Morris, M. H., Schindehutte, M., & LaForge, R. W. (2002). Entrepreneurial marketing: A construct for integrating emerging entrepreneurship and marketing perspectives. *Journal of Marketing Theory and Practice*, *10*(4), 1–19. https://doi.org/10.1080/10696679.2002.11501922

Morrish, S. C., Miles, M. P., & Deacon, J. H. (2010). Entrepreneurial marketing: Acknowledging the entrepreneur and customer-centric interrelationship. *Journal of Strategic Marketing*, *18*(4), 303–316. https://doi.org/10.1080/09652541003768087

Murray, J. A. (1981). Marketing is home for the entrepreneurial process. *Industrial Marketing Management*, *10*(2), 93–99.

Narver, J., Slater, S., & Tietje, B. (1998). Creating a market orientation. *Journal of Market-Focused Management*, *2*, 241–255.

Ngo, T., Hales, R., & Lohmann, G. (2019). Collaborative marketing for the sustainable development of community-based tourism enterprises: A reconciliation of diverse perspectives. *Current Issues in Tourism*, *22*(18), 2266–2283.

Niroula, R. (2018). Internationalisation readiness: The case of handicrafts-based firms from Nepal. https://nordopen.nord.no

Nwankwo, C. A., & Kanyangale, M. I. (2022). The evolution from pre-academic marketing thought to the new paradigm of entrepreneurial marketing. *Academy of Strategic Management Journal*, *21*(2), 1–15.

Oates, L., Kasaija, P., Sseviiri, H., Sudmant, A., Ersoy, A., & Van Bueren, E. (2023). Pluralising the urban waste economy: Insights from community-based enterprises in Ahmedabad (India) and Kampala (Uganda). *Environment & Urbanization*, *35*(2), 411–432.

Ouragini, I., & Lakhal, L. (2024). The effect of entrepreneurial marketing education on the determinants of students' entrepreneurial intention. *The International Journal of Management Education*, *22*(1), 100903.

Pandit, B., Albano, A., & Kumar, C. (2009). Community-based forest enterprises in Nepal: An analysis of their role in increasing income benefits to the poor. *Small-Scale Forestry*, *8*, 447–462.

Pathak, B., Xie, Y., & Bohara, R. (2017). Community-based forestry in Nepal: Status, issues and lessons learned. *International Journal of Sciences*, *6*, 119–129. https://doi.org/10.18483/ijSci.1232

Paudel, N. S., Adhikary, A., Mbairamadji, J., & Nguyen, T. Q. (2018). *Small-Scale forest enterprise development in Nepal: Overview, issues and challenges*. Food and Agricultural Organisation.

Pedersen, T. (2000). The internationalisation process of Danish firms: Gradual learning or discrete rational choices?. *Journal of Transnational Management Development*, *5*(2), 75–89.

Peredo, A. M., & Chrisman, J. J. (2006). Toward a theory of community-based enterprise. *Academy of Management Review*, *31*(2), 309–328. https://doi.org/10.5465/AMR.2006.20208683

Pokharel, R., & Acharya, S. (2015). Sustainable transport development in Nepal: Challenges, opportunities and strategies. *Journal of the Eastern Asia Society for Transportation Studies*, *11*, 209–226.

Pradhan, S., Dyson, L. E., & Lama, S. (2022). The nexus between cultural tourism and social entrepreneurship: A pathway to sustainable community development in Nepal. *Journal of Heritage Tourism*, *17*(6), 615–630.

Pradhan, S., & Samanta, S. (2022). Global research on community-based enterprise: A bibliometric portrait. *Journal of Enterprising Communities: People and Places in the Global Economy*, *17*.

Prahalad, C. K., & Hamel, G. (1990). The core competence and the corporation. *Harvard Business Review*, *3*, 71–91.

Prihadini, D. (2021). Role of entrepreneurial marketing in increasing product innovation during a pandemic: A case study on MSMEs managed by students in Jakarta. *Technium Social Sciences Journal*, *24*, 468.

Rahman, M., Uddin, M., & Lodorfos, G. (2017). Barriers to entering foreign markets: Evidence from SMEs in emerging markets. *International Marketing Review*, *34*(1), 68–86.

Rathnasiri, M. S. H., & Gunathilaka, D. H. P. M. (2024). Net zero policies for sustainable future: Issues and challenges in the Asia Pacific region. In R. Singh & D. Crowther (Eds.), *Transition towards a sustainable future. Approaches to global sustainability, markets, and governance*. Springer. https://doi.org/10.1007/978-981-97-5756-5_12

Sadiku-Dushi, N., Dana, L.-P., & Ramadani, V. (2019). Entrepreneurial marketing dimensions and SMEs performance. *Journal of Business Research*, *100*, 86–99. https://doi.org/10.1016/j.jbusres.2019.03.025

Schweizer, R., Vahlne, J. E., & Johanson, J. (2010). Internationalisation as an entrepreneurial process. *Journal of International Entrepreneurship*, *8*(4), 343–370.

Seixas, C. S., & Davy, B. (2008). Self-organisation in integrated conservation and development initiatives. *International Journal of the Commons*, *2*(1), 99–125.

Sharma, B. (2006). A new product development process was used in Nepal's consumer product manufacturing units. *Journal of Nepalese Business Studies*, *1*(1). https://doi.org/10.3126/jnbs.v1i1.35

Stuart, T. E., & Sorenson, O. (2005). Social networks and entrepreneurship. In S. A. Alvarez, R. Agarwal, & O. Sorenson (Eds.), *Handbook of entrepreneurship Research, International Handbook Series on Entrepreneurship* (Vol. 2). Springer. https://doi.org/10.1007/0-387-23622-8_11

Subedi, B. P. (2006). *Linking plant-based enterprises and local communities to biodiversity conservation in Nepal Himalaya*. ANSAB. Adroit Publishers.

Subedi, B., & Khanal, C. S. (2017). *Sikre: A village in Nepal Mountain on the path of transformation to sustainable rural development*. ANSAB.

Suryani, A., Soedarso, S., Utomo, C., Endarko, E., & Ahmad, I. S. (2022). Strengthening community-based entrepreneurship: The significance of community capacity building and enabling ecosystem. *Indonesian Journal of Development Studies*, *1*(2), 1–12.

Ta'Amnha, M. A., Magableh, I. K., Asad, M., & Al-Qudah, S. (2023). Open innovation: The missing link between the synergetic effect of entrepreneurial orientation and knowledge management over product innovation performance. *Journal of Open Innovation: Technology, Market, and Complexity*, *9*(4), 100147.

Whalen, P., Uslay, C., Pascal, V. J., Omura, G., McAuley, A., Kasouf, C. J., Jones, R., Hultman, C. M., Hills, G. E., Hansen, D. J., Gilmore, A., Giuliano, J., Eggers, F., & Deacon, J. (2015). Anatomy of competitive advantage: Towards a contingency theory of entrepreneurial marketing. *Journal of Strategic Marketing*, *24*(1), 5–19. https://doi.org/10.1080/0965254x.2015.1035036

Chapter 3

Overview of Managing Digital Agility Among South Asian Family Business Firms During the Ongoing Economic Crisis

Thilini Chathurika Gamage

Sabaragamuwa University of Sri Lanka, Sri Lanka

Abstract

Despite increasing scholarly attention to managing digital agility amid the current economic crisis, attention to specific organizational forms, particularly family business firms, is still scarce. A better understanding of how family business firms manage digital agility in a crisis is crucial for their future survival. This qualitative inquiry addresses this void by providing an overview of how family business firms in the South Asian region manage digital agility during the economic crisis. A qualitative, exploratory study was conducted using 26 semi-structured interviews with family business owners and managers from four South Asian countries to collect data. Thematic analysis was used to analyze the data. The findings reveal that fostering and managing digital agility in family business firms primarily relies on a digital-first mindset and long-term orientation. Four success pillars related to distinctive family business firm characteristics that can collectively strengthen digital agility were identified: resource orchestration capabilities, workforce transformation, technology orientation and digital risk strategy. A framework for fostering and managing digital agility in family business firms, leveraging these insights, was proposed. This study offers actionable recommendations for South Asian family business owners and managers to foster and manage digital agility during the ongoing economic crisis.

Keywords: Digital agility; digital transformation; economic crisis; family business firms; South Asia

Shaping Entrepreneurial Marketing, Volume 1, 29–43

Published under exclusive licence by Emerald Publishing Limited
doi:10.1108/978-1-83708-852-220251003

Introduction

The rapid proliferation of digitalization has catalyzed profound transformations across the contemporary business landscape, ushering in novel modes of communication, collaboration and cooperation (Al Jabri et al., 2024). This unprecedented paradigm shift has pressured firms to reinvent their business strategies in response to digital disruptions. To this end, the ability to continuously adjust and adapt to digital disruption, known as digital agility, is paramount for the survival of business firms (Gamage, 2022), particularly for family business firms aiming to thrive across multiple generations (Jayawardena et al., 2023). Digital agility refers to a business firm's ability to adapt swiftly to changing business requirements using digital technologies (Srivastava et al., 2023). This encompasses digitalizing key business processes, upgrading technological infrastructure and embracing frontier digital technologies (Srivastava et al., 2023).

Family business firms constitute the majority of business firms globally and play a vital role in fostering economic and social prosperity worldwide, a reality that holds even in the South Asian region (Jayawardena et al., 2023). A family business firm distinguishes itself from a non-family business firm through several unique characteristics, notably its strong emphasis on long-term orientation, emotional attachment to the firm and personalized involvement of family members (Kallmuenzer et al., 2022). With their often-relentless attention to long-term orientation and the personalized participation of family members, family business firms are well-positioned to embrace digital disruptions more than non-family businesses (Jayawardena et al., 2023; Zapata-Cantu et al., 2023). Consequently, there has been a growing interest among family business firms in effectively utilizing digital technologies to enhance competitiveness, especially in these post-pandemic times (Zapata-Cantu et al., 2023).

However, despite family businesses' potential to embrace digital disruptions, most family business firms in South Asia are still at the embryonic stage of adopting digital technologies (Jayawardena et al., 2023). It is disheartening to witness such a reactive response from family business firms in the South Asian region, considering that digital agility could offer them the means to economically navigate their business operations while enhancing performance, particularly amid the ongoing economic crisis (Saura et al., 2023). The South Asian region was selected as the research setting for this study, as family business firms form the backbone of the South Asian economy (Teixeira et al., 2020). However, amid the ongoing economic crisis, many South Asian family business firms are grappling with unprecedented challenges in managing their businesses effectively, primarily due to difficulties in demonstrating digital agility (Jayawardena et al., 2023; Saura et al., 2023).

On the other hand, digital transformation in family business firms in the South Asian region remains relatively unexplored (e.g. Jayawardena et al., 2023; Saura et al., 2023) and demands increased scholarly attention and empirical investigation. Further, there has been limited exploration (e.g., Jayawardena et al., 2023; Kass-Hanna et al., 2022) regarding how family business firms can manage digital agility to enhance competitiveness during the ongoing economic crisis, particularly in the South Asian region. Building on this backdrop and to address the void in prior literature, the research question of this study is thereby formulated as follows:

- How do family business firms in the South Asian region manage digital agility during the ongoing economic crisis?

This study addresses the research question by proposing a model for fostering digital agility in family businesses based on 26 semi-structured interviews with family business owners and managers from four South Asian countries. By delving into the intricacies of how family business firms navigate digital agility amid the prevailing economic downturn, this study seeks to enrich and complement the existing literature. Additionally, it provides valuable insights and actionable recommendations for academics, family business owners and managers to bolster their capabilities for managing digital agility to enhance competitiveness.

Literature Review and Theoretical Underpinning

Digital Agility

The origin of agility in strategic management literature traces back to the 1990s (Walter, 2021). Organizational agility, a cornerstone concept, is commonly perceived as a multifaceted capability encompassing two fundamental dimensions: the ability to (1) detect or foresee shifts in internal and external business environments and (2) respond promptly, efficiently and economically (Walter, 2021). Since digital technologies today have become an increasingly integral component of business firms' value propositions, a new concept known as digital agility has been introduced, stemming from the broader concept of organizational agility (Salmela et al., 2022).

Based on a comprehensive review of agility in previous literature, Srivastava et al. (2023) define digital agility as a business firm's ability to seize opportunities or mitigate threats by utilizing transformative digital technologies. Central to their definition is acknowledging that risk and risk-taking are intrinsic to digital agility. Building upon prior literature, this study defines digital agility as a combination of a family business firm's adaptability and propensity for risk-taking by effectively utilizing digital technologies to enhance competitiveness.

As implied, digital agility encompasses not only a business firm's readiness and ability to change but also the capability to adapt to those changes swiftly. Risk-taking, an integral component of digital agility, denotes a business firm's willingness to make decisions and take action despite lacking technical expertise and potentially facing risks. Mrugalska and Ahmed (2021) conducted a systematic review examining how organizational agility influences digitalization, revealing a crucial insight: Organizational learning flourishes through experimentation and embracing risk-taking when employing digital technologies. Similarly, Tian et al. (2022) underscore risk-taking as a critical determinant of successful digital transformation, emphasizing the need to foster an organizational culture that encourages calculated risk-taking and embraces frontier digital technologies. As digitalization continues to reshape the business landscape, business firms must cultivate new capabilities, particularly flexibility and risk-taking, which have assumed heightened significance in navigating this evolving terrain. Thus, to understand how family business firms in South Asia navigate digital agility amid the ongoing economic crisis, this study decided to frame it theoretically based on the dynamic capabilities view.

Dynamic Capabilities View

From the resource-based view, the dynamic capabilities view elucidates how business firms can achieve and maintain competitive advantages. Dynamic capabilities can be categorized into three core dimensions: (1) the aptitude to discern and proactively influence market opportunities and threats, (2) the proficiency to harness opportunities through effective utilization of resources and competencies and (3) the capability to evolve organizational capacities to outperform competitors continually (Teece, 2017). This theory extends conventional strategic management frameworks by embracing greater flexibility and responsiveness, highlighting the ability of individuals or business firms to cultivate and deploy capabilities in response to evolving market dynamics. Central to the dynamic capabilities view is creating and sustaining competitive advantages by nurturing and fostering dynamic capabilities, which include adapting to fluid market conditions, assimilating new technologies and responding adeptly to shifts in the business environment. The theory emphasizes that these dynamic capabilities involve leveraging strategic firm resources such as knowledge, skills and technologies to drive innovation. This process ultimately enhances digital agility, bolstering competitiveness in the marketplace. It further encompasses capabilities essential for technology adoption and digital transformation practices, enabling business firms to navigate digital shifts adeptly by fostering digital agility.

Family Business Firms

Family business firms are the cornerstone of virtually every economy worldwide (Saura et al., 2023). Distinguished by their unique strategies, these entities set themselves apart from non-family counterparts through long-term orientation, risk aversion, inclination towards equity financing and dedication to frugal innovation (Kallmuenzer et al., 2022). The synergy between family dynamics and business operations endows these firms with distinctive resources and capabilities, potentially yielding a competitive advantage.

Amid the imperative for adaptability in the face of change and adversity, it has become equally crucial for family business firms to formulate flexible strategies that leverage firm resources and capabilities. Family businesses have demonstrated a remarkable ability to pivot and adapt swiftly, often on par with or outpacing non-family business firms. Their intimate involvement in the firm's management and business processes facilitates rapid decision-making and empowers them to respond promptly to evolving market demands and shifts. Thus, family business firms are well-positioned to embrace digital transformation than their non-family counterparts.

Fostering Digital Agility in Family Business Firms

Embracing digital technologies has become a significant enabler, offering family business firms exciting opportunities to transform, innovate and evolve their value propositions, structures and business strategies (Ano & Bent, 2022). Consequently, digital transformation in family businesses has emerged as a recent research domain due to compelling theoretical reasons suggesting that the impacts of digital technologies differ significantly in family business firms than non-family business firms (Jayawardena et al., 2023). For instance, unlike non-family business firms, digital technology adoption in family business firms is facilitated by solid collaborations among family members and key stakeholders and their long-term orientation (Ano & Bent, 2022). Additionally, the emotional attachment to the firm and the personalized involvement of family members fosters an organizational culture that encourages workforce transformation in deploying technologies effectively in family business firms (Soluk & Kammerlander, 2021). Further, technology-oriented family businesses take proactive approaches to embracing digital agility. These examples demonstrate that family business firms are more likely to demonstrate digital agility, which is paramount for a successful digital transformation.

To this end, there is no doubt that family business firms are in a better position to manage ongoing economic crises effectively by managing digital agility through which effective digital transformation can be implemented. However, recently, it was found that, unlike family firms in developed countries, most family business firms in the South Asian region find it difficult to effectively implement digital transformation, mainly due to issues inherent to the region. Given that the South Asian region is still emerging and many member countries are grappling with economic challenges, family businesses often struggle to demonstrate digital agility (Jayawardena et al., 2023; Kass-Hanna et al., 2022). This struggle primarily stems from distinctive obstacles like a dearth of technical know-how, limited financial resources and underdeveloped technology infrastructure. However, this issue has not yet received adequate scholarly attention, and only a few studies (e.g., Jayawardena et al., 2023; Saura et al., 2023) have been conducted focusing on managing digital agility in family firms in the South Asian region.

Methodology

Research Approach and Data Collection

Given the limited research on fostering and managing digital agility in family business firms in South Asia, this study adopts an interpretive qualitative approach (Tomaszewski et al., 2020). Twenty-six in-depth interviews were conducted with family business owners/managers from four South Asian countries:

India, Pakistan, Bangladesh and Sri Lanka (see Table 3.1 for the respondent profile). These four countries were chosen because they significantly drive economic development within the South Asian region. Furthermore, they are home to most regional family business firms (Teixeira et al., 2020).

Table 3.1. Respondent Profile.

Code	Country	Industry	Digital Technology Deployment and Usage (Years)
I1	India	Agriculture	7
I2	India	Iron and steel	12
I3	India	Food processing	10
I4	India	Retail	8
I5	India	Information technology	17
I6	India	Apparel	11
I7	India	Retail	9
P1	Pakistan	Food processing	6
P2	Pakistan	Retail	9
P3	Pakistan	Agriculture	7
P4	Pakistan	Apparel	12
P5	Pakistan	Agriculture	6
P6	Pakistan	Tourism and hospitality	10
B1	Bangladesh	Agriculture	7
B2	Bangladesh	Agriculture	6
B3	Bangladesh	Retail	9
B4	Bangladesh	Retail	6
B5	Bangladesh	Apparel	10
B6	Bangladesh	Apparel	11
SL1	Sri Lanka	Agriculture	6
SL2	Sri Lanka	Agriculture	7
SL3	Sri Lanka	Tourism and hospitality	12
SL4	Sri Lanka	Tea	6
SL5	Sri Lanka	Apparel	10
SL6	Sri Lanka	Retail	8
SL7	Sri Lanka	Tourism and hospitality	10

Source: Author's own.

The online interviews typically lasted between 50 and 80 minutes and lasted 2 months, commencing in February 2024. Before commencement, explicit consent was obtained from the respondents to record the responses. Subsequently, each interview was transcribed verbatim and supplemented with detailed field notes. On average, each transcription yielded approximately 20 typed pages.

Data Analysis

Data collection and analysis preceded concurrently, with the researcher and her two research assistants actively participating in the analysis process. The thematic analysis explored the concepts from the interviews (Braun & Clarke, 2022). This approach combined inductive and deductive methodologies, initially employing a *theory-driven* perspective where themes and codes were identified a priori, followed by a *data-driven approach* wherein additional codes emerged organically from the collected data (Braun & Clarke, 2022).

The research team initiated the process by thoroughly reading and reviewing interview transcripts and supplementary field notes multiple times to understand the content comprehensively. Subsequently, employing an inductive approach, the team meticulously identified in-vivo codes emerging directly from the data by thoroughly scrutinizing the interview transcripts and field notes. The team utilized a shared codebook to facilitate collaboration, simplifying the review process. Before finalizing the codes, extensive detailed discussions were conducted to ensure consensus on the identified codes. Additionally, inter-coder reliability was assessed to gauge the consistency and validity of the shared codebook, yielding a substantial inter-coder reliability value of 0.79 (Landis & Koch, 1977).

This meticulous process facilitated the identification of first-order categories through in-vivo codes, classifying these categories into second-order themes, delineating theme boundaries, and summarizing the content in each theme through iterative rounds of intense discussions (Braun & Clarke, 2006). Throughout this phase, particular attention was paid to the contextual nuances in which respondents shared their experiences to ensure an accurate coding interpretation (Braun & Clarke, 2006).

After completing the inductive coding for the initial 12 interviews, the team established a preliminary coding framework. Subsequently, the remaining interview transcripts and supplementary materials were analyzed using a deductive approach. Despite the deductive framework, the team thoroughly examined the remaining data to identify any additional emergent themes or categories not captured by the preliminary coding framework.

Findings and Discussion

Drawing on the dynamic capabilities view (Teece, 2017), a critical literature review and insights from qualitative interviews, this study presents a comprehensive framework for fostering and managing digital agility within family business firms (refer to Fig. 3.1). At the core of this model lies the pivotal interplay

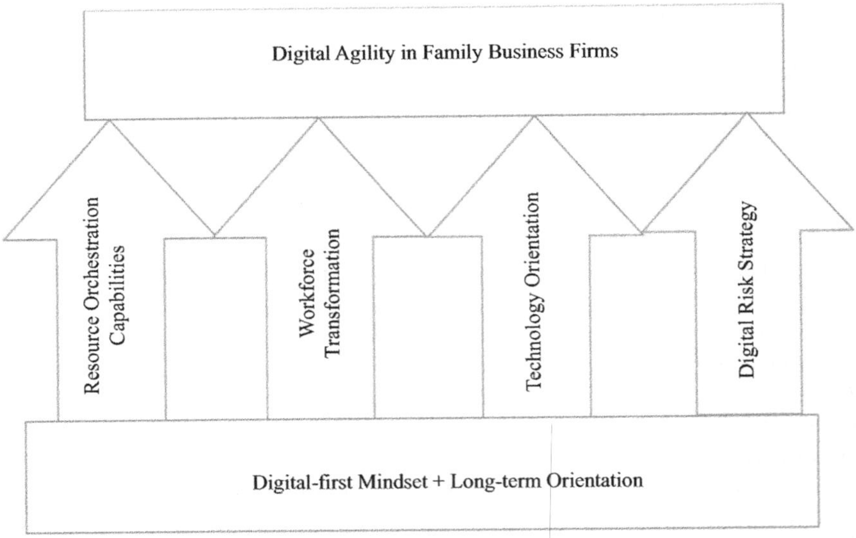

Fig. 3.1. Framework for Fostering and Managing Digital Agility in Family Business Firms. *Source:* Author's own.

between the digital-first mindset and a steadfast long-term orientation, which serves as the founding stepping stone for effectively fostering and managing digital agility. From this foundational standpoint, the framework delineates four key success pillars, as depicted in Fig. 3.1, each intricately tied to the unique characteristics of family business firms. These pillars encompass resource orchestration capabilities, workforce transformation, technology orientation and digital risk strategy. Further, these four pillars may unfold at varying paces and stages, with their interdependence and mutual reinforcement playing a crucial role in shaping a family business firm's overall digital agility trajectory.

Digital-First Mindset

The findings reveal that adopting a digital-first mindset is a cornerstone for fostering and managing digital agility in family business firms. A digital-first mindset is characterized by an inclination among family business owners and managers to prioritize digital solutions when addressing new challenges or opportunities. From the interviews, it is evident that all respondents unanimously stressed the importance of family businesses embracing frontier digital technologies to become competitive during the ongoing economic crisis. According to the managing director of a fully digitalized family business firm operating in the retail sector in India:

> Surviving and managing in the economic crisis hinges on crafting more potent business strategies that encourage effective digital transformation rather than merely implementing technology. True victory necessitates embracing a digital-first mindset, where conducting business digitally becomes the sole approach. (I7)

From the interviews, it is also evident that some family business firms in South Asia view digitalization merely as a technological add-on to their existing operations, aiming to become 'more digital' without fundamentally altering their conventional business processes. This reactive stance categorizes them as digital laggards. Many firms hesitate to overhaul their traditional business practices for efficiency and agility. Instead, they prefer to automate or optimize existing processes. Conversely, family business firms with a digital-first mindset embark on a distinct trajectory towards fostering digital agility. Their journey does not commence with the simple deployment of technology. Instead, they transform their business strategies to expedite product and service delivery while minimizing friction and disrupting the status quo. Our findings resonate with Salmela et al. (2022) and Srivastava et al. (2023), underscoring the imperative of integrating frontier digital technologies in implementing effective digital transformation. This approach not only accelerates processes but also minimizes friction. Consequently, in today's fiercely competitive landscape, the digital-first mindset is swiftly emerging as the norm, enabling family business firms to fuller digital agility, thus maintaining competitiveness and avoiding being sidelined. As emphasized by the owner of a tourism and hospitality family business firm in Sri Lanka:

> A digital-first mindset gives a business firm the optimal opportunity to not only catch up with industry leaders but also ascend to the position of industry leadership itself. (SL3)

Long-Term Orientation

The findings reveal that long-term orientation has been instrumental in guiding family business firms to acknowledge the necessity of implementing more formalized structures and processes conducive to effective digital transformation. These efforts not only bolster firm capabilities that foster digital agility but also enhance their resilience, thus bolstering their prospects for survival amid ongoing economic crises. As emphasized by an agricultural family business firm owner from Pakistan:

> I think that is one of the challenges for a family business, especially in the South Asian region, to have a far-sighted vision and try to be professional and not too much of a family when capitalising on technological developments. (P5)

In agreement with the above quotes, five other respondents also said that the collectivist culture in the South Asian region, in some instances, prevents family businesses from adopting professional management approaches, eventually inhibiting successful digital transformation. Thus, most respondents emphasized the importance of maintaining a delicate balance in the long-term orientation of family business firms for fostering and managing digital agility. As exemplified by the managing director of a retail family business firm in Sri Lanka:

> Balancing the long-term perspective with the fast-changing business world triggered by unprecedented technological development requires family business firms to be digitally agile. (SL6)

The findings echoed those of Ano and Bent (2022), who emphasized that family businesses lay the groundwork for their digital transformation by strongly emphasizing long-term orientation.

Resource Orchestration Capabilities

Insights from the interviews reveal a prevalent awareness among most family business firms in South Asia regarding the benefits of effective digital transformation. However, many cannot fully engage in such transformation initiatives despite this awareness. This limitation predominantly stems from resource constraints, a characteristic inherent to family business firms in the region (Jayawardena et al., 2023; Kass-Hanna et al., 2022). Hence, family business firm owners and managers face the imperative of strategically structuring, bundling and leveraging available resources within their organizations in innovative and cost-effective ways when embarking on digital transformation endeavours to enhance competitiveness. As emphasized by the owner and managing director of a well-known apparel manufacturing family firm in Bangladesh:

> Since only a few family business firms can claim to have all the technological resources and capabilities necessary to implement an effective digital transformation, orchestrating resources is critical to fostering and managing digital agility. (B6)

As highlighted in the quote above, this study reveals that the resource orchestration capability of family business firms has emerged as a dynamic capability in managing digital agility. Surprisingly, this has been largely overlooked in previous literature.

Workforce Transformation

Aligned with the dynamic capabilities view (Teece, 2017), insights from interviews emphasize that the success of digital transformation initiatives hinges on the dynamic capabilities inherent within family business firms. Given the pivotal role of the workforce in shaping these capabilities, it is evident that a family business firm aspiring to achieve digital agility must not confine its notion of the workforce solely to internal employees. Instead, it should adopt a broader perspective, recognizing the invaluable contributions of principal stakeholders – employees, customers, suppliers and business partners – is essential. These stakeholders collectively play indispensable roles in the fabric of a family business firm.

As technology evolves, family business firms, leveraging their long-term orientation and digital-first mindset, actively seek collaborative opportunities within and beyond organizational boundaries. This collaborative ethos fosters seamless communication and interaction, facilitating data-driven decisions at lightning speed with insights that are always up-to-date and relevant (Ano & Bent, 2022). To get the maximum benefits out of these collaborations and to achieve business excellence, family business firms need to transform their employees' conventional work behaviours and habits, demonstrating flexibility and resilience. As emphasized by the family business owner of a reputed apparel manufacturing family business firm in Pakistan:

> In the contemporary landscape, family businesses must build a resilient workforce adept at embracing change and dedicated to continuous learning. Such a workforce is better equipped to adapt positively and productively amidst the perpetual evolution of the digital sphere. (P4)

Interestingly, this finding is consistent with that of Soluk and Kammerlander (2021), who highlighted that the workforce and their ability to demonstrate flexibility and resilience play a vital role in fostering digital agility and digital transformation in family business firms.

Technology Orientation

Most respondents echoed a common sentiment throughout the interviews: technologically oriented family business firms prioritize allocating resources to acquiring frontier digital technologies and developing innovative business processes that facilitate effective digital transformation while demonstrating digital agility. Sharing his success story in embracing digital technology, the owner and managing director of a renowned agricultural family business firm in Bangladesh stated:

> Previously, I was sluggish about embracing digital technologies. Digital technology deployment was never on my agenda as I was into agriculture. However, becoming technologically oriented is now essential for every business firm, regardless of the industry in which you operate. My firm has outperformed its competitors

> since becoming technology-oriented in my business processes. It is essential to foster digital agility to become competitive. (B2)

The findings largely align with those of Upadhyay et al. (2023), who emphasized that becoming technologically oriented is crucial to embarking on effective digital transformation.

Digital Risk Strategy

Insights from the interviews emphasized the critical importance of implementing a digital risk strategy for family business firms in effectively managing digital agility, particularly amid the ongoing economic crisis. Digital risk encompasses the unforeseen consequences arising from digital transformation that impede the achievement of business objectives. As a business expands, its attack surface broadens, heightening susceptibility to cyber threats. For instance, with increased social media presence, digital risks such as phishing and account hacking emerge, threatening a business firm's existence and damaging its reputation. Consequently, digital risk emerges as an inevitable outcome of technological advancement and the evolution of digital landscapes. Thus, as emphasized by the family business owner of a renowned IT family business firm in India:

> Today, it has become imperative to broaden the scope of risk assessment beyond traditional boundaries. All family business firms must fine-tune their risk management strategies to mitigate digital risks so that digital transformation can continue without any disturbances. (I5)

Most respondents concurred with this viewpoint, emphasizing that implementing a digital risk management strategy offers significant advantages to family business firms amid the current economic crisis. Such a strategy mitigates the potential threats posed by cybersecurity issues and cybercrime. The findings echo Tian et al. (2022), emphasizing risk-taking as a pivotal factor in driving successful digital transformation. In line with Tian et al. (2022), most respondents also underscore the necessity of cultivating an organizational climate that promotes calculated risk-taking to navigate the complexities of digital agility effectively.

Implications, Limitations and Future Research Directions

Theoretical Implications

This study's findings significantly contribute to the dynamic capabilities view (Teece, 2017). Grounded on the dynamic capabilities view (Teece, 2017), this study represents one of the pioneering efforts to comprehensively examine the management of digital agility within South Asian family business firms amid the ongoing economic crisis. This study extends the dynamic capability view by introducing a novel theoretical framework for fostering and managing digital agility within family business firms. In doing so, this study validates the applicability of the dynamic capability view in delving into the intricacies of how family business firms navigate digital agility amid the prevailing economic downturn in the South Asian region.

Managerial Implications

While the path to successful digital transformation varies for each family business firm, the interview findings highlight that shared experiences are crucial for family business owners and managers embarking on this journey. They must recognize that resource orchestration capabilities, workforce transformation, technology orientation and digital risk strategy form the backbone of this transformation. Thus, initiating change management efforts becomes imperative to ensure the shift from traditional mindsets, practices and resources towards long-term orientation and digital mindsets across all levels and functions of the family business firm.

Built on the solid foundation of both long-term orientation and digital mindset, a family business firm should integrate resource orchestration capabilities, workforce transformation, technology orientation and digital risk strategy to foster and manage digital agility. Moreover, family business owners and managers can utilize the proposed framework (see Fig. 3.1) to manage their digitalization journey and demonstrate digital agility.

Given the uniqueness of each family business firm's digital journey, developing a one-size-fits-all model poses challenges. However, the proposed framework allows family business firms to assess their progress and identify shared experiences and concerns among peers in similar circumstances. Any family business firm can adopt this model as it embarks on its journey towards digitalization, fostering digital agility to enhance inclusivity and diversity within the organization. In summary, family business owners and managers should anticipate a classic 'S-curve' pattern during their digitalization journey: starting gradually, accelerating improvement and eventually stabilizing at a new level of digital agility.

Conclusion

As with any research, this study has limitations delineating avenues for future investigation. Remarkable among these limitations is adopting a mono-method qualitative approach and utilizing a limited number of respondents. While qualitative methodologies offer rich insights, mono-method qualitative studies may lack methodological rigour and trustworthiness of the findings. Thus, future researchers can enhance the robustness of their findings by adopting a mixed-methods research design, thereby triangulating data from various sources to enrich the analysis. Moreover, the relatively small sample size of respondents warrants attention in future studies. Scholars may consider expanding respondents to encompass a broader spectrum of family business firms across all South Asian countries, thereby enhancing the representativeness and depth of the findings.

Furthermore, while the proposed framework outlines key constructs relevant to managing digital agility, there remains a need to delve deeper into the cohesion and interrelationships among these constructs. Future researchers should consider measuring the strength of these interrelationships and elucidate cause–effect relations, thus furnishing family business owners and managers with actionable recommendations to bolster their firms' capacity for fostering and managing digital agility. Additionally, given the dynamic nature of managing digital agility, longitudinal studies represent a promising avenue for future inquiry. Such studies would offer insights into the evolving trajectories of digital agility within family business firms, thereby enriching our understanding of this multifaceted phenomenon.

Acknowledgements

I want to express our sincere gratitude to the reviewers and editors of this book. The editors' diligent efforts and reviewers' sensible feedback shaped this work. We are incredibly thankful to these folks for the attention to detail and dedication to quality they brought to this book.

References

Al Jabri, M. A., Shaloh, S., Shakhoor, N., Haddoud, M. Y., & Obeidat, B. Y. (2024). The impact of dynamic capabilities on enterprise agility: The intervening roles of digital transformation and IT alignment. *Journal of Open Innovation: Technology, Market, and Complexity*, *10*(2), 100266.

Ano, B., & Bent, R. (2022). Human determinants influencing the digital transformation strategy of multigenerational family businesses: A multiple-case study of five French growth-oriented family firms. *Journal of Family Business Management*, *12*(4), 876–891.

Braun, V., & Clarke, V. (2006). Using thematic analysis in psychology. *Qualitative Research in Psychology*, *3*(2), 77–101.

Braun, V., & Clarke, V. (2022). Conceptual and design thinking for thematic analysis. *Qualitative Psychology*, *9*(1), 3.

Gamage, T. C. (2022). The journey towards harnessing frontier technologies: Becoming a digital firm with digital capability and dexterity. In G. Singh, R. Goel, & V. Garg (Eds.), *Promoting inclusivity and diversity through Internet of Things in organisational settings* (pp. 60–81). IGI Global.

Jayawardena, N. S., Chavali, K., Dewasiri, N. J., Perera, C. H., Koswatte, I., Pereira, V., Gupta, M., & Mardani, A. (2023). Exploring the challenges in developing and managing digital agility among Sri Lankan family business owners during the economic crisis. *Journal of Global Information Management*, *31*(8), 1–22.

Kallmuenzer, A., Tajeddini, K., Gamage, T. C., Lorenzo, D., Rojas, A., & Schallner, M. J. A. (2022). Family firm succession in tourism and hospitality: An ethnographic case study approach. *Journal of Family Business Management*, *12*(3), 393–413.

Kass-Hanna, J., Lyons, A. C., & Liu, F. (2022). Building financial resilience through financial and digital literacy in South Asia and Sub-Saharan Africa. *Emerging Markets Review*, *51*, 100846. https://doi.org/10.1016/j.ememar.2021.100846

Landis, J. R., & Koch, G. G. (1977). An application of hierarchical kappa-type statistics in the assessment of majority agreement among multiple observers. *Biometrics*, 363–374. https://doi.org/10.2307/2529786

Mrugalska, B., & Ahmed, J. (2021). Organisational agility in Industry 4.0: A systematic literature review. *Sustainability*, *13*(15), 8272.

Salmela, H., Baiyere, A., Tapanainen, T., & Galliers, R. D. (2022). Digital agility: Conceptualizing agility for the digital era. *Journal of the Association for Information Systems*, *23*(5), 1080–1101.

Saura, J. R., Palacios-Marqués, D., & Barbosa, B. (2023). A review of digital family businesses: Setting marketing strategies, business models and technology applications. *International Journal of Entrepreneurial Behavior & Research*, *29*(1), 144–165.

Soluk, J., & Kammerlander, N. (2021). Digital transformation in family-owned Mittelstand firms: A dynamic capabilities perspective. *European Journal of Information Systems*, *30*(6), 676–711.

Srivastava, A. P., Yadav, M., Yadav, R., Singh, B., & Dewasiri, N. J. (2023). Exploring digital agility and digital transformation leadership: A mixed method study. *Journal of Global Information Management*, *31*(8), 1–23.

Teece, D. J. (2017). Dynamic capabilities and (digital) platform lifecycles. In *Entrepreneurship, innovation, and platforms* (Vol. 37, pp. 211–225). Emerald Publishing Limited. https://doi.org/10.1108/S0742-332220170000037008

Teixeira, S., Mota Veiga, P., Figueiredo, R., Fernandes, C., Ferreira, J. J., & Raposo, M. (2020). A systematic literature review on family business: Insights from an Asian context. *Journal of Family Business Management*, *10*(4), 329–348.

Tian, G., Li, B., & Cheng, Y. (2022). Does digital transformation matter for corporate risk-taking? *Finance Research Letters*, *49*, 103107. https://doi.org/10.1016/j.frl.2022.103107

Tomaszewski, L. E., Zarestky, J., & Gonzalez, E. (2020). Planning qualitative research: Design and decision making for new researchers. *International Journal of Qualitative Methods*, *19*. https://doi.org/10.1177/1609406920967174

Upadhyay, N., Upadhyay, S., Al-Debei, M. M., Baabdullah, A. M., & Dwivedi, Y. K. (2023). The influence of digital entrepreneurship and entrepreneurial orientation on the intention of family businesses to adopt artificial intelligence: Examining the mediating role of business innovativeness. *International Journal of Entrepreneurial Behavior & Research*, *29*(1), 80–115.

Walter, A. T. (2021). Organisational agility: Ill-defined and somewhat confusing? A systematic literature review and conceptualisation. *Management Review Quarterly*, *71*(2), 343–391.

Zapata-Cantu, L., Sanguino, R., Barroso, A., & Nicola-Gavrilă, L. (2023). Family business adapting a new digital-based economy: Opportunities and challenges for future research. *Journal of the Knowledge Economy*, *14*(1), 408–425.

Chapter 4

Antecedents of Knowledge-Hiding Behaviour Among Sri Lankan Entrepreneurial Undergraduates: An Empirical Study

Vilasini De Silva

Sabaragamuwa University of Sri Lanka, Belihuloya, Sri, Lanka

Abstract

This study aims to identify the factors explaining the knowledge-hiding behaviour (KHB) of Sri Lankan entrepreneurial undergraduates. Using a survey strategy and convenience sampling, data was collected from 250 undergraduates from Sri Lankan universities that offer entrepreneurial degree programs. The research established that distrust, mutual reciprocity and psychological ownership positively affect KHB for university students. However, social interaction and social identification were not found to have a significant influence. Thus, this study contributes theoretically to the domain of knowledge hiding in an academic setting within the Sri Lankan context to encourage further research. In practical terms, the study implies that university management must create a favourable learning environment to control KHB and enhance knowledge sharing among learners through increased social interactions, attention to psychological ownership and cooperation. To the author's knowledge, only a few studies have examined the antecedents of KHB in the context of Sri Lanka.

Keywords: Knowledge-hiding behaviour; undergraduates; Sri Lanka; distrust; mutual reciprocity; psychological ownership

Shaping Entrepreneurial Marketing, Volume 1, 45–63

doi:10.1108/978-1-83708-852-220251004

Introduction

'Jnana,' a Sanskrit word found in Indian philosophy and some religions (mostly in Buddhism), has been used to denote knowledge that centres on a cognitive event. Similarly, other Sanskrit words like *Pajna*, *Prajna* and *Vidya* are also used in Sri Lanka instead of the word *knowledge*. These words are related to religious beliefs, which are always based on profound knowledge that human beings may possess. It is deeply believed that humans were civilized by discovering and advancing new knowledge. Civilization developed rapidly after new knowledge was shared in society. Thus, it is apparent that knowledge sharing plays a vital role in moulding individuals and society.

Since the second wave of industrialization in the 1900s, knowledge continues to be an essential modification in any organizational achievement (de Falco, 2019) and a driver of competitive advantage. The contemporary digitalized world promotes knowledge for the betterment of the establishment regardless of its nature, and knowledge and knowledge management (KM) are considered core activities (Fauzi, 2023). The arrival of KM many decades ago and its crucial position have supported entities in setting strategically fitted goals with properly organized knowledge, enabling them to clinch unbeaten competitive positions in the marketplace (Howell & Annansingh, 2013; Nonaka & Takeuchi, 1995). Accordingly, KM is more predominant in higher education institutions, as its prime focus is to create, nurture and disseminate knowledge to society (Al-Kurdi et al., 2018). The literature on knowledge and KM emphasizes that knowledge expands into innovative areas when appropriately utilized (Giustiniano et al., 2016; Škerlavaj et al., 2018). Religious leaders, authors, academics and other philosophers remind us that knowledge is valuable when shared.

Fullwood and Rowley (2017) highlight that knowledge sharing (KS) can be considered the most crucial piece of the KM spectrum, as it sets the direction for the flow and continuity of knowledge. Though the gravity and incalculable results of KS are known to individuals and organizations, some people are reluctant to share their knowledge with their colleagues (Connelly & Zweig, 2015; Fong et al., 2018; Renzl, 2008; Zhao & Xia, 2017). Possible causes could be different personalities, the threat of losing power or status (Ulrike et al., 2005), or the fear of being underestimated (Bordia et al., 2006). Hence, people hide their thoughts and ideas but pretend to prefer and promote KS (Arain et al., 2020; Babic et al., 2019; Connelly & Zweig, 2015; Karim, 2020).

The constructive impact of KM on the upliftment of higher education institutions (HEI) could be diminished by students' knowledge-hiding behaviour (KHB). It is highlighted that KHB should be given sufficient research attention, while a study by Connelly et al. (2012) led to profound productive discussions on KHB. Their studies shed light on a different sphere of the KM domain, and scholars also realized the need to examine KHB, its determinants and its consequences. Knowledge hiding, defined as 'an intentional attempt by an individual to withhold or conceal task information, ideas, and know-how that another person has requested' (Connelly et al., 2012, p. 65), can significantly damage the prospects of any establishment, especially HEIs. As Davenport and Prusak (1998) point out, people concealing what they learn is an act of falsity and an issue within the context of acquiring knowledge. University researchers are destined to generate and share knowledge with peers and learners to uphold academic progress in specific fields and improve society (Hernaus et al., 2019).

Therefore, exploring the drivers of KHB in HEIs is pivotal to demolishing barriers for future knowledge leaders. These explorations will enhance KM systems and their effectiveness as the drivers of KS (Al-Kurdi et al., 2018). KH can occur when goal-oriented individuals consider knowledge a weapon to hold power (Johannessen, 2018) in HEIs. Al-Husseini and Elbeltagi (2018) and Ghani et al. (2020) mention that KH is hazardous since it can affect intellectual thinking, innovation and healthy relationships, including strategic partnerships. Further, Connelly and Zweig (2015) added that KH could also hinder knowledge seekers, damaging the HEIs, including reduced creative ability, innovativeness and academic performance. Based on their perceptions of university culture, students in HEIs are inclined to think of knowledge as power or a tool for gaining a competitive edge (Chaudhry, 2005). Hence, they exhibit KHB, especially where graded academic tasks are involved (Yuen & Majid, 2007).

Studies such as Garg and Anand (2020), Demirkasımoğlu (2016), Ghani et al. (2020) and Hernaus et al. (2019) have highlighted that the body of knowledge about KH and KS shows a prominent upward trend in the form of studies related to general organizational behaviour and their KM efforts; however, investigations and explorations related to the academic context remain scarce. Thus, the KH domain is a potential area of study for researchers to concentrate on, which would be pivotal for knowledge transfer and management within the context of academic institutions (Annansingh et al., 2018; Bari et al., 2019; Connelly et al., 2012). Thus, understanding the drivers of KHB would help HEI administration enhance the management of students' KHB effectively and simultaneously be of practical value to society. This study focuses on the Sri Lankan context since the literature on KH in the country is not very encouraging. The literature survey could only pick very few studies in the Sri Lankan context, including the deep motivation and the rationale behind the current study.

Literature Review and Hypothesis Development

Among several theories available to explain individuals' behaviour in various settings, a list of theories, namely the theory of reasoned action (TRA), the social capital theory (SCT), the social exchange theory (SET), the theory of planned behaviour (TPB), the psychological ownership theory (POT) and the big five personality theory (BFPT) were noticed in the KHB literature (Omotayo & Akintibubo, 2024). The present study utilizes SET, SCT and POT to explore the determinants of university students' KHB.

Social Exchange Theory

The first scholar to study social behaviour based on exchange was Homans (1968), as stated by Omotayo and Akintibubo (2024). However, according to Homan, it is also essential to note that material/tangible items are complemented by recognition, respect, trust, knowledge and approval. The literature identifies the SET, initially developed from the economic exchange theory (Liao, 2008; Wang et al., 2015), as a prominent theory for exploring an individual's KHB (Blau, 1964; Connelly et al., 2012) as it entails intrinsic rewards (Blau, 1964). Bock and Kim (2002) also stressed that social exchange, in contrast to economic exchange, cannot be priced and that the nature of return cannot be measured and bargained. In the same light, Tsai and Cheng (2012) noted that while social exchange creates inner pressure, patrons feel obligated, grateful and trusting. According to the SET, behaviour in the social context is best explained in terms of an exchange process.

Many distinguished scholars, such as Connelly et al. (2012), Liao (2008), Liang et al. (2008), Wang et al. (2015), Yan et al. (2016), Jinyang (2015), Tsai and Cheng (2012) and Bock et al. (2005), have used the SET to analyse KHB in organizations. Based on the above literature review, the present exploratory study will seek to conduct the research by integrating the SET with two other theories.

Distrust

Abrams et al. (2003) note that trust is significant in supporting KS of persons, groups and communities in any setting. According to Blau (1964), trust is evident when the social exchange is healthy. Therefore, trust is a crucial concept in social exchange, as it forms its nucleus. Moreover, the literature review of KSB and KHB states that trust is an essential positive factor in KS (Khamseh & Jolly, 2014; Khan et al., 2022; Molm et al., 2000; Norman, 2004; Panteli & Sockalingam, 2004). Consequently, it can be readily appreciated that most people do not share knowledge without a proper reason or good vibes about the knowledge requestor (Ellis, 2001). Likewise, Geoffrey (1997) posited on the same line that the brain will not work to its maximum capacity when there is no trust. Trust can directly and indirectly affect KS through relationships and culture, as postulated by McNeish and Mann (2010). Furthermore, Nelson and Cooprider (1996), Gray (2001) and Usoro et al. (2007) support the notion of trust as the predictor of KS.

Distrust can be explained as a specific feeling of insecurity about the other, a belief that the other may try to get at one and that the other has no interest in one's well-being, wants to be unfavourable and is antagonistic (Govier, 1994). According to Molm et al. (2000) and Blau (1964), interpersonal distrust is a potent incentive that makes people feel that unfair individuals are untruthful. Khan et al. (2022) also mention that when an individual is distrustful towards another in a relationship, other people become distrustful. Distrust can compel people to conceal their knowledge and to react to acts done to them or punish such a person (Yuan et al., 2021). Connelly et al. (2012) and Wu et al. (2022) also stated that interpersonal distrust provokes KHB in institutions.

Several works have confirmed that knowledge creators or possessors conceal knowledge from seekers if they do not trust them (Afshan et al., 2022; Černe et al., 2014; Peng et al., 2019). Hence, distrust is one of the aspects that could be used to predict KH among undergraduates, and therefore, the following hypothesis has been developed for this study.

H1. Distrust has a positive impact on KHB among undergraduates.

Reciprocity

The social exchange theory states that 'the relationship and mutual interaction behaviour among people requires a process in which different parties exchange valuable resources in relevant activities' (Su et al., 2021, p. 3). The positive reciprocity principle of social exchange theory asserts that people interact at the social level and aim at positive interpersonal communication lines and reciprocal norms (Miles et al., 2017).

Ben-Ari and Enosh (2013, p. 426) described reciprocity as a 'process whereby each research party believes that he or she contributes not necessarily to the other party, but to a matter of common interest, an issue of concern, a social phenomenon, or a personal matter.' This definition accounts for the flow of information and knowledge, which is fair and reasonable, and reciprocity, which justifies the efforts exerted in sharing knowledge (Molm et al., 2007; Tamjidyamcholo et al., 2013). Therefore, reciprocity is inherent in healthy relationships, which are considered more valuable than those that involve only the sender's communication (Linton, 2000). Adding to the knowledge, Davenport and Prusak (1998) conclude that reciprocity is essential to knowledge sharing.

The theory of reciprocity is good for social exchange and structure (Mohsin et al., 2022; Zaheer et al., 2022). From the social perspective, reciprocity may be described as a state whereby an individual is supposed to support other people if those people have offered support to him/her first. In addition, in many instances, social and interpersonal behaviour reflects the process of students' mutual reciprocation, which ensures positive relations. Reciprocity is of two types: positive and negative reciprocity, according to Caliendo et al. (2010). Positive or mutual reciprocity is an individual's predisposition to compensate others according to what he/she receives. Positive reciprocity refers to people paying back positively to instrumentally perceived friendliness. Negative or absence of mutual reciprocity is demonstrated where one's behavioural predisposition is to return ill-treatment for ill-treatment or hostility (Caliendo et al., 2010; Shaw et al., 2019). Mitchell et al. (2012) affirm that people may be willing to suppress possessed knowledge and display KHB whenever a signal of perceived unfriendliness is detected. Therefore, it was postulated that any form of non-reciprocity or lack of mutual reciprocity on the part of the undergraduates (being studied) could dissuade them from sharing knowledge. Thus, the following hypothesis was formulated:

> *H2*. Negative or lack of mutual reciprocity has a positive impact on KHB among undergraduates.

Lack of Social Interaction (SI)

Lin (2011) confirms SI as strengthening reciprocity among people by satisfying the need to share knowledge in information, experience or ideas. Several researchers (Bell, 2005; Brachos et al., 2007; Sparrowe et al., 2001) who have studied social networks state that the density of contact between individuals enhances organizational inventiveness and dissemination. Adding to the literature, Chen and Huang (2007) also stress the relative importance of interpersonal SI as a means of sharing and fortifying the inventory of knowledge and the cycle of resources. Tsai and Ghoshal (1998) also state that facilitating social communication among people can generate more than ordinary value in managerial work.

SI theory was introduced in 1964 by Blau and was linked to establishing the grounds for people's KSB. According to Razak et al. (2016), an individual may anticipate larger profit margins out of his/her transactions even where no gains are evident. Contacts between people are seen as solid media of information and resource exchange. Therefore, if more people use a particular channel to interact, the flow of information could be enriched and bring about positive 'side effects.' Thus, interactions between people are among the primary information and knowledge-sharing sources.

Larson (1992) also found that the level, frequency and extent of knowledge or information transferred are superior where there are numerous SIs. The opinion of other people and their behaviour (Hasgall, 2012; Wasko & Faraj, 2005) can be regarded as a significant impact of SI on the behaviour displayed by an individual towards knowledge. A similar, even more developed picture emerges among communities in the virtual world where 'social interaction ties' provide access to knowledge at minimum cost (Liang et al., 2008). Tsai and Ghoshal (1998) also point out that the latest literature supports this contention. On this premise, the study assumed the following hypothesis.

> *H3*. Lack of social interaction has a positive impact on KHB among undergraduates.

Social Capital Theory (SCT)

It was Nahapiet and Ghoshal (1998) who introduced the management domain to the concept of social capital, which they defined as the 'sum of the actual and potential resources embedded within, available through, and derived from the network of relationships possessed by an individual or social unit' (p. 243). SCT has been used to elucidate ideas of KS and KH (Silva de Garcia et al., 2022).

Social capital may be viewed as tangible stock-in-trade in social relations, which can also be accumulated and is priceless (Adler & Kwon, 2002). It must be noted that social capital does not necessarily have to be context-bounded. A network developed in one context may be reconfigured in another (Adler & Kwon, 2002; Nahapiet & Ghoshal, 1998). For instance, the network created in the academic context of a university may be employed by a student in his/her working career. As with the other types of capital, social capital is also considered productive and oriented towards achieving specific goals. It can be described, though it cannot be exchanged in the same way that other capital assets in the balance sheet can be (Nahapiet & Ghoshal, 1998). Some forms of social capital likely to influence knowledge transfer include trust, norms, network relations, identification, language and goals.

Lack of Social Identification

Human beings prefer associating with colleagues or social groups, creating a kind of identity, and utilizing it as an investment to obtain tangible or intangible benefits. Recognizing an individual with a group or a community creates the need for affection or belongingness (mentioned in Maslow's hierarchy of needs). The abovementioned identity is perceived as a capital facilitating the cross-flow of knowledge (Nahapiet & Ghoshal, 1998). Having achieved compatibility with other members, people prove their readiness to demonstrate the knowledge they possess within the group. Thus, social identification with the community must induce KSB (Chiu et al., 2006). The author concludes a positive correlation between social identification and KS. Therefore, the following hypothesis has been formulated for the current study among university undergraduates.

> *H4*. Lack of social identification has a positive impact on KHB among undergraduates.

Psychological Ownership

The psychological ownership theory postulates that psychological ownership (PO) is a significant aspect of an individual's engagement to protect and sustain his/her belongings (Pierce et al., 2001). The author notes that PO is a cognitive-affective concept derived from peoples' perception of ownership and being psychologically bonded or anchored to concrete and abstract items. Avey et al. (2009) and Li et al. (2015) showed that PO implies that employees own an organization. Hence, it is apparent that people feel connected to other groups or community members when they possess a sense of ownership, which triggers KSB.

According to Van Dyne and Pierce (2004), perceptions of ownership may prompt employees' selfless spirit, which has been regarded as a positive characteristic of extra-role behaviour, for instance, KS. PO may influence individuals to extend knowledge, persuade people to study, solve problems in groups, embrace and promote organizational values and ideas, and accept and further the values and ideas of the organization. In a similar study, Hameed et al. (2019) showed that employees who are highly charged with psychological ownership and demonstrating an altruistic tendency can boost KS. The authors regard it as one of the most essential antecedent variables of KS.

PO is classified into two categories: promotion and prevention. Sharing knowledge with colleagues is a promotive PO. Such individuals are willing to perform actions that lead to improvements in a particular setting. However, others tend to avoid sharing knowledge they deem to be reserved. It was discovered that individuals tend to hide knowledge when they feel a strong PO of it. Pierce et al. (2003) also mention that sometimes people are unwilling to share knowledge, assuming they may lose their status.

Similarly, Batool et al. (2022) concluded that high levels of PO encourage positive work behaviour, such as knowledge sharing, and hostile work behaviour, such as knowledge hiding. Mangold (2017) identified that PO is one of the sources of KHB. Kumar Jha and Varkkey (2018) also assert that PO will likely lead to KHB due to this territoriality. Based on the findings mentioned above, the following hypothesis has been formulated:

H5. Psychological ownership has a positive impact on KHB among undergraduates.

Methodology

This study employs a descriptive research design because it describes the factors that predict students' KHB. The unit of analysis is an undergraduate enrolled in an undergraduate degree program in entrepreneurship in Sri Lanka. The subjects for the study were selected using convenient sampling since the students were studying online during the data collection period. The sample size of 250 was chosen in a natural setting to justify previous literature (Omotayo & Babalola, 2016; Serenko & Bontis, 2016) and research methodology guidelines from Sekaran and Bougie (2016).

The survey instrument consisted of two sections. The first section was devoted to gathering the socio-demographic information of respondents. The subsequent section encompassed all the measurement scales employed to operationalize each dimension from the conceptual framework in Fig. 4.1, proposed for the study and adopted from the literature. Since these measurement scales (distrust, psychological ownership, mutual reciprocity, SI, social identification and KHB) were developed to be deployed in varied research settings associated with KHB, minor changes were incorporated in the survey instrument. The questionnaire, which contained closed-ended questions, had items adapted from previous studies. Previously validated items were adapted to measure distrust (Jessup et al., 2020), psychological ownership (Peng, 2013), damaging or lack of mutual reciprocity (Serenko & Bontis, 2016), lack of SI (Lasode & Ogunsola, 2019), lack of social identification (Chiu et al., 2006) and KHB (Demirkasımoğlu, 2016).

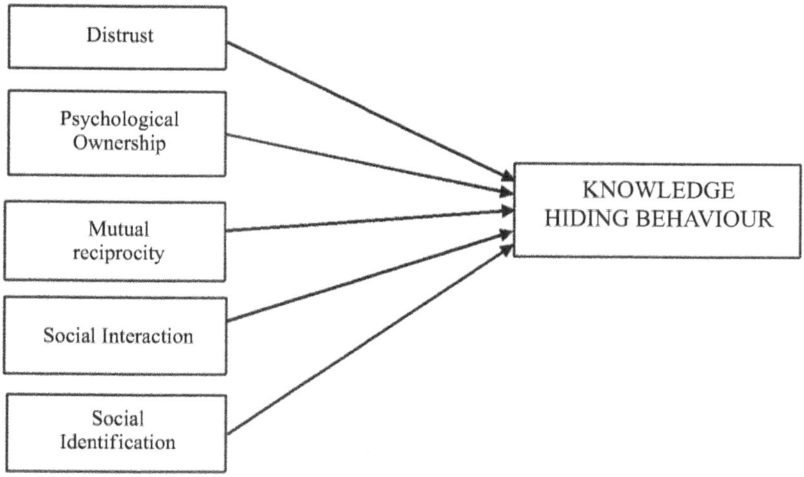

Fig. 4.1. Conceptual Framework. *Source:* Author's own.

A five-point Likert scale, in which one indicates 'strongly disagree' and five 'strongly agree,' was utilized to obtain responses for each measure of variables in the conceptual framework. Multiple regression analysis in SPSS was the analytical tool deployed to investigate the phenomenon and derive conclusions.

Results From the Data Analysis

Approximately two-thirds of those who responded (62.2%) were female since most Faculty of Management Studies undergraduates were female. The age of the respondents was not included in the questionnaire as all undergraduates fall into the 20–24 age category. The majority of the respondents (97.6%) were unmarried.

The hypotheses portrayed in the conceptual framework shown in Fig. 4.1 were statistically tested by deploying multiple regression in SPSS 21. Then, the researcher assessed the internal consistency using Cronbach's alpha, which measures reliability based on the interrelationships of the observed variables. In this study, Cronbach alpha values exceeded 0.7; the threshold level was achieved (Hair et al., 2014). The researcher did not conduct any tests to identify convergent, discriminant, concurrent or predictive validity because all variables were measured using a well-established scale. However, the researcher established content and face validity before conducting the survey. The researcher distributed the questionnaire to selected subject experts, got their feedback and made the necessary changes.

The present investigation employed multiple regression to test the suggested hypotheses for the study. The modified R^2 value quantifies the level of explanation in the dependent variable. The value of the adjusted R square is 0.589 (Table 4.1). The analysis reveals that 58.9% of the KHB is determined by three antecedents,

Table 4.1. Model Summary.

Model	*R*	*R* Square	Adjusted *R* Square	The Std. Error of the Estimate	Durbin–Watson
1	0.774	0.599	0.589	0.47465	1.837

Source: Survey data (2024).

namely distrust, mutual reciprocity and psychological ownership. Table 4.1 demonstrates the statistical importance of the regression model. Given that the *P*-value of the ANOVA test is below 0.05, the researcher determined that the model is statistically significant.

Please refer Table 4.2 for the results from the ANOVA.

Table 4.3 carries the test results of the multiple regression analysis run to test suggested hypotheses for the present study. The β value generated by the regression analysis measures the extent to which every independent variable impacts the dependent variable, assuming that all other variables are held constant. According to the test results in Table 4.3, three of the posited hypotheses for the present exploration have been supported since the significance values are below 0.05. Therefore, it can be concluded that distrust, mutual reciprocity and psychological ownership predict the KHB of undergraduates in the context of Sri Lanka.

Table 4.2. Results From the ANOVA.

Models	Sum of Squares	Df	Mean Square	*F*	Sig.
Regression	68.673	5	13.735	60.964	0.000
Residual	45.959	204	0.225		
Total	114.632	209			

Source: Survey Data (2024).

Table 4.3. Coefficient Table.

	Unstandardized Coefficient		
Model	*B*	Std. Error	Sig.
Constant	0.857	0.146	0.000
Distrust	0.146	0.067	0.031
Psychological ownership	0.341	0.062	0.000
Mutual reciprocity	0.164	0.066	0.014

Source: Survey data (2024).

Discussion of Findings

This study may be classified as one of the few investigations in the Sri Lankan context. Data show that students in a university environment may exhibit three types of KHB (playing dumb, evasive hiding and rationalized hiding) as defined by Omotayo and Akintibubo (2024), Connelly et al. (2012) and other researchers like Garg and Anand (2020) and Garg et al. (2021). This first-of-its-kind research identified several favourable results, some of which can be considered future study areas and guidelines for encouraging KSH and discouraging KHB. In addition, of the five variables, distrust, psychological ownership and lack of mutual reciprocity had a significant positive correlation with KHB.

The current analysis reveals that the variable distrust had a significant positive correlation with KHB, which corroborates the previous research literature on distrust, including Kumar Jha and Varkkey (2018), Afshan et al. (2022), Černe et al. (2014), Mangold (2017), Peng et al. (2019) and Omotayo and Akintibubo (2024). Therefore, the author concluded that distrust could be one of the indicators that explain KHB among undergraduates. In other words, students withhold knowledge from individuals they do not trust. Gibbs (2009) and Connelly et al. (2012) note that distrust in an organization is a critical predicting factor of KHB. Individuals intentionally indulge in KHB for their benefit and do not trust others.

This study also supports the previous findings on the impact of psychological ownership on KHB (Batool et al., 2022; Kumar Jha & Varkkey, 2018; Mangold, 2017; Omotayo & Akintibubo, 2024; Pierce et al., 2003; Peng, 2013). A study by Hernaus et al. (2019) established that personal competitiveness motivates KHB, especially in academic settings with mistrust. In simple terms, the findings suggest that when students attain a high level of psychological ownership over the knowledge they possess, they convince themselves that the 'owned' knowledge is vital to their academic accomplishment. The reasonable justification for these results could be that since students expend funds, time and effort acquiring knowledge, they feel they own it.

The findings reveal that mutual reciprocity enhances healthy relationships and generates more significant results than one-way communication (Linton, 2000). Enriching existing literature, the present study also reveals that a lack of mutual reciprocity contributes significantly to KHB. Davenport and Prusak (1998) also affirm that reciprocity is a significant determinant of KS. Cropanzano and Mitchell (2005), Omotayo and Akintibubo (2024) and Mitchell et al. (2012) also contributed to the literature on mutual reciprocity by revealing its predictability concerning KHB. The results from the present exploration concerning the ability to predict the impact of the lack of SI on KHB are contrary to the existing literature. The results reveal no association between the absence of SI and KHB among entrepreneurship undergraduates in Sri Lanka. Similarly, there is no significant relationship between the lack of social identification and KHB. A study by Omotayo and Akintibubo (2024) also found no impact of social identification or interpersonal affiliation on KHB among university students.

Conclusion

This exploration attempts to study the determinants underlying the KHB of entrepreneurship undergraduates in Sri Lanka, a novel concept in this context. Accordingly, five hypotheses were posited to test the direct effects of all independent variables, namely distrust, mutual reciprocity, psychological ownership, SI and social identification, on KHB among undergraduates. Data were collected from undergraduate students of a Sri Lankan university to test the formulated hypotheses and achieve research objectives. Convenience sampling, a non-probability sampling technique, was used to arrive at a sample size of 250. Cronbach's alpha values were used to assess reliability, and multiple regression was deployed to test the hypotheses statistically.

Based on the study's outcomes, the researcher concluded that distrust, mutual reciprocity and psychological ownership significantly positively impact KHB among university students. In addition, SI and social identification do not significantly impact KHB among undergraduates.

Theoretical and Practical Implications

There are several theoretical and practical implications from this study, a pioneer in the KHS and KHB domain in the Sri Lankan context, that can provide a solid platform for future research undertakings and a conducive learning environment in academic institutions. The present exploration was designed to investigate the antecedents that determine the KHB of undergraduates by borrowing constructs from the SET, the SCT and the POT. The study unveils some exciting directions for theorizing about KHB and more investigations in the Sri Lankan context. Similarly, the research framework deployed in the study would be an excellent foundation for further studies.

The outcomes shed light on an area university management must focus on to create a conducive learning environment. Creating a conducive environment will help reduce KHB and promote KHS among students. Measures should be explained to help reduce an individual's estimate of his/her knowledge. Perhaps the most concerning outcome was psychological ownership, which could be offset by explaining to the student that no one knows everything. If knowledge is strength, it is much mightier when shared; knowledge is not erased by sharing. It is also recommended that tutors encourage and increase student engagement by incorporating more classroom discussions and participation, classroom and online forums, group assignments, and study group sessions to create contact hours. These activities may increase the amount and the frequency of communication with other individuals and facilitate the appreciation of the importance of reciprocity that will in turn prompt KSB. The findings imply that communicating with students through purposefully planned social discourse and interaction leads to creating knowledge/information and generates social capital and user interactivity, leading to KS and discouraging KHB. The research has meaningful managerial consequences because it acknowledges that interaction and social capital influence knowledge sharing.

Acknowledgements

I want to extend my heartfelt thanks to the editors and reviewers for the attention to detail and quality they brought to this book. Their invaluable comments, suggestions and feedback have helped shape this work.

References

Abrams, L. C., Cross, R., Lesser, E., & Levin, D. Z. (2003). Nurturing interpersonal trust in knowledge-sharing networks. *The Academy of Management Executive*, *17*(4), 64–77.

Adler, P. S., & Kwon, S.-W. (2002). Social capital: Prospect for a new concept. *Academy of Management Review*, *27*(1), 17–40.

Afshan, G., Sahibzada, U. F., Rani, H., Mughal, Y. H., & Kundi, G. M. (2022). Supervisor's knowledge hiding and knowledge-based trust: From the lens of social impact theory. *Aslib Journal of Information Management*, *74*(2), 332–353.

Al-Husseini, S., & Elbeltagi, I. (2018). The role of knowledge sharing in enhancing innovation: A comparative study of public and private higher education institutions in Iraq. *Innovations in Education and Teaching International*, *55*(1), 23–33.

Al-Kurdi, O., El-Haddadeh, R., & Eldabi, T. (2018). Knowledge sharing in higher education institutions: A systematic review. *Journal of Enterprise Information Management*, *31*(2), 226–246.

Annansingh, F., Howell, K. E., Liu, S., & Baptista Nunes, M. (2018). Academics' perception of knowledge sharing in higher education. *International Journal of Educational Management*, *32*(6), 1001–1015.

Arain, G. A., Hameed, I., Umrani, W. A., Khan, A. K., & Sheikh, A. Z. (2020). Consequences of supervisor knowledge hiding in organisations: A multilevel mediation analysis. *Applied Psychology*, *11*(2), 57–77.

Avey, J. B., Avolio, B. J., Crossley, C. D., & Luthans, F. (2009). Psychological ownership: Theoretical extensions, measurement and relation to work outcomes. *Journal of Organisational Behavior*, *30*(2), 173–191. https://doi.org/10.1002/job.583

Babic, K., Cerne, M., Connelly, C. E., Dysvik, A., & Škerlavaj, M. (2019). Are we in this together? Knowledge hiding in teams, collective prosocial motivation, and leader-member exchange. *Journal of Knowledge Management*, *23*(8), 1502–1522.

Bari, M. W., Abrar, M., Shaheen, S., Bashir, M., & Fanchen, M. (2019). Knowledge hiding behaviours and team creativity: The contingent role of perceived mastery motivational climate. *SAGE Open*, *9*(3). https://doi.org/10.1177/2158244019876297

Batool, U., Raziq, M. M., Obaid, A., & Sumbal, M. S. U. K. (2022). Psychological ownership and knowledge behaviours during a pandemic: Role of approach motivation. *Current Psychology*, *42*, 25089–25099. https://doi.org/10.1007/s12144-022-03450-y

Bell, G. G. (2005). Clusters, networks, and firm innovativeness. *Strategic Management Journal*, *26*(3), 287–295. https://doi.org/10.1002/smj.458

Ben-Ari, A., & Enosh, G. (2013). Power relations and reciprocity: Dialectics of knowledge construction. *Qualitative Health Research*, *23*(3), 422–429.

Blau, P. (1964). *Power and exchange in social life*. John Wiley & Sons.

Bock, G., & Kim, Y. (2002). Breaking the myths of rewards: An exploratory study of attitudes about knowledge sharing. *Information Resources Management Journal*, *15*(2), 14–21.

Bock, G.-W., Zmud, R. W., Kim, Y.-G., & Lee, J.-N. (2005). Behavioural intention formation in knowledge sharing: Examining the roles of extrinsic motivators, social-psychological forces, and organisational climate. *MIS Quarterly*, *29*(1), 87–111. https://doi.org/10.2307/25148660

Bordia, P., Irmer, B. E., & Abusah, D. (2006). Differences in sharing knowledge interpersonally and via databases: The role of evaluation apprehension and perceived benefits. *European Journal of Work and Organisational Psychology*, *15*(3), 262–280.

Brachos, D., Kostopoulos, K., Soderquist, K. E., & Prastacos, G. (2007). Knowledge effectiveness, social context, and innovation. *Journal of Knowledge Management*, *11*(5), 31–44.

Caliendo, M., Fossen, F., & Kritikos, A. (2010). *Trust, positive reciprocity, and negative reciprocity: Do these traits impact entrepreneurial dynamics?* IZA Discussion Paper No. 5370, 1–37. https://doi.org/10.2139/ssrn.1728327

Černe, M., Nerstad, C. G. L., Dysvik, A., & Škerlavaj, M. (2014). What goes around comes around: Knowledge hiding perceived motivational climate and creativity. *Academy of Management Journal*, *57*(1), 172–192. https://doi.org/10.5465/amj.2012.0122

Chaudhry, A. B. (2005). Knowledge sharing practices in Asian institutions: A multi-cultural perspective from Singapore [Conference session] *World Library and Information Congress: 71st IFLA General Conference and Council Libraries*. http://www.ifla.org/IV/ifla71/Programme.htm

Chen, C. J., & Huang, J. W. (2007). How organisational climate and structure affect knowledge management–the social interaction perspective. *International Journal of Information Management*, *27*(2), 104–118. https://doi.org/10.1016/j.ijinfomgt.2006.12.003

Chiu, C. M., Hsu, M. H., & Wang, E. T. (2006). Understanding knowledge sharing in virtual communities: An integration of social capital and social cognitive theories. *Decision Support Systems*, *42*(3), 1872–1888. https://doi.org/10.1016/j.dss.2006.04.001

Connelly, C. E., & Zweig, D. (2015). How perpetrators and targets construe knowledge hiding in organisations. *European Journal of Work and Organisational Psychology*, *24*(3), 479–489.

Connelly, C. E., Zweig, D., Webster, J., & Trougakos, J. P. (2012). Knowledge hiding in organisations. *Journal of Organisational Behavior*, *33*(1), 64–88. https://doi.org/10.1002/job.737

Cropanzano, R., & Mitchell, M. S. (2005). Social exchange theory: Interdisciplinary review. *Journal of Management*, *31*(6), 874–900. https://doi.org/10.1177/0149206305279602

Davenport, T. H., & Prusak, L. (1998). *Working knowledge: How organisations manage what they know*. Harvard Business School Press.

de Falco, S. (2019). From Silicon Valley to Africa Valley: Which paradigms are needed in the transition from II to IV industrial revolution? Knowledge roadmap and technological track. *Innovation: The European Journal of Social Science Research*, *35*(4), 675–703. https://doi.org/10.1080/13511610.2019.1595538

Demirkasımoğlu, N. (2016). Knowledge hiding in academia: Is personality a key factor? *International Journal of Higher Education*, *5*(1), 128–140. https://doi.org/10.5430/ijhe.v5n1p128

Ellis, K. (2001). Dare to share. *Training*, *32*(2), 74–80.

Fauzi, M. A. (2023). Knowledge hiding behaviour in higher education institutions: A scientometric analysis and systematic literature review approach. *Journal of Knowledge Management*, *27*(2), 302–327. https://doi.org/10.1108/JKM-07-2021-0527

Fong, P. S. W., Men, C., Luo, J., & Jia, R. (2018). Knowledge hiding and team creativity: The contingent role of task interdependence. *Management Decision*, *56*(2), 329–343. https://doi.org/10.1108/MD-09-2017-0917

Fullwood, R., & Rowley, J. (2017). An investigation of factors affecting knowledge sharing amongst UK academics. *Journal of Knowledge Management*, *21*(5), 1254–1271.

Garg, N., & Anand, P. (2020). Knowledge hiding, conscientiousness, loneliness and affective commitment: A moderated mediation model. *International Journal of Educational Management*, *34*(9), 1417–1437.

Garg, N., Talukdar, A., Ganguly, A., & Kumar, C. (2021). Knowledge hiding in academia: An empirical study of Indian higher education students. *Journal of Knowledge Management*, *25*(9), 2196–2219. https://doi.org/10.1108/JKM-10-2020-0783

Geoffrey, C. (1997). *The changing art of becoming unbeatable* (p. 229). Fortune.

Ghani, U., Zhai, X., Spector, J. M., Chen, N.-S., Lin, L., Ding, D., & Usman, M. (2020). Knowledge hiding in higher education: Role of interactional justice and professional commitment. *Higher Education*, *79*(2), 325–344.

Gibbs, G. (2009). *Qualitative data analysis*. Artmed.

Giustiniano, L., Lombardi, S., & Cavaliere, V. (2016). How knowledge collecting fosters organisational creativity. *Management Decision*, *54*(6), 1464–1496.

Govier, T. (1994). An epistemology of trust. *International Journal of Moral and Social Studies*, *8*, 155–174.

Gray, P. H. (2001). The impact of knowledge repositories on power and control in the workplace. *Information Technology & People*, *14*(4), 368–384.

Hair, Jr., J. F., Sarstedt, M., Hopkins, L., & Kuppelwieser, V. G. (2014). Partial least squares structural equation modelling (PLS-SEM): An emerging tool in business research. *European Business Review*, *26*(2), 106–121. https://doi.org/10.1108/EBR-10-2013-0128

Hameed, Z., Khan, I. U., Sheikh, Z., Islam, T., Rasheed, M. I., & Naeem, R. M. (2019). Organisational justice and knowledge sharing behaviour. *Personnel Review*, *48*(3), 748–773. https://doi.org/10.1108/pr-07-2017-0217

Hasgall, A. E. (2012). The effectiveness of social networks in complex adaptive working environments. *Journal of Systems and Information Technology*, *14*(3), 220–235.

Hernaus, T., Cerne, M., Connelly, C., Vokic, N. P., & Škerlavaj, M. (2019). Evasive knowledge hiding in academia: When competitive individuals are asked to collaborate. *Journal of Knowledge Management*, *23*(4), 597–618.

Homans, G. C. (1968). A life of synthesis. *American Behavioural Scientist*, *12*(1), 2–8.

Howell, K. E., & Annansingh, F. (2013). Knowledge generation and sharing in UK universities: A tale of two cultures? *International Journal of Information Management*, *33*(1), 32–39. https://doi.org/10.1016/j.ijinfomgt.2012.05.003

Jessup, S. A., Alarcon, G. M., Capiola, A., & Ryan, T. J. (2020). Multi-method approach measuring trust, distrust, and suspicion in information technology. In A. Moallem (Ed.), *HCI for cybersecurity, privacy, and trust. HCII 2020. Lecture notes in computer science* (Vol. 12210). Springer. https://doi.org/10.1007/978-3-030-50309-3_27

Jinyang, L. (2015). Knowledge sharing in virtual communities: A social exchange theory perspective. *Journal of Industrial Engineering and Management*, *8*(1). https://doi.org/10.3926/jiem.1389

Johannessen, H. T. D. (2018). The need to grow, learn, and develop – How does management affect motivation for professional development? *LIBER Quarterly*, *28*, 1–16.

Karim, D. N. (2020). Effect of dark personalities on knowledge hiding behaviour at higher education institutions. *Journal of Information & Knowledge Management*, *19*(4), 1–20.

Khamseh, H. M., & Jolly, D. (2014). Knowledge transfer in alliances: The moderating role of the alliance type. *Knowledge Management Research & Practice*, *12*(4), 409–420. https://doi.org/10.1057/kmrp.2014.13

Khan, M. A., Malik, O. F., & Shahzad, A. (2022). Social undermining and employee creativity: The mediating role of interpersonal distrust and knowledge hiding. *Behavioral Sciences*, *12*(2), 25. https://doi.org/10.3390/bs12020025

Kumar Jha, J., & Varkkey, B. (2018). Are you a cistern or a channel? Exploring factors triggering knowledge-hiding behaviour at the workplace: Evidence from the Indian R and D professionals. *Journal of Knowledge Management*, *22*(4), 824–849. https://doi.org/10.1108/JKM-02-2017-0048

Lasode, D. O., & Ogunsola, K. (2019). Predicting knowledge sharing by professional architects in architectural firms in Ibadan, Nigeria. *Information Development*, *35*(5), 749–766. https://doi.org/10.1177/0266666918793927

Larson, A. (1992). Network dyads in entrepreneurial settings: A study of the governance of exchange relationships. *Administrative Science Quarterly*, *37*(1), 76–104. https://doi.org/10.2307/2393531

Li, J., Yuan, L., Ning, L., & Li-Ying, J. (2015). Knowledge sharing and affective commitment: The mediating role of psychological ownership. *Journal of Knowledge Management*, *19*(6), 1146–1166.

Liang, T.-P., Liu, C.-C., & Wu, C.-H. (2008). Can social exchange theory explain individual knowledge-sharing behaviour? A meta-analysis. In *International Conference on Information Systems 2008 Proceedings* (p. 171). https://aisel.aisnet.org/icis2008/171

Liao, L. F. (2008). Knowledge-sharing in R&D departments: A social power and social exchange theory perspective. *The International Journal of Human Resource Management*, *19*(10), 1881–1895.

Lin, F. (2011). The effects of employee motivation, social interaction, and knowledge management strategy on KM implementation level. *Knowledge Management Research & Practice*, *9*, 263–275. https://doi.org/10.1057/kmrp.2011.24

Linton, J. D. (2000). The role of relationships and reciprocity in implementing process innovation. *Engineering Management Journal*, *12*(3), 34–38.

Mangold, S. (2017). *Knowledge hiding in organisations: A multilevel analysis of antecedents and consequences*. Doctoral dissertation. Technische Universitat Munchen.

McNeish, J., & Mann, I. J. S. (2010). Knowledge sharing and trust in organisations. *The IUP Journal of Knowledge Management*, *8*(1&2), 18–38.

Miles, J. A., Xu, S., & Li, C. (2017). *Management and organisation theory*. Peking University Press.

Mitchell, M. S., Cropanzano, R. S., & Quisenberry, D. M. (2012). Social exchange theory, exchange resources, and interpersonal relationships: A modest resolution of theoretical difficulties. In K. Törnblom & A. Kazemi (Eds.), *Handbook of social resource theory: Critical issues in social justice* (pp. 99–118). Springer.

Mohsin, M., Jamil, K., Naseem, S., Sarfraz, M., & Ivascu, L. (2022). Elongating nexus between workplace factors and knowledge hiding behaviour: Mediating role of job anxiety. *Psychology Research and Behavior Management*, *15*, 441–457. https://doi.org/10.2147/PRBM.S348467

Molm, L. D., Schaefer, D. R., & Collett, J. L. (2007). The value of reciprocity. *Social Psychology Quarterly*, *70*(2), 199–217.

Molm, L. D., Takahashi, N., & Peterson, G. (2000). Risk and trust in social exchange: An experimental test of a classical proposition. *American Journal of Sociology*, *105*, 1396–1427.

Nahapiet, J., & Ghoshal, S. (1998). Social capital, intellectual capital, and organisational advantage. *The Academy of Management Review*, *23*(2), 242–266. https://doi.org/10.2307/259373

Nelson, K., & Cooprider, J. (1996). The contribution of shared knowledge to IS group performance. *MIS Quarterly*, *20*(4), 409–432.

Nonaka, I., & Takeuchi, H. (1995). *The knowledge-creating company: How Japanese companies create the dynamics of innovation*. Oxford University Press.

Norman, P. (2004). Knowledge acquisition, knowledge loss, and satisfaction in high technology alliances. *Journal of Business Research*, *57*(6), 610–619. https://doi.org/10.1016/S0148-2963(02)00395-8

Omotayo, F. O., & Akintibubo, A. O. (2024). Knowledge hiding in the academia: Individual and social Factors predicting knowledge hiding behaviour of Nigerian university undergraduates. *Journal of Librarianship and Information Science*, *56*(1), 145–163. https://doi.org/10.1177/09610006221133564

Omotayo, F. O., and Babalola, S. O. (2016). Factors influencing knowledge sharing among information and communication technology artisans in Nigeria. *Journal of Systems and Information Technology*, *18*(2), 148–169.

Panteli, N., & Sockalingam, S. (2004). Trust and conflict within virtual inter-organisational alliances: A framework for facilitating knowledge sharing. *Decision Support Systems*, *39*, 599–617. https://doi.org/10.1016/S0167-9236(04)00004-7

Peng, H. (2013). Why and when do people hide knowledge? *Journal of Knowledge Management*, *17*(3), 398–415.

Peng, W., Fangwei, Z., Haoyang, S., & Xiaona, B. (2019). Interpersonal trust and knowledge hiding behaviour: The joint moderating effects of personal reputation concern and perceived uncertainty. *Management Review*, *31*(1), 155–170.

Pierce, J. L., Kostova, T., & Dirks, K. T. (2001). Toward a theory of psychological ownership in organisations. *Academy of Management Review*, *26*(2), 298–310.

Pierce, J. L., Kostova, T., & Dirks, K. T. (2003). The state of psychological ownership: Integrating and extending a century of research. *Review of General Psychology*, *7*(1), 84–107. https://doi.org/10.1037/1089-2680.7.1.84

Razak, N. A., Pangil, F., Zin, M. L. M., Yunus, N. A. M., & Asnawi, N. H. (2016). Theories of knowledge sharing behaviour in business strategy. *Procedia Economics and Finance*, *37*, 545–553. https://doi.org/10.1016/S2212-5671(16)30105-7

Renzl, B. (2008). Trust in management and knowledge sharing: The mediating effects of fear and knowledge documentation. *Omega*, *36*(2), 206–220.

Su, X., Lin, W., Wu, J., Zheng, Q., Chen, X., & Jiang, X. (2021). Ethical leadership and knowledge sharing: The effects of positive reciprocity and moral efficacy. *SAGE Open*, *11*(2). https://doi.org/10.1177/21582440211021823

Sekaran, U., & Bougie, R. (2016). *Research methods for business: A skill-building approach* (7th ed.). Wiley & Sons.

Serenko, A., & Bontis, N. (2016). Understanding counterproductive knowledge behaviour: Antecedents and consequences of intra-organisational knowledge hiding. *Journal of Knowledge Management*, *20*, 1199–1224. https://doi.org/10.1108/JKM-05-2016-0203

Shaw, A., Barakzai, A., & Keysar, B. (2019). When and why do people evaluate negative reciprocity as more fair than positive reciprocity? *Cognitive Science: A Multidisciplinary Journal*, *43*(8), 1–35. https://doi.org/10.1111/cogs.12714

Silva de Garcia, P., Oliveira, M., & Brohman, K. (2022). Knowledge sharing, hiding, and hoarding: How are they related? *Knowledge Management Research & Practice*, *20*(3), 339–351.

Škerlavaj, M., Connelly, C. E., Cerne, M., & Dysvik, A. (2018). Tell me if you can: Time pressure, prosocial motivation, perspective taking, and knowledge hiding. *Journal of Knowledge Management*, *22*(7), 1489–1509.

Sparrowe, R. T., Liden, R. C., & Kraimer, M. L. (2001). Social networks and the performance of individuals and groups. *Academy of Management Journal*, *44*(2), 316–325.

Tamjidyamcholo, A., Baba, M. S. B., Tamjid, H., & Gholipour, R. (2013). Information security–professional perceptions of knowledge-sharing intention under self-efficacy, trust, reciprocity, and shared language. *Computers and Education*, *68*, 223–232. https://doi.org/10.1016/j.compedu.2013.05.010

Tsai, M.-T., & Cheng, N.-C. (2012). Understanding knowledge sharing between IT professionals–an integration of social cognitive and social exchange theory. *Behaviour & Information Technology*, *31*(11), 1069–1080.

Tsai, W., & Ghoshal, S. (1998). Social capital and value creation: An empirical study of interfirm networks. *Academy of Management Journal*, *41*(4), 464–476.

Ulrike, C., Beatriz, B., Jurgen, B., & Friedrich, H. W. (2005). Social dilemma in knowledge communication via shared databases. *Barriers and Biases in Computer-Mediated Knowledge Communication*, *5*(1), 143–167.

Usoro, A., Sharratt, M. W., Tsui, E., & Shekhar, S. (2007). Trust as an antecedent to knowledge sharing in virtual communities of practice. *Knowledge Management Research & Practice*, *5*, 199–212.

Van Dyne, L., & Pierce, J. L. (2004). Psychological ownership and feelings of possession: Three field studies predicting employee attitudes and organisational citizenship behaviour. *Journal of Organisational Behavior*, *25*(4), 439–459. https://doi.org/10.1002/job.249

Wang, H.-K., Yen, Y.-F., & Tseng, J.-F. (2015). Knowledge sharing in knowledge workers: The roles of social exchange theory and the theory of planned behaviour. *Innovation*, *17*(4), 450–465. https://doi.org/10.1080/14479338.2015.1129283

Wasko, M. M., & Faraj, S. (2005). Why should I share? Examining social capital and knowledge contribution in electronic networks of practice. *MIS Quarterly*, *29*, 35–57. https://doi.org/10.2307/25148679

Wu, Q., Saqib, S., Sun, J., Xiao, Y., & Ma, W. (2022). Incivility and knowledge hiding in academia: Mediating role of interpersonal distrust and rumination. *Frontiers in Psychology*, *12*, 769282. https://doi.org/10.3389/fpsyg.2021.769282

Yan, Z., Wang, T., Chen, Y., & Zhang, H. (2016). Knowledge sharing in online health communities: A social exchange theory perspective. *Information and Management*, *53*(5), 643–653. https://doi.org/10.1016/j.im.2016.02.001

Yuan, Y., Yang, L., Cheng, X., & Wei, J. (2021). What is bullying hiding? Exploring antecedents and potential dimension of knowledge hiding. *Journal of Knowledge Management*, *25*, 1146–1169.

Yuen, J. T., & Majid, S. M. (2007). Knowledge-sharing patterns of undergraduate students in Singapore. *Library Review*, *56*(6), 485–494.

Zaheer, H., Karim, J., & Bibi, Z. (2022). Actions dictate the consequences: Workplace incivility, knowledge hiding, and psychological entitlement. *Journal of Business and Social Review in Emerging Economies*, *8*(1), 25–38.

Zhao, H., & Xia, Q. (2017). An examination of the curvilinear relationship between workplace ostracism and knowledge hoarding. *Management Decision*, *55*(2), 331–346.

Chapter 5

Quest for Student Engagement and Loyalty From a Private Higher Education Perspective

Konalingam Kajenthiran, Mahadevan Karunanithy and Sivarajah Rajumesh

University of Jaffna, Sri Lanka

Abstract

This research examines how service quality influences student loyalty within higher education and scrutinizes its impact by assessing student satisfaction and engagement. The study consists of valid data from 346 students from private higher education institutions. The data were analyzed utilizing PLS-SEM to assess the proposed framework and test hypotheses. A positive relationship exists between service quality and student loyalty. Student satisfaction and engagement significantly mediate this relationship, demonstrating their indirect influence on loyalty. These findings provide valuable insights for higher education institutions, particularly private ones. By enhancing service quality, institutions can foster student satisfaction, engagement and loyalty, leading to stronger student relationships and improved marketing strategies.

Keywords: Student loyalty; service quality; student satisfaction; student engagement; private higher education; mediating effect

Introduction

Higher education institutions employ fundamental marketing techniques for generating and retaining loyalty among students. This, in turn, encourages institutions to create ongoing, mutually beneficial connections with their current and prospective students (Amegbe et al., 2019). The education sector, specifically higher education, directly impacts socio-economic growth and development more than all other service sectors (Annamdevula & Bellamkonda, 2016).

Shaping Entrepreneurial Marketing, Volume 1, 65–83

Published under exclusive licence by Emerald Publishing Limited
doi:10.1108/978-1-83708-852-220251005

Authorities in higher education should assess the effectiveness of their academic programs to ensure a high level of student service and experience and implement a service culture in the environment. Many studies over the last few decades have focused on the calibre of services provided by institutions of higher learning (Najimdeen et al., 2021). Further, the educational sector is gradually evolving into a more dynamic one, with several options available to prospective students looking to further their studies (Chandra et al., 2019).

Accommodating students' expectations has become more critical for today's universities (Alvarez-Risco et al., 2021). Therefore, private universities need to figure out how to get new students in and retain the ones they already have. This aspect is paramount in determining their overall success in the educational landscape (Muzammil et al., 2020). Reeve et al. (2020) argue that if educational establishments can provide solutions to their student's needs, it will lead to increased student engagement, a continuation of studies, favourable word of mouth about the organization and ultimately, increased student loyalty. The existing literature does not provide comprehensive research on the correlation between service quality and customer loyalty (Chandra et al., 2019). Although a clear cause-and-effect connection between service quality and student loyalty to educational institutions is plausible, it has been claimed that this relationship is unlikely to hold up under closer examination (Keshavarz & Jamshidi, 2018).

Amidst higher education's dynamic and competitive landscape, securing student loyalty has become a crucial differentiator for institutions (Paposa & Paposa, 2022). While student satisfaction and engagement are widely acknowledged as key drivers of competitive advantage (Santos et al., 2020). Our understanding of their interplay with service quality remains incomplete – existing research, though exploring various facets of this relationship, leaves several critical gaps. Firstly, studies investigating the direct link between service quality and student loyalty in private higher education are limited. Secondly, existing evidence regarding this connection is often inconclusive, with inconsistencies and nuances demanding further examination. Finally, the potential mediating role of factors like student satisfaction and engagement within this relationship has received insufficient attention.

In response to these gaps, this study has adopted a comprehensive approach. A comprehensive analysis of the entire model meticulously examines the direct and indirect impacts of service quality on student loyalty. The investigation considers the critical mediating roles of student satisfaction and engagement, offering a nuanced understanding of their interaction. Furthermore, the study is situated within the context of private higher education institutions in Jaffna district, Sri Lanka, enabling valuable insights to be gained from a potentially understudied setting.

An Examination of the Literature and the Formulation of Hypotheses

Service Quality

The text discusses the 'Service Quality' (SERVQUAL) framework introduced by Parasuraman, Zeithaml and Berry in 1985, widely used in various service contexts. Despite criticism and debates about its unity, SERVQUAL is recognized as a diverse and systematic framework applied in different service industries, including education. Over the last 30 years, service quality has gained significance in international business due to widespread adoption by academics and corporate professionals (Chandra et al., 2019). The framework includes precursors such as 'Tangibility,' focusing on resources and staff appearance. Moreover, 'Assurance' pertains to workers' abilities, politeness and the establishment of trust. Reliability, responsiveness and empathy are critical components in evaluating a firm's service quality, consistency in delivering advertised services, readiness to assist customers and the level of care and attention provided to individual customers, respectively (Sugiarto & Octaviana, 2021).

Service Quality and Student Loyalty

Over the years, several scholars have refined the theoretical foundation connecting the perceived quality of service and the loyalty of customers (Özkan et al., 2020). Nevertheless, few are in the independent college and university sector (Borishade et al., 2021; El Ahmad & Kawtharani, 2021). Another study highlights the importance of service quality in building and sustaining a faithful clientele. The quality of the services students are loyal to affects the higher education sector. It is widely believed that improving the quality of services offered may encourage students to remain loyal to their schools (Chandra et al., 2019). Making useful academic programs that foster and build long-term bonds enhances students' loyalty (Annamdevula & Bellamkonda, 2016). Students who show loyalty to their teachers tend to be engaged in their studies, exhibit high standards of citizenship behaviour and achieve academic success (Sökmen, 2021). When students like their time at institutions, they are more inclined to tell their peers about it and spread goodwill (Ali et al., 2021). The preceding logic allows us to postulate that:

H1. Service quality positively affects student loyalty.

Service Quality and Student Satisfaction

The ability of higher education institutions to maintain their students' satisfaction may be attributed, in part, to the quality of the services they provide. Customers' level of satisfaction may be gauged by contrasting the actual advantages they have received from service with their expectations of those benefits (Parasuraman et al., 1985). In several studies, researchers found that high-achieving students' satisfaction levels were impacted by the quality of the services they received (Chaudhary & Dey, 2021), and researchers have consistently demonstrated a substantial correlation between service quality and student satisfaction (Singh & Jasial, 2021). We propose the following hypothesis:

H2. Service quality positively affects student satisfaction.

Student Satisfaction and Student Engagement

Earlier research indicates a positive correlation between high consumer involvement and elevated customer satisfaction, suggesting that customer satisfaction precedes active participation, with satisfied consumers often becoming more engaged with the purchased goods or services (Eslami et al., 2022). When consumers have a positive experience with a company's offering, they are more likely to promote it to others actively (Abror et al., 2020). High-engagement children succeed academically (Klinkenberg et al., 2023), exhibit good citizenship (Emirie & Gebremeskel, 2022), are involved in the service delivery method and engage well with others in the classroom and the faculty (Thakur, 2019). What follows is a working hypothesis derived from the preceding discussion:

H3. Student satisfaction positively affects student engagement.

Student Satisfaction and Student Loyalty

The proliferation of domestic and international universities has increased, raising the value placed on students' loyalty to their alma mater. The likelihood of an individual remaining with an offer is significantly influenced by their level of satisfaction with a product or service (Upamannyu et al., 2021). If consumers are pleased with what they purchase and utilize, they will continue to do so long-term (Keshavarz & Jamshidi, 2018). Several research projects in various business contexts have confirmed the favourable correlation between customer satisfaction and loyalty (Kataria & Saini, 2020; Khan et al., 2022). Relationships between student satisfaction and loyalty were established in university research (Kaushal & Ali, 2020; Latif et al., 2021). The following hypothesis will thus demonstrate the connection between student satisfaction and loyalty towards the institution.

H4. Student satisfaction positively affects student loyalty.

Student Engagement and Student Loyalty

Research has shown that student engagement and loyalty are positively related (Snijders et al., 2020). Several studies have indicated that a heightened interest in market offerings correlates with an increased inclination towards purchasing (Ghali-Zinoubi & Toukabri, 2019). 'Customer engagement' describes an approach to analyzing client actions beyond simple purchases and passive browsing (Monferrer et al., 2019). It entails establishing an emotional and rational connection between a customer and a product or service (Ng et al., 2020). In addition, high-intent buyers consistently exhibit the most devoted brand loyalty (Abror et al., 2020). Considering these factors, the following hypothesis was formulated:

H5. Student engagement positively affects student loyalty.

Service Quality, Student Satisfaction and Student Loyalty

Higher education institutions primarily focus on students (Findler et al., 2019), aiming to provide them with a high-quality education by balancing the demands of instruction with those of the institution's physical and social settings (Shin & Hickey, 2021). Based on the findings from a literature review examining the association between service quality and customer loyalty, it is concluded that service quality alone does not influence loyalty (Annamdevula & Bellamkonda, 2016). Besides, Boonlertvanich (2019) argues that service quality may not influence customer loyalty alone. Loyalty is more likely to be retained by customers who experience exceptional service (Tzavlopoulos et al., 2019). Specifically, a hypothesis to probe this intermediary connection has been drawn as follows:

H6. Student satisfaction mediates the link between service quality and student loyalty.

Student Satisfaction, Student Engagement and Student Loyalty

There are many ongoing discussions at the university level about the meaning of 'student engagement' and its relevance to improving educational outcomes. Customer experience throughout the service delivery mechanism is seen as a precursor to the customer's subsequent engagement with the service (Monferrer et al., 2019). The connection between customer satisfaction and loyalty can be influenced by the extent of student engagement (Annamdevula & Bellamkonda, 2016; Harimurti & Suryani, 2019). Students are more likely to stay committed to an institution if they are pleased with the education they are receiving (Abror et al., 2020). Therefore, student involvement mediates the connection between service quality and student loyalty. As a result, here is what we suggest:

H7. Student engagement mediates the link between student satisfaction and student loyalty.

Conceptual Framework

Fig. 5.1 shows the proposed conceptual framework based on the literature above and prior assumptions.

Research Methods

Data for the study was gathered by having respondents complete a questionnaire independently. Prior research had validated the scales used to assess the study components. Five dimensions, Tangibility, Assurance, Reliability, Responsiveness and Empathy, were tested using 05, 06, 05, 06 and 04 items, respectively. These 26 questions were used to measure the quality of services among private institutions of higher learning (Annamdevula & Bellamkonda, 2016; Parasuraman et al., 1985).

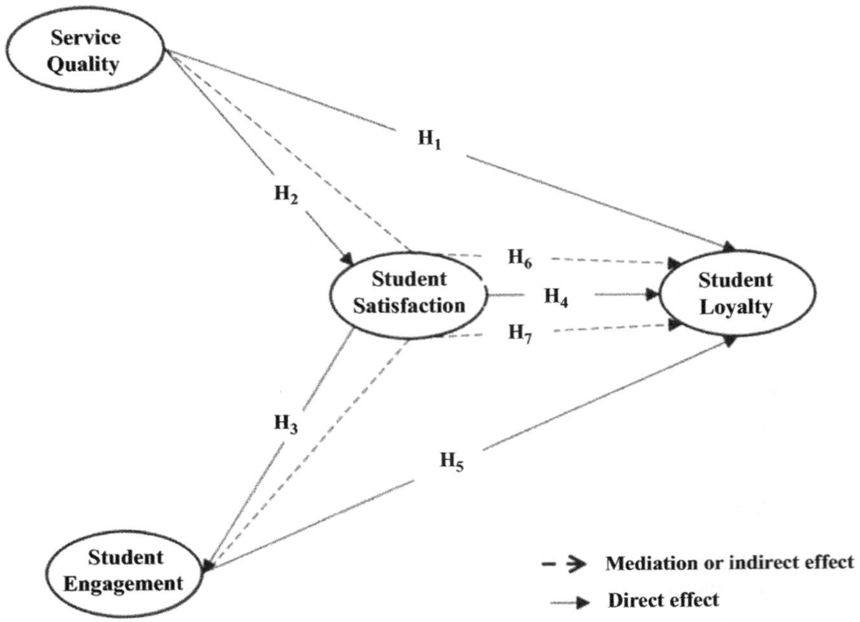

Fig. 5.1. Conceptual Framework. *Source:* Author's own.

Three measures assessing student satisfaction and four scales (04) for assessing student loyalty were taken from Annamdevula and Bellamkonda (2016), while student engagement was operationalized with a five-item scale (05) derived from Abror et al. (2020) and Carini et al. (2006). Except for student demographics, all questions assessing research components were operationalized using a Likert scale with five preferences (where '1' indicates strongly disagree and '5' strongly agree).

The respondents' native language was Tamil; thus, an English survey translation was made. A pilot study involving 35 Faculty of Management Studies and Commerce students at the University of Jaffna was conducted before the primary survey was administered. The survey instrument underwent minor tweaks as a result of the pilot test. Four hundred responses were received from students in this research, 346 of which were chosen for analysis. These students attended either New College of High Studies Jaffna or Jaffna College Undergraduate Department, two outstanding privately owned higher education institutions in Jaffna. In addition, the poll was conducted before the COVID-19 epidemic (from July 2019 to August 2019). Therefore, the analysis ignored the effect that COVID-19 would have on private institutions.

Most of the 346 legitimate responses (54.9%) came from women, while men (45.1%) comprised the rest. Statistics suggest that 29.2% of the sample population falls within the age bracket of 22–24 years. The age demographic of the rest of the respondents is as follows: 28.3% of the population is under the age of 19, 24.6%

between the ages of 25 and 27, 6.6% between the ages of 28 and 30, 6.1% between the ages of 18 and 19 and 5.2% were over the age of 30. Regarding communities, 88.4% of respondents identify as Tamil and 11.6% identify as Muslim. The data also show that 60.4% are enrolled in bachelor's degree programs elsewhere and 39.6% are doing professional coursework. Further, 73.3% of respondents are Tamil speakers, while 27.7% are English speakers.

Results and Findings

PLS, a variance-based SEM method, was employed to evaluate the research hypotheses. SmartPLS 3.0 was used to carry out the PLS analysis for this study. The measurement model and the structural model of the PLS model underwent two independent iterations. Table 5.1 summarizes the findings from evaluating first-order components using the reflective measurement model. Factor loadings for every item used to assess the study's constructs were far more significant than

Table 5.1. The Measurement Model in Summary.

Construct	Statement	FL
Tangibility AVE (0.540), CR (0.853), α = 0.791	Lecturers always come with a smart dress.	0.703
	Arrangements in the classrooms are always good.	0.827
	Lighting arrangements are enough.	0.810
	I like the building structure and setups.	0.695
	The classroom/surroundings are clean and comfortable.	0.620
Assurance AVE (0.605), CR (0.902), α = 0.869	Lecturers are friendly and courteous.	0.803
	Research efficiency/productivity of the lecturers is good.	0.735
	The academic credentials of the lecturers are good.	0.707
	Lecturers are innovative agents of change.	0.787
	Staff are aware of rules and regulations.	0.849
	Communication skills: Courses are well taught in this institution.	0.778
Reliability AVE (0.691), CR (0.918), α = 0.888	The institution keeps its records accurately.	0.807
	The staff shows sincere involvement in solving student problems.	0.847
	This institution meets its promises in service-providing.	0.798

(Continued)

Table 5.1. *(Continued)*

Construct	Statement	FL
	Dependable teaching capability/proficiency of lecturers.	0.857
	Lecturers show their concern in solving student problems.	0.847
Responsiveness AVE (0.574), CR (0.890), $\alpha = 0.852$	Staff are available when you need help, if any.	0.748
	Lecturers are available to clear your doubts.	0.742
	Lecturers are knowledgeable in solving student problems.	0.784
	Staff show interest in solving student problems.	0.788
	Students can raise their problems at any time.	0.754
	Queries are dealt with efficiently and promptly.	0.728
Empathy AVE (0.573), CR (0.841), $\alpha = 0.753$	The administration has students' best interests as a priority.	0.704
	Staff are willing to give students individual attention.	0.631
	The institution is fair and unbiased in the treatment of individual student.	0.838
	Lecturers are sympathetic and supportive of the needs of students.	0.836
Student satisfaction AVE (0.829), CR (0.936), $\alpha = 0.897$	I think I did the right thing when I chose to study at this institution.	0.888
	My choice to enrol in this institution is a wise one.	0.907
	I am happy about my decision to enrol in this institution.	0.937
Student engagement AVE (0.774), CR (0.945), $\alpha = 0.929$	I intend to stay on as a student of this institution.	0.853
	I want to help other students with their questions.	0.873
	I want to help the institution to improve its service.	0.869
	I wish to maintain good relationships with people at my institution.	0.920

Table 5.1. *(Continued)*

Construct	Statement	FL
	I wish to active participation and collaborative learning.	0.882
Student loyalty AVE (0.728), CR (0.914), α = 0.876	I feel proud to study at this institution.	0.893
	I care about the university.	0.888
	I would continue at the same institution if I wanted to start a new course.	0.840
	I will recommend this institution to my friends and family.	0.787

Source: Authors' own.

0.5 (Hair et al., 2010). Hence, none of them were eliminated from the final analysis. Further demonstrating convergent validity and construct reliability, the AVE value and composite reliability are more significant than the corresponding minimum threshold of 0.5 and 0.7 (Hair et al., 2013).

The findings in Table 5.2 further demonstrate that the square root of the AVE value of the research constructs is higher than the correlation with other variables. This shows that the constructs can be used to differentiate one variable from another (Fornell & Larcker, 1981). Also, the estimated values of the construct-to-construct correlations in the heterotrait-monotrait ratio of correlations (HTMT) analysis are much lower than 0.9. (Hair et al., 2013).

Consequently, the indications for individual constructs are checked to ensure they do not have a strong relationship with other constructs. The researchers confirm that the higher-order construct (Service Quality) was valid throughout validating the measurement model by comparing it to different first-order constructs. Table 5.2 illustrates the outcomes of these comparisons. Table 5.3 summarizes the indicators for construct reliability and convergent validity of higher-order constructs, both of which meet the threshold value.

Hypothesis Testing

In the final phase of the investigation, we employed a SmartPLS structural equation modelling approach for hypothesis testing. This method highlights the structural model by providing all the model requirements that were met. The results indicate that all constructs in this research exhibited VIF values less than the cut-off value of 5, showing no multicollinearity. Fig. 5.2 displays the structural model's R^2 and Q^2 values, standardized coefficients and corresponding *p*-values. It shows that the proportion of variation in students' allegiances that can be accounted for by controlling for other factors is 53.1% (adjusted $R^2 = 0.526$). The endogenous latent variables are classified as substantial (0.67), moderate (0.33) or weak (0.19) (Chin et al., 2003) to guarantee the model's validity. The suggested

Table 5.2. Fornell & Larcker Criterion Analysis and HTMT Statistics for Checking Discriminant Validity.

	ASS	EMP	SEN	SLT	REL	RES	SAT	TAN
ASS	0.778[a]							
EMP	0.600**(***0.710***)	0.757[a]						
SEN	0.040** (***0.051***)	0.024** (***0.058***)	0.880[a]					
SLT	0.068** (***0.089***)	0.025** (***0.061***)	−0.020**(***0.041***)	0.853[a]				
REL	0.754**(***0.846***)	0.649**(***0.776***)	0.008**(***0.047***)	0.055**(***0.082***)	0.831[a]			
RES	0.759**(***0.874***)	0.631**(***0.779***)	0.013**(***0.056***)	0.093**(***0.106***)	0.742**(***0.853***)	0.758[a]		
SAT	0.626**(***0.698***)	0.521**(***0.611***)	0.039**(***0.041***)	0.018**(***0.050***)	0.573**(***0.638***)	0.583**(***0.663***)	0.911[a]	
TAN	0.606**(***0.687***)	0.420**(***0.520***)	−0.060**(***0.082***)	−0.052**(***0.103***)	0.533**(***0.595***)	0.441**(***0.526***)	0.427**(***0.474***)	0.735[a]

Source: Authors' own.

Note: ASS, Assurance; EMP, Empathy; REL, Reliability; RES, Responsiveness; SAT, Student Satisfaction; SEN, Student Engagement; SLT, Student Loyalty; TAN, Tangibility.

Bold and italics represent the HTMT statistics.

**Correlation is significant at $p < 0.01$.

[a]Diagonal value indicates the square root of AVE of the individual latent construct.

Table 5.3. Construct Reliability and Convergent Validity of Higher-Order Constructs.

	Cronbach's Alpha	**Composite Reliability**	**Average Variance Extracted (AVE)**
Service quality (SQL)	0.896	0.924	0.710

Source: Authors' own.

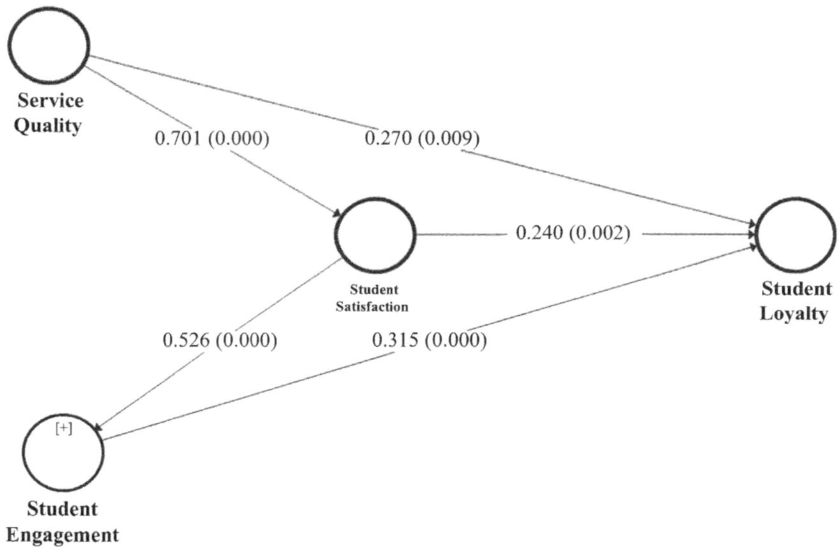

Fig. 5.2. Structural Model. *Source:* Authors' own.

model provides enough explanatory power on student loyalty if this variation is well explained.

In addition to R^2, the predictive sample reuse technique (Q^2) is an adequate criterion for assessing predictive relevance (Akter et al., 2011; Chin, 2010). According to Fornell and Cha (1993), the value of Q^2 should be greater than 0 for a model to be relevant. The findings indicate that the Q^2 scores for student satisfaction, engagement and loyalty are, sequentially, 0.395, 0.07 and 0.142, all above 0, suggesting satisfactory predictive relevance. According to Wong (2013), when endogenous variables are predicted by multiple predicting/exogenous variables, the researcher(s) should determine the model's effect size (f^2). Cohen (1988) mentioned that 'a f2 value of 0.02 shows a small effect, 0.15 shows a medium effect, and 0.35 shows a large effect.' In this research, the scores are as follows: service quality (f^2 = 0.044), student satisfaction (f^2 = 0.063) and student engagement (f^2 = 0.085).

Table 5.4. Fornell–Larcker Criterion Analysis and HTMT Statistics for Checking Discriminant Validity.

	SAT	SEN	SLT	SQL
SAT	0.916[a]			
SEN	0.526 ***(0.387)***	0.883[a]		
SLT	0.595 ***(0.671)***	0.65 ***(0.447)***	0.862[a]	
SQL	0.701 ***(0.782)***	0.773 ***(0.588)***	0.682 ***(0.712)***	0.843[a]

Source: Authors' own.

Note: RES = Responsiveness, SAT = Student Satisfaction, SEN = Student Engagement, SLT = Student Loyalty, SQL = Service Quality, TAN = Tangibility.

Bold and italics represent the HTMT statistics.

[a]Diagonal value indicates the square root of AVE of the individual latent construct.

Please refer Table 5.4 for the Fornell–Larcker criterion analysis and HTMT statistics for checking discriminant validity.

Table 5.5 shows the structural estimates which support the anticipated link. Student loyalty was found to be strongly influenced by service quality ($\beta = 0.270$, $t = 2.618$, $p = 0.012$). There is a statistically significant relationship between service quality and student satisfaction ($\beta = 0.701$, $t = 14.347$, $p = 0.000$). Satisfied students make a difference in how involved they are in class ($\beta = 0.526$, $t = 8.662$, $p = 0.000$). The correlation between student satisfaction and retention is substantial ($\beta = 0.240$, $t = 3.05$, $p = 0.003$). A substantial positive relationship

Table 5.5. Structural Estimates (Hypothesis Testing).

Path	**Beta Value (β)**	***T*-Statistics**	**Decision**
H1: Service quality → student loyalty	0.270**	2.618	Supported
H2: Service quality → student satisfaction	0.701**	14.347	Supported
H3: Student satisfaction → student engagement	0.526**	8.662	Supported
H4: Student satisfaction → student loyalty	0.240**	3.04	Supported
H5: Student engagement → student loyalty	0.315**	3.862	Supported
H6: Service quality → student satisfaction → student loyalty	0.168**	2.918	Supported
H7: Student satisfaction → student engagement → student loyalty	0.165**	3.510	Supported

Source: Authors' own.

Note: ** significant at $p < 0.01$.

exists between student involvement and loyalty ($\beta = 0.315$, $t = 3.862$, $p = 0.000$). We conclude that the evidence strongly supports all five of our research hypotheses (H1–H5).

The mediatory function of (1) student satisfaction between service quality and student loyalty and (2) student engagement between student satisfaction and student loyalty was also analyzed using mediational analysis. The results reveal that service quality's direct and indirect effects on student loyalty are statistically significant ($\beta = 0.168$, $t = 2.918$, $p = 0.003$). As a result, hypothesis H6 was also confirmed: a positive student experience may increase a school's reputation and boost loyalty among former students. In addition, the direct paths between student satisfaction and student loyalty were confirmed to be significant, and the indirect effect (mediation effect) between student satisfaction and student loyalty was found to be positive and statistically significant ($\beta = 0.165$, $t = 3.51$, $p = 0.001$). This finding lends credence to the notion that student engagement plays a role in mediating the relationship between student satisfaction and student loyalty, supporting H7.

Discussion

This paper aimed to empirically investigate the relationship between service quality and loyalty among students in private higher education institutions. The standard practice is to use student satisfaction as a proxy for service quality in gauging loyalty. Engagement was defined as a proxy for student satisfaction to examine its potential impact on retention. Many studies have examined the correlation between service quality and student loyalty. (Annamdevula & Bellamkonda, 2016; Chandra et al., 2019; El Ahmad & Kawtharani, 2021; Keshavarz & Jamshidi, 2018). However, few studies have explored the specific context of private higher education or examined the mediating role of student engagement. The present study aligns with recent calls for further exploration of this relationship (Innab & Alqahtani, 2023; Khan & Hemsley-Brown, 2021). Thus, the research established a link between service quality, student satisfaction, student involvement and student loyalty.

There is a need for private universities to understand better how to draw in new students and retain the ones they already have. If private universities want to stay competitive, they may need to focus first on ensuring their students are satisfied and actively participating in their studies. Confirming earlier studies like Latif et al. (2021), our findings underscore the crucial role of student satisfaction in fostering loyalty. Building on this, we demonstrated that engagement further strengthens this relationship. Furthermore, suppose educational institutions are successful in engaging their students. In that case, they may increase the number of satisfied students, motivate the never-ending learning process and increase positive word of mouth about the institution, ultimately improving student loyalty and attracting more potential pupils.

From a theoretical perspective, many concepts in the higher education service quality model work together to foster student loyalty. Furthermore, our findings resonate with recent calls for studying student engagement as a crucial factor in building loyalty in higher education. (Bowden et al., 2021), expanding the existing service quality model within this context. This research expands our knowledge by examining student involvement as a moderator in private higher education. The current study also offers a thorough conceptual framework detailing how service quality leads to student satisfaction and engagement, which further leads to student loyalty.

Conclusion and Implications

This study delved into the complex interconnections between service quality, student satisfaction, student engagement and student loyalty within private higher education institutions. The comprehensive model employed and its meticulous analysis yielded robust evidence for both direct and indirect effects of service quality on loyalty. Notably, student satisfaction and engagement emerged as crucial mediating factors, illustrating their significant contributions to fostering long-lasting commitment and positive word of mouth among private university students.

These findings resonate with substantial theoretical and practical implications for private higher education institutions. From a theoretical standpoint, our research expands the conceptual understanding of service quality in the context of higher educational institutions by demonstrating the mediating roles of student satisfaction and engagement in the student loyalty relationship. It bolsters the case for studying student engagement as a vital factor in building loyalty within the competitive landscape of private education. The proposed comprehensive model also offers a valuable framework for future research on student loyalty in diverse educational settings.

From a practical standpoint, universities can leverage these findings to prioritize service quality enhancements that directly foster student satisfaction and engagement, ultimately leading to greater student loyalty. By investing in strategies involving students in the learning process, curriculum development and feedback mechanisms, institutions can significantly boost engagement and satisfaction, thereby contributing to loyalty and retention. Understanding students' specific needs and expectations within the private higher education context is paramount for tailoring service quality initiatives and marketing strategies to maximize their impact on student loyalty.

Private higher education institutions seeking loyal students must prioritize holistic service quality while actively engaging students in learning and feedback. Engaging stakeholders, from academic staff offering responsive support to administrators streamlining processes, is crucial. Adequate marketing highlighting student satisfaction and tailored support will further solidify loyalty, ensuring long-term success in a competitive landscape.

Limitations and Future Directions

While this study successfully examined the interplay between service quality, satisfaction, engagement and loyalty in Jaffna's private universities, its limitations demand further exploration. Adapting existing scales and relying solely on self-reported data could introduce bias, and the pre-pandemic timeframe overlooks the impact of COVID-19. Replicating the study with broader samples and context-specific tools while incorporating objective data and examining the pandemic's influence would strengthen generalizability and offer richer insights.

The future landscape of research in this domain presents exciting possibilities. The influence of specific service quality dimensions, like technology integration or administrative efficiency, on student satisfaction and engagement in rural, urban or international settings can provide valuable context-specific solutions. Additionally, investigating the role of cultural factors and individual student characteristics, such as learning styles or socio-economic background, as moderators in these relationships can offer a nuanced understanding of loyalty drivers. Finally, exploring the long-term consequences of student loyalty for private universities, encompassing student engagement and financial sustainability, holds immense practical value.

Acknowledgements

We would like to express our heartfelt gratitude to the editors and reviewers whose valuable suggestions and comments helped make this chapter publishable. We also extend our gratitude to the Team ICMR, Sabaragamuwa University of Sri Lanka, for all the support given throughout this process.

References

Abror, A., Patrisia, D., Engriani, Y., Evanita, S., Yasri, Y., & Dastgir, S. (2020). Service quality, religiosity, customer satisfaction, customer engagement, and Islamic bank's customer loyalty. *Journal of Islamic Marketing*, *11*(6), 1691–1705. https://doi.org/10.1108/JIMA-03-2019-0044

Akter, S., D'ambra, J., & Ray, P. (2011). *An evaluation of PLS-based complex models: the roles of power analysis, predictive relevance, and GoF index*. Paper presented at the *AMCIS 2011 Proceedings*.

Ali, M., Amir, H., & Ahmed, M. (2021). The role of university switching costs, perceived service quality, perceived university image, and student satisfaction in shaping student loyalty. *Journal of Marketing for Higher Education*, 1–22. https://doi.org/10.1080/08841241.2021.1975184

Alvarez-Risco, A., Del-Aguila-Arcentales, S., Rosen, M. A., García-Ibarra, V., Maycotte-Felkel, S., & Martínez-Toro, G. M. (2021). Expectations and interests of university students in COVID-19 times about sustainable development goals: Evidence from Colombia, Ecuador, Mexico, and Peru. *Sustainability*, *13*(6), 3306.

Amegbe, H., Hanu, C., & Mensah, F. (2019). Achieving service quality and student loyalty through intimacy and trust of university employees. *International Journal of Educational Management, 33*(2), 359–373. https://doi.org/10.1108/IJEM-09-2017-0251

Annamdevula, S., & Bellamkonda, R. S. (2016). The effects of service quality on student loyalty: The mediating role of student satisfaction. *Journal of Modelling in Management, 11*(2), 446–462. https://doi.org/10.1108/JM2-04-2014-0031

Boonlertvanich, K. (2019). Service quality, satisfaction, trust, and loyalty: The moderating role of main-bank and wealth status. *International Journal of Bank Marketing, 37*(1), 278–302. https://doi.org/10.1108/IJBM-02-2018-0021

Borishade, T. T., Ogunnaike, O. O., Salau, O., Motilewa, B. D., & Dirisu, J. I. (2021). Assessing the relationship among service quality, student satisfaction, and loyalty: The Nigerian higher education experience. *Heliyon, 7*(7), e07590. https://doi.org/10.1016/j.heliyon.2021.e07590

Bowden, J. L.-H., Tickle, L., & Naumann, K. (2021). The four pillars of tertiary student engagement and success: A holistic measurement approach. *Studies in Higher Education, 46*(6), 1207–1224. https://doi.org/10.1080/03075079.2019.1672647

Carini, R. M., Kuh, G. D., & Klein, S. P. (2006). Student engagement and student learning: Testing the linkages. *Research in Higher Education, 47*(1), 1–32. https://doi.org/10.1007/s11162-005-8150-9

Chandra, T., Hafni, L., Chandra, S., Purwati, A. A., & Chandra, J. (2019). The influence of service quality and university image on student satisfaction and student loyalty. *Benchmarking: An International Journal, 26*(5), 1533–1549. https://doi.org/10.1108/BIJ-07-2018-0212

Chaudhary, S., & Dey, A. K. (2021). Influence of student-perceived service quality on sustainability practices of university and student satisfaction. *Quality Assurance in Education, 29*(1), 29–40. https://doi.org/10.1108/QAE-10-2019-0107

Chin, W. W., Marcolin, B. L., & Newsted, P. R. (2003). A partial least squares latent variable modeling approach for measuring interaction effects: Results from a Monte Carlo simulation study and an electronic-mail emotion/adoption study. *Information Systems Research, 14*(2), 189–217. https://doi.org/10.1287/isre.14.2.189.16018

Chin, W. W. (2010). How to write up and report PLS analyses. In V. Esposito Vinzi, W. W. Chin, J. Henseler, & H. Wang (Eds.), *Handbook of partial least squares: Concepts, methods and applications* (pp. 655–690). Springer Berlin Heidelberg.

Cohen, J. (1988). *Statistical power analysis for the behavioural sciences* (2nd ed.). Erlbaum.

El Ahmad, A. H., & Kawtharani, A. M. (2021). Service quality and students' satisfaction in private Lebanese higher education institutions: The case of X university. *Journal of Higher Education Policy and Leadership Studies, 2*(3), 100–118. https://doi.org/10.52547/johepal.2.3.100

Emirie, T. B., & Gebremeskel, M. M. (2022). How do primary school teachers practice organisational citizenship behaviour in Amhara regional state, Ethiopia? The case of Bahir Dar city. *Education, 3–13*, 1–15. https://doi.org/10.1080/03004279.2022.2150064

Eslami, S. P., Ghasemaghaei, M., & Hassanein, K. (2022). Understanding consumer engagement in social media: The role of product lifecycle. *Decision Support Systems, 162*, 113707. https://doi.org/10.1016/j.dss.2021.113707

Findler, F., Schönherr, N., Lozano, R., Reider, D., & Martinuzzi, A. (2019). The impacts of higher education institutions on sustainable development. *International Journal of Sustainability in Higher Education*, *20*(1), 23–38. https://doi.org/10.1108/IJSHE-07-2017-0114

Fornell, C., & Cha, J. (1993). *Partial least squares (PLS)*. Unpublished working paper (p. 16). University of Michigan Business School.

Fornell, C., & Larcker, D. F. (1981). Structural equation models with unobservable variables and measurement error: Algebra and statistics. *Journal of Marketing Research*, *18*(3), 382–388. https://doi.org/10.1177/002224378101800313

Ghali-Zinoubi, Z., & Toukabri, M. (2019). The antecedents of the consumer purchase intention: Sensitivity to price and involvement in organic product: Moderating role of product regional identity. *Trends in Food Science & Technology*, *90*, 175–179. https://doi.org/10.1016/j.tifs.2019.02.028

Hair, Jr., J. F., Black, W. C., Babin, B. J., & Anderson, R. E. (2010). *Multivariate data analysis* (7th ed.). Prentice-Hall Publication.

Hair, Jr., J. F., Ringle, C. M., & Sarstedt, M. (2013). Partial least squares structural equation modelling: Rigorous applications, better results, and higher acceptance. *Long Range Planning*, *46*(1–2), 1–12. https://ssrn.com/abstract=2233795

Harimurti, R., & Suryani, T. (2019). The impact of total quality management on service quality, customer engagement, and customer loyalty in banking. *Jurnal Manajemen dan Kewirausahaan*, *21*(2), 95–103. https://doi.org/10.9744/jmk.21.2.95-103

Innab, A., & Alqahtani, N. (2023). The mediating role of E-learning motivation on the relationship between technology access and satisfaction with E-learning. *Nursing Open*, *10*(4), 2552–2559. https://doi.org/10.1002/nop2.1513

Kataria, S., & Saini, V. (2020). The mediating impact of customer satisfaction on brand equity and brand loyalty. *South Asian Journal of Business Studies*, *9*(1), 62–87. https://doi.org/10.1108/SAJBS-03-2019-0046

Kaushal, V., & Ali, N. (2020). University reputation, brand attachment, and brand personality as antecedents of student loyalty: A study in the higher education context. *Corporate Reputation Review*, *23*(4), 254–266. https://doi.org/10.1057/s41299-019-00084-y

Keshavarz, Y., & Jamshidi, D. (2018). Service quality evaluation and the mediating role of perceived value and customer satisfaction in customer loyalty. *International Journal of Tourism Cities*, *4*(2), 220–244. https://doi.org/10.1108/IJTC-09-2017-0044

Khan, J., & Hemsley-Brown, J. (2021). Student satisfaction: The role of expectations in mitigating the pain of paying fees. *Journal of Marketing for Higher Education*, 1–23. https://doi.org/10.1080/08841241.2021.1973646

Khan, R. U., Salamzadeh, Y., Iqbal, Q., & Yang, S. (2022). The impact of customer relationship management and company reputation on customer loyalty: The mediating role of customer satisfaction. *Journal of Relationship Marketing*, *21*(1), 1–26. https://doi.org/10.1080/15332667.2020.1840904

Klinkenberg, E. F., Versteeg, M., & Kappe, R. F. (2023). Engagement and emotional exhaustion among higher education students: A mixed-methods study of four student profiles. *Studies in Higher Education*, 1–15. https://doi.org/10.1080/03075079.2023.2281533

Latif, K. F., Bunce, L., & Ahmad, M. S. (2021). How can universities improve student loyalty? The roles of university social responsibility, service quality, and "customer" satisfaction and trust. *International Journal of Educational Management, 35*(4), 815–829. https://doi.org/10.1108/IJEM-11-2020-0524

Monferrer, D., Moliner, M. A., & Estrada, M. (2019). Increasing customer loyalty through customer engagement in the retail banking industry. *Spanish Journal of Marketing - ESIC, 23*(3), 461–484. https://doi.org/10.1108/SJME-07-2019-0042

Muzammil, M., Sutawijaya, A., & Harsasi, M. (2020). Investigating student satisfaction in online learning: The role of student interaction and engagement in distance learning university. *Turkish Online Journal of Distance Education, 21*, 88–96. https://doi.org/10.17718/tojde.770928

Najimdeen, A. H. A., Amzat, I. H., & Ali, H. B. M. (2021). The impact of service quality dimensions on students' satisfaction: A study of international students in Malaysian public universities. *IIUM Journal of Educational Studies, 9*(2), 89–108. https://doi.org/10.31436/ijes.v9i2.324

Ng, S. C., Sweeney, J. C., & Plewa, C. (2020). Customer engagement: A systematic review and future research priorities. *Australasian Marketing Journal, 28*(4), 235–252. https://doi.org/10.1016/j.ausmj.2020.05.004

Özkan, P., Süer, S., Keser, İ. K., & Kocakoç, İ. D. (2020). The effect of service quality and customer satisfaction on customer loyalty. *International Journal of Bank Marketing, 38*(2), 384–405. https://doi.org/10.1108/IJBM-03-2019-0096

Paposa, K. K., & Paposa, S. S. (2022). From brick to click classrooms: A paradigm shift during the pandemic—Identifying factors influencing service quality and learners' satisfaction in click classrooms. *Management and Labour Studies, 48*(2), 182–196. https://doi.org/10.1177/0258042X211066234

Parasuraman, A., Zeithaml, V. A., & Berry, L. L. (1985). A conceptual model of service quality and its implications for future research. *Journal of Marketing, 49*(4), 41–50. https://doi.org/10.1177/002224298504900403

Reeve, J., Cheon, S. H., & Jang, H. (2020). How and why students make academic progress: Reconceptualizing the student engagement construct to increase its explanatory power. *Contemporary Educational Psychology, 62*, 101899. https://doi.org/10.1016/j.cedpsych.2020.101899

Santos, G., Marques, C. S., Justino, E., & Mendes, L. (2020). Understanding social responsibility's influence on service quality and student satisfaction in higher education. *Journal of Cleaner Production, 256*, 120597. https://doi.org/10.1016/j.jclepro.2020.120597

Shin, M., & Hickey, K. (2021). Needs a little TLC: Examining college students' emergency remote teaching and learning experiences during COVID-19. *Journal of Further and Higher Education, 45*(7), 973–986. https://doi.org/10.1080/0309877X.2020.1847261

Singh, S., & Jasial, S. S. (2021). The moderating effect of perceived trust on service quality – Student satisfaction relationship: Evidence from Indian higher management education institutions. *Journal of Marketing for Higher Education, 31*(2), 280–304. https://doi.org/10.1080/08841241.2020.1825029

Snijders, I., Wijnia, L., Rikers, R. M. J. P., & Loyens, S. M. M. (2020). Building bridges in higher education: Student-faculty relationship quality, student engagement, and student loyalty. *International Journal of Educational Research, 100*, 101538. https://doi.org/10.1016/j.ijer.2020.101538

Sökmen, Y. (2021). The role of self-efficacy in the relationship between the learning environment and student engagement. *Educational Studies, 47*(1), 19–37. https://doi.org/10.1080/03055698.2019.1665986

Sugiarto, S., & Octaviana, V. (2021). Service quality (SERVQUAL) dimensions on customer satisfaction: Empirical evidence from bank study. *Golden Ratio of Marketing and Applied Psychology of Business, 1*(2), 93–106. https://doi.org/10.52970/grmapb.v1i2.103

Thakur, R. (2019). The moderating role of customer engagement experiences in customer satisfaction–loyalty relationship. *European Journal of Marketing, 53*(7), 1278–1310. https://doi.org/10.1108/EJM-11-2017-0895

Tzavlopoulos, I., Gotzamani, K., Andronikidis, A., & Vassiliadis, C. (2019). Determining the impact of e-commerce quality on customers' perceived risk, satisfaction, value, and loyalty. *International Journal of Quality and Service Sciences, 11*(4), 576–587. https://doi.org/10.1108/IJQSS-03-2019-0047

Upamannyu, N. K., Rajput, S., & Bhakar, S. S. (2021). Antecedents of customer loyalty and word of mouth: A study on consumer durables in emerging economies. *FIIB Business Review, 12*(4), 439–458. https://doi.org/10.1177/23197145211053398

Wong, K. K.-K. (2013). Partial least squares structural equation modelling (PLS-SEM) techniques using SmartPLS. *Marketing Bulletin, 24*(1), 1–32.

Chapter 6

The Moderating Effects of Transformational Leadership Behaviour and Firm Performance of SMEs in Sri Lanka

Sonali Diyamanthi Jayasooriya, Wanninayake Mudiyanselage Chandrarathne Bandara Wanninayake and Kaushalya Yatigammana

University of Kelaniya, Sri Lanka

Abstract

The fundamental goal of this research is to explore how transformational leadership (TL) influences the relationship between entrepreneurial orientation (EO) and the business performance of small and medium-sized enterprises (SMEs) in developing countries, with a specific emphasis on Sri Lanka. This study adopted a deductive-quantitative strategy and a cross-functional survey design. The sampling approach used was a simple random selection of SMEs registered in multiple databases in Sri Lanka. The survey consisted of 58 self-administered questions and received 150 valid responses from SME owner-managers, yielding a response rate of 37.5%. The results emphasize that EO and organizational success positively correlate with SMEs' leadership style. In addition, a strong and moderately positive relationship was found between EO and the financial performance of SMEs. This investigation enhances and validates the resource-based view (RBV) theory and the full-range leadership theory (FRLT) for managing SMEs. This study contributes to the existing scientific literature on small business management by examining the impact of EO and TL on the business performance of SMEs in developing markets, with a primary emphasis on Sri Lanka.

Shaping Entrepreneurial Marketing, Volume 1, 85–101

Published under exclusive licence by Emerald Publishing Limited
doi:10.1108/978-1-83708-852-220251006

Keywords: Entrepreneurial orientation (EO); transformational leadership (TL); small and medium enterprises (SMEs); firm performance; RBV theory

Introduction

In the dynamic and highly competitive industry environment, businesses must continuously seek new talent and opportunities to maintain their market position (Isichei et al., 2020; Nguyen et al., 2023). Covin and Miller (2014) said that firms that strive for exceptional performance should prioritize their internal behaviour, namely, entrepreneurial orientation (EO). EO refers to an organization's internal drive to ensure longevity through innovation, knowledge acquisition, originality, cultural transformation and dedication. Furthermore, it allows firms to enhance their competitive edge by utilizing internal and external resources (Isichei et al., 2020).

In developed and developing nations, small to medium-sized businesses (SMEs) are critical to creating wealth, jobs, entrepreneurship, innovation and advancing skills and technology (Chatterjee & Kumar Kar, 2020; Madushanka & Sachitra, 2021). There is a consensus that SMEs contribute substantially to countries' economic growth at various stages of development. However, SMEs in most developing economies encounter substantial challenges that hinder their growth and perpetuate their position at lower levels of development. These challenges include the inability to benefit from economies of scale, limited access to financial resources and infrastructure, reliance on outdated technology, deficiency of modern management and entrepreneurial skills, inadequate leadership qualities, scarcity of skilled labour, restricted access to market information and sociocultural factors (Diabate et al., 2019). This sector of the economy is particularly significant, especially during an economic downturn like the present. In emerging nations like Sri Lanka, almost 90% of all businesses fall under the category of SMEs. These companies represent 45% of the labour force and contribute 20% to the overall value generated by the industrial sector. In addition, they substantially influence the country's gross domestic product (GDP; Gunawardana, 2016; Wijetunge & Pushpakumari, 2014).

Despite the significant literature showing a strong association between EO and the success of SMEs in Sri Lanka, most studies have used the 1983 Miller scale to quantify EO (Fairoz et al., 2010; Wijetunge & Pushpakumari, 2014). There have been varied perspectives regarding the relevance of EO to SME performance. Certain scholars have observed significantly better results, while others have identified adverse effects, and some have discovered limited favourable connections. According to Isichei et al. (2020), leadership style is an internal factor that significantly enhances innovation and competitive advantage.

This study, too, highlights the significance of leadership, as innovation is a critical predictor of business growth and SME success. Many researchers suggest innovation is critical to improving organizational processes and leadership strategies (Rasheed et al., 2021). Hence, transformational leadership (TL) has a more significant effect than other leadership styles (Nguyen et al., 2023). The primary intent of this research is to explore the impact of TL styles on the relationship between EO and SME success and to fill existing gaps in knowledge in this subject area. This study provides insights into how SME leaders can effectively manage EO while achieving financial success through TL. This study intends to provide answers to the following questions:

- In the context of Sri Lankan SMEs, does TL have the potential to act as a moderating influence on the relationship between EO and company performance?
- What insights can be derived from these associations to guide strategies for improving the performance of SMEs in emerging countries such as Sri Lanka?

The suggested research and conceptual approaches significantly enhance current knowledge by including the TL style of top management as a moderating variable for SMEs in Sri Lanka. This study offers a comprehensive conceptual understanding of the correlation between employee ownership and positive company outcomes.

Theoretical Background and Hypothesis Development

Firms should maintain a competitive advantage using their valuable, scarce, unique and non-replaceable resources. The central concept is expressed in Barney's (1991) resource-based view (RBV) framework, which serves as the primary theoretical basis for this study. The economic success of SMEs is strongly dependent on their talents and competencies, which are crucial for developing performance and gaining a competitive advantage. Internal capabilities are essential components that enhance an organization's capacity to produce novel concepts, embrace risks and exhibit proactive behaviour. The primary differentiation is in Miller's (1983) three-dimensional framework and Lumpkin and Dess's (1996) concept, which incorporates two additional dimensions: competitive aggressiveness and autonomy. Avolio and Bass introduced the full-range leadership theory (FRLT) in 1991, considered a groundbreaking leadership approach (Bass et al., 2003). The FRLT constructs categorize leadership behaviour into three categories: transformational, transactional and non-transactional laissez-faire leadership. Each category is composed of nine distinct components. The Multifactor Leadership Questionnaire (MLQ) was the primary survey tool utilized to evaluate the nine components of the FRLT (Bass et al., 2003). Nguyen et al. (2023) suggest that transformational leaders are more likely to generate better results than the other two leadership styles.

Transformational Leadership

The behaviours and approaches to the decision-making of high-ranking managers and senior executives, recognized as intrapreneurs, substantially influence the firm's growth (Razavi & Ab Aziz, 2017). In order to enhance performance, corporates must groom executives who exhibit intrapreneurial attributes and leadership characteristics. TL is intrapreneurs' most appropriate leadership style

(Nguyen et al., 2023). Transformative leaders are recognized for their capacity to motivate team members to achieve objectives by identifying their opinions while considering their views and requirements, fostering mutual trust, incentivizing them to exceed expectations, and assisting them in pursuing and realizing an appealing vision (Klein, 2023). Burns (1978, cited in Arham et al., 2017) first identified the differences between transformative and transactional leadership. Leaders who use self-interest as a significant incentive are known as transactional leaders. Transformative leaders foster trust and confidence in their followers, inspiring them to collaborate to satisfy their higher-level self-actualization requirements rather than chasing self-centred ambitions (Boukamcha, 2019). Proactive transformational leaders elevate the awareness of their followers and support them in achieving exceptional goals.

The term 'transformational leadership' comprises five main elements. *Idealized influence* is the institutionalized charisma of leaders who are confident and strong and give greater importance to relatively high principles and ethics (Engelen et al., 2015). *Idealized influence (behaviour)* refers to leadership that inspires followers to have confidence in their capacity to accomplish set objectives. They serve as role models, emphasize ethics, exhibit pride among team members, and establish mutual trust. *Inspiring motivation* includes choosing an appealing, intriguing vision, motivating people to achieve it and inspiring them to go above and beyond what is anticipated. This pertains to how leaders motivate their followers by maintaining a positive outlook on the future, emphasizing ambitious objectives, presenting an idealized vision and attempting to reassure them that the vision is achievable (Antonakis et al., 2003). *Intellectual stimulation* refers to leadership that provides inspirational motivation; stimulates and encourages staff to rethink old problems and develop new solutions; welcomes unique methods of work; and promotes innovation, creativity and adaptability among their team members (Antonakis et al., 2003). The fourth aspect, *individualized consideration*, was addressed in this article. These leaders demonstrate concern for their employees' needs, delegate duties, provide resources based on their skills and concentrate on their professional growth. Other research has raised doubts about a firm's possible continuous concentration on EO. Appropriate organizational behaviour must be adequately matched to translate EO into benefits for firm performance (Engelen et al., 2015). EO gives firms guidance on taking advantage of emerging market opportunities, yet successful EO implementation calls for transformative leadership at the executive level.

H1. Transformational leadership significantly moderates the positive effect on the relationship between EO and business success in Sri Lanka.

Entrepreneurial Orientation

The term EO was initially proposed by Miller in 1983 and was later refined by Covin and Slevin (1989). At the organizational level, it has evolved into a sophisticated idea researched by people engaged in strategic management and entrepreneurship. EO includes a variety of factors, such as firm-level outcomes, managerial perspectives, overall company perspectives, responsiveness to consumer requests and requirements, product offerings and relationships with competitors (Covin & Slevin, 1989). EO is responsible for the survival of an organization while helping advance its culture. Covin and Slevin (1989) argue that to improve performance, organizations must take a more imaginative and proactive approach to strategic decision-making.

An organization that embraces an entrepreneurial mindset exhibits innovation through developing novel products and services. It also takes proactive steps to recognize and respond to changing consumer preferences, monitors and responds to competing actions, takes reasonable risks when exploring new endeavours and enables its employees to make sound decisions (Diabate et al., 2019). Putniņš and Sauka (2020) suggest that individual results and managerial preferences significantly impact a company's overall performance, product offerings, competitive interactions, risk-taking and management structure.

According to Covin and Miller (2014), the critical objective of EO is to help participants develop new internal traits. An organization can achieve this goal in various ways, including setting up new goods or ventures within or without and comprehensively reorganizing its operational and functional divisions. Miller (1983) emphasized two fundamental principles: creative thinking and willingness to take risks. Lumpkin and Dess (1996) further developed this concept by incorporating two additional dimensions: competitive assertiveness and autonomy. Furthermore, they urged enterprises to continue exploring market-related possibilities by actively participating in the open market. Moreover, businesses must grasp how to manage competitive market changes effectively and match consumer wants (Soomro & Shah, 2020).

H2. EO is favourably associated with the business success of SMEs in Sri Lanka.

H2a. The performance of SMEs in Sri Lanka is significantly related to the innovativeness of their entrepreneurial mindset.

H2b. The performance of SMEs in Sri Lanka is significantly related to their proactive entrepreneurial direction.

H2c. SMEs in Sri Lanka perform significantly better when they take risks and are entrepreneurial.

H2d. A direct relationship exists between the level of autonomy and its performance in small to medium-sized enterprises (SMEs) in Sri Lanka.

H2e. The performance of Sri Lankan SMEs has a positive relationship with EO's competitive aggressiveness.

The Impact of EO and TL on Firm Performance

Entrepreneurs offer unique ideas for their products or services, meaning EO positively and significantly impacts a firm's performance. They add new product features, review their packaging, improve current items and design distinctively and appealingly to distinguish their products from their business rivals. Consequently, firms' total sales may increase, improving their performance. According to Putniņš and Sauka (2020), developing new products and services contributes to transforming knowledge and ideas into more efficient business practices or improved goods and services that the community values.

Multiple research articles have outlined numerous approaches to assess the growth and performance of SMEs. Measuring the success and growth of SMEs must become increasingly complex, rigorous and hard. There are practical constraints to getting quality data since business owners have been less inclined to submit and share financial information. An empirical study assessed the growth of small businesses based on multiple factors, including market expansion, sales volume, market share increase, employment growth, profitability, staffing ratio, customer base and market share expansion. Lumpkin and Dess (1996) discovered that the association with EO differs based on the specific performance indicators used to evaluate the multifaceted notion of performance.

Most research studies include a range of performance indicators, distinguishing between financial and non-financial metrics. This study focuses on non-financial metrics. As indicated in Fig. 6.1, a study model was created to investigate the multidimensional links between small and medium-sized firms and

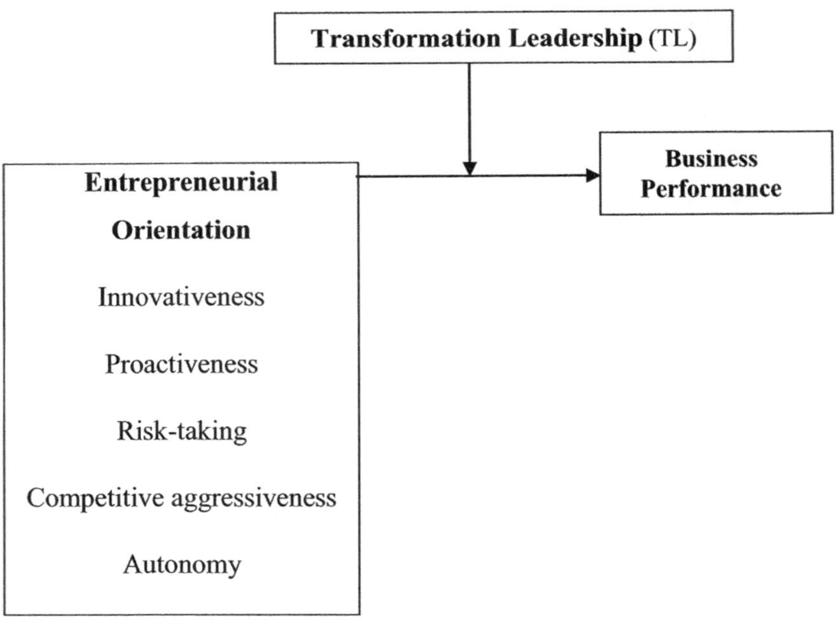

Fig. 6.1. Theoretical Framework – Entrepreneurial Orientation, Transformation Leadership and Firm Performance of SME.
Source: Authors' own.

their performance. This study treats EO and dimensions as independent variables, with performance measures as dependent variables. The literature analysis found that TL would elicit more entrepreneurial responses. Therefore, this study incorporated TL as a moderating variable (Deligianni et al., 2016; Fairoz et al., 2010).

The suggested model emphasizes key TL characteristics considered significant in the correlation between EO and SMEs' consistent and profitable operations. Prior research has demonstrated a clear and favourable correlation between TL and performance. This alliance is advantageous for TL. Nevertheless, only a few researchers have examined the correlation between EO and corporate success, considering TL a moderator. The central hypothesis has been derived from the conceptual framework proposed by Dionne et al. (2004), Matzler et al. (2012) and Yang (2008).

Prior research has demonstrated that EO is necessary to enhance a company's performance and competitive positioning. Empirical research has shown that firms with higher EO demonstrate superior performance and exhibit a more pronounced association with sales growth. Covin et al. (2006) found a high correlation between the EO of manufacturing enterprises and their sales growth. It can be compared to how individuals manage their businesses and achieve growth by seizing opportunities and implementing strategic changes (Dess & Lumpkin, 2005). The primary research inquiry outlined in the preceding paragraph forms the basis for the central hypothesis and its accompanying sub-hypotheses.

Methodology

The quantitative survey evaluated the impact of TL on SME performance by examining the specific EO aspect that contributed to their success. The data gathered from Sri Lankan SME entrepreneurs and senior executives across several sectors, such as manufacturing, service, packaging, information technology (IT), power and energy, retail, hotels, footwear and textiles, retail outlets and trading, were exceptionally comprehensive. The SMEs in this sample employed between 5 and 300 people. According to statistics from the Sri Lanka Chamber of Small and Medium Industries, the Export Development Board, the National Chamber of Exporters and the Sri Lanka Association for Software and Services Company, 400 SME businesses were chosen using a simple random selection method. The model was tested with IBM SPSS Statistics 23.

As of the data collection deadline, 160 questionnaires were collected manually, resulting in a response rate of 37.5%. Upon data analysis, 10 incomplete and biased questions were excluded. Data were processed utilizing SPSS 23v, and its reliability was assessed employing Cronbach's alpha, a measure of internal consistency. The components were evaluated using a standardized five-point Likert scale; the questionnaire was drafted in English. EO encompasses five key dimensions: innovation, risk-taking, proactivity, competition and fostering independent behaviour. The items were generated utilizing questionnaires outlined in prior research conducted by Covin and Slevin (1989) and Lumpkin and Dess (2001). Modifications were made to items based on the particular circumstances or settings of the study. Bass et al. (2003) created the MLQ to evaluate different leadership styles, such as transformative and passive leadership behaviours. The questionnaire consisted of 45 elements (Rowold, 2005). The MLQ evaluates transformative leadership. The previous study demonstrates that business performance is a multifaceted concept that may be assessed using financial and non-financial indicators. Due to the unwillingness of SMEs to reveal financial data, this study used subjective metrics to estimate profitability and growth. Firms' performance was evaluated using the multidimensional performance scale developed by Wiklund and Shepherd (2005). The items were evaluated using a five-point scale, where one represented 'strongly disagree' and five represented 'strongly agree.'

Data Analysis and the Results

According to frequent research, 62% of businesses are in the manufacturing sector, 20% are in IT and BPO, 8.67% are in sales and marketing, 8.00% are in service and 1.33% are in retail. After completing market research, it was discovered that half of the enterprises operate in domestic and export markets. At the same time, 36% of SMEs predominantly focus on the local market. The remaining 14% only target the export market. This study specifically targeted the SMEs that meet the criterion regarding workforce size. Of the total, 62.7% of companies had a workforce size ranging from 101 to 150 employees. Twelve percent of companies had 5–10 employees, 11.33% had 51–100 employees and 8.67% had 11–50 employees. The rest of the companies had more than 150 employees. Upon analyzing the demographic information of the owners and managers, it was found that 92% of the respondents were male, while 8% were female. Age-wise, 22% of the participants belonged to the age bracket of 41–45, 15.33% were within the age range of 46–50, 14% fell into the age group of 36–40 and 6.67% were in the age category of 31–35. A majority of respondents (42%) were aged 51 or older. Although a minority of owner-managers (19.33%) did not, the majority (80.67%) had received prior training before joining the current business.

Descriptive Results

Cronbach's alpha is a statistical metric used to assess the internal consistency and reliability of a set of items on a scale. After a review, the alpha value of each variable exceeded 0.7, as indicated in Table 6.1.

The Effects of Each EO Element on the Performance of the Company

The Pearson correlation coefficient quantifies the degree of linear correlation between two variables. The Pearson correlation matrix is shown in Table 6.2. The

Table 6.1. Internal Consistency of the Model Variable.

Model Variables	Cronbach's Alpha Values	*N* Items
Innovativeness	0.754	4
Proactiveness	0.783	4
Risk-taking	0.705	5
Competitive aggressiveness	0.757	4
Autonomy	0.797	6
Idealized influence	0.861	5
Inspirational motivation	0.865	4
Intellectual stimulation	0.823	4
Individualized consideration	0.825	4
Growth	0.907	5
Performance	0.897	4

Source: Authors' own.

values marked with ** signify a significance level lower than 0.01, as stated in the correlation matrix output. The absolute values vary from 0.3 to 0.7. All values exhibiting moderate correlations are statistically significant at $p < 0.001$, indicating a positive relationship between all elements in the EO model and the business's overall success.

Multiple linear regression was used to analyze the impact of each EO construct on SMEs' performance. The study produced a multiple regression equation with an F statistic of 16.174, degrees of freedom (5, 144) and a significance level of 0.01. The R-squared value was calculated to be 0.360. The formula for calculating the performance of SMEs is as follows: 0.886 plus 0.083 multiplied by RST, 0.235 multiplied by PRA, 0.343 multiplied by COA, 0.104 multiplied by INV and 0.002 multiplied by AUT the performance of SMEs can be calculated using the following formula: 0.886 + 0.083 multiplied by RST + 0.235 * PRA + 0.343 * COA + 0.104 *INV + 0.002 * AUT. Each aspect of EO, which encompasses innovativeness, proactivity, risk-taking, competitive aggressiveness and autonomy, was determined to be a predictor of the commercial success of SMEs.

Overall Effects of EO on Firm Performance

The total impact of EO on business performance was evaluated using multiple linear regression (Table 6.3) – the value calculated by assessing SMEs' performance in all market segments. The regression equation was discovered to have a significant level of importance, with an R^2 value of 0.334 (F (1, 148) = 74.102, p 0.01). The ultimate results can be calculated by adding 0.791–0.801 times the EO value. Table 6.4 indicates that the R^2 value is lower than the R^2 values of the multidimensional EO constructs.

Table 6.2. Correlation Matrix.

		AVG_ INV	AVG_ PRA	AVG_ RST	AVG_ COA	AVG_ AUT	Business Performance
AVG_INV	Pearson correlation	1					
	Sig. (2-tailed)						
AVG_PRA	Pearson correlation	**0.686****	1				
	Sig. (2-tailed)	**0.000**					
AVG_RST	Pearson correlation	**0.403****	**0.585****	1			
	Sig. (2-tailed)	**0.000**	**0.000**				
AVG_COA	Pearson correlation	**0.598****	**0.708****	**0.453****	1		
	Sig. (2-tailed)	**0.000**	**0.000**	**0.000**			
AVG_AUT	Pearson correlation	**0.482****	**0.625****	**0.535****	**0.601****	**1**	
	Sig. (2-tailed)	**0.000**	**0.000**	**0.000**	**0.000**		
Business-performance	Pearson correlation	**0.455****	**0.537****	**0.376****	**0.558****	**0.404****	**1**
	Sig. (2-tailed)	**0.000**	**0.000**	**0.000**	**0.000**	**0.000**	

Source: Authors' own.

Note: **Correlation is significant at the 0.01 level (2-tailed).

Table 6.3. Model Summary – Multiple Linear Regression.

Model	*R*	*R* Square	Adjusted *R* Square	Std. Error of the Estimate
1	0.600[a]	0.360	0.337	0.56331

Source: Authors' own.

[a]Predictors: (Constant), AVG_AUT, AVG_INV, AVG_RST, AVG_COA, AVG_PRA.

The Moderating Effect of TL

The correlation analysis in Table 6.4 shows that all measurement results fall within the allowed range of 0.3–0.7. All values show moderate relationships with total EO and are statistically significant at $p < 0.001$. All TL variables demonstrate a moderately favourable correlation between overall EO and business performance. The second model was employed to examine the moderating impact of TL. The original model employed an accurate regression equation ($F\,(1, 148) = 74.102$, $p < 0.01$) and an R^2 value of 0.334 to assess the impact of EO on corporate performance. After accounting for the mild variable, the regression equation produced a significant $F\,(4, 144) = 3.019$, with a p-value of less than 0.02. The p-value was found to be statistically significant at the 0.05 level. Upon introducing the TL as a moderator variable, the value of R^2 increased substantially from 0.334 to 0.385. Therefore, the influence of TL on the correlation between EO and the financial performance of Sri Lankan SMEs is apparent.

Discussion of the Findings

The fundamental purpose of this study was to assess how TL, as demonstrated by top managers, influences the success of SMEs in Sri Lanka. Prior research on organizational behaviour in Sri Lanka ignored this particular aspect of leadership. Furthermore, the study aimed to assess the effectiveness of five-factor EO measures in promoting SME success (Lumpkin & Dess, 2001). The investigation found that top managers' TL behaviour has a positive but minor impact on the association between EO and business performance. The introduction of the TL variable increased the correlation coefficient by 0.051. According to Table 6.4, Model 1 has an R^2 value of 0.334, indicating a relationship between EO and corporate performance. Adding TL to the EO link improved commercial success by 0.385. Several researchers have undertaken similar analyses in diverse circumstances, and their

Table 6.4. Model Summary – Overall Effects of EO on Firm Performance.

Model	*R*	*R* Square	Adjusted *R* Square	Std. Error of the Estimate
1	0.578[a]	0.334	0.329	0.56681

[a]Predictors: (Constant), Overall_EO.

conclusions are congruent with the current findings (Engelen et al., 2015). The findings from this study indicate that TL has a beneficial influence on the relationship between EO and corporate performance.

The results are consistent with previous studies, indicating a beneficial relationship between EO and SME growth. Forward-thinking SMEs adapt their offers and take calculated risks to capitalize on market opportunities. EO's impact on market share and sales growth demonstrates the favourable association between EO and growth. All five EO attributes (innovation, proactivity, risk-taking, competitive aggressiveness and autonomy) positively relate to SMEs' business outcomes. The findings from this study closely mirror those of Fairoz et al. (2010), which focused explicitly on SMEs in the Hambantota region in Sri Lanka. As previously indicated, the amount of EO influences the success of SMEs. Furthermore, it has been discovered that the owner-manager's innovativeness influences the level of EO. According to the article, the firm's overall industry performance determines the level of EO. This research indicates that producers who employ incremental advancements rather than radical inventions achieve better results than their rivals. Owner-managers were urged to exhibit innovation and possess robust technical expertise and deep industry knowledge.

Wijetunge and Pushpakumari (2014) discovered a slightly positive link between EO and business performance in an empirical study on manufacturing SMEs in Sri Lanka's Western Province. A small positive correlation (0.404) was discovered between total EO and corporate performance. Additionally, the business performance of each dimension of EO was assessed. The researchers argue that pro-activeness and risk-taking have a moderately positive relationship, and the level of innovation is highly related to firm performance. Nonetheless, other investigations have targeted all SMEs in Sri Lanka, regardless of their industry or sector. Wijetunge and Pushpakumari (2014) and Fairoz et al. (2010) applied a three-dimensional EO scale. Unlike previous research, the current study utilized the five-dimensional EO scale proposed by Lumpkin and Dess (1996). A thorough examination of the data showed a relatively positive (0.578) relationship between the level of EO across five categories and the success of firm performance.

The outcomes of this study partially contradict the research undertaken by Wijetunge and Pushpakumari (2014). Competitive aggressiveness (0.598) and proactiveness (0.537) positively correlated with corporate performance. Autonomy and innovativeness, traits of EO, showed moderately favourable correlation coefficients of 0.482 and 0.455, respectively. Both researchers discovered a slight positive correlation between risk-taking and business performance. The present study discovered a correlation between aspects of EO: proactiveness, innovation, risk-taking and their overall impact on market share growth. It found a favourable association between proactivity, competitive aggressiveness and corporate performance, consistent with prior research (Lumpkin & Dess, 1996).

Conclusion and Implications of the Study

The primary objective of this study was to determine TL's influence on EO and corporate performance. Boukamcha (2019) emphasized that TL impacts the correlation between corporate entrepreneurship and company success. The findings show that top management's behaviour influences organizational effectiveness and performance outcomes in Sri Lankan SMEs. Entrepreneurs aim to foster innovation with their leadership style, and TL is particularly appropriate for top management. This strategy aids in identifying employees' motivations for creativity and product development, establishing the foundation for their work and giving a vision. Leaders of transformation are required to learn the following five competencies: (1) proficiency in analytical thinking and problem-solving techniques, along with feedback; (2) improved techniques for idea generation; (3) ability to communicate effectively; (4) exceptional management abilities concerning body language, verbal skills and behavioural patterns; and (5) empowerment through communicating high-performance expectations, involving employees in decision-making, goal setting and effectively implementing rewards for achievement (Conger & Kanungo, 1998, as cited in Matzler et al., 2012).

According to this study, there is some evidence that EO helps organizations succeed. The secondary purpose of this study was to examine how the EO traits of initiative, creativity, risk-taking, competitive aggressiveness and independence influence the growth and success of SMEs in Sri Lanka. Businesses must manage EO properly to realize its benefits thoroughly. Statistics show a direct association between EO and economic performance. However, compared to entrepreneurs of SMEs in other nations, entrepreneurs in Sri Lanka exhibit less innovation and risk-taking behaviour. This is owing to the country's status as a developing economy. Innovation, support and development of fresh ideas, experimentation with new concepts and creative processes are some avenues for generating new products and services (Wijetunge & Pushpakumari, 2014).

Firms might undergo much trial and error while testing new ideas and utilizing financial and non-financial resources. Companies assume risks by involving themselves in more uncertain industries, committing to projects utilizing exceptional resources and incurring substantial liabilities through massive loans. The risk-taking of SMEs adds to their level of innovativeness. Businesses, particularly in developing nations such as Sri Lanka, must take measures to strengthen their organizations by motivating and supporting entrepreneurship. Owner-managers/entrepreneurs of firms should stimulate innovativeness, new ideas and creativity within their organizations because product innovation is crucial to their existence worldwide (Putniņš & Sauka, 2020).

The pro-activeness and competitive aggressiveness factors demonstrated a reasonably high link between performance. These critical components suggest a forward-thinking perspective, followed by innovative or new venture activities (or firms that take the initiative in the marketplace/market area). The findings show that entrepreneurs in Sri Lankan SMEs anticipate future difficulties and needs or changes by creating an environment achieved by introducing new products, technology and administrative processes rather than just reacting to market variations. This contrasts sharply with many other countries, where business owners are more likely to react to market developments (Altinay et al., 2016; Lumpkin & Dess, 1996). SMEs in Sri Lanka show slightly higher proactivity, competitive aggressiveness and autonomy than their larger competitors (SMEs).

Implications

The study has both theoretical and managerial consequences. Previous research on entrepreneurship used Barney's (1991) RBV as their theoretical framework. The research on leadership styles relied on Avolio and Bass's FRLT theory as a solid theoretical framework for studying corporate entrepreneurship (Bass et al., 2003). According to this study, the abovementioned theories may apply to SMEs in developing nations such as Sri Lanka. As a result, this study contributes theoretically to the existing literature on the impact of leadership style on the corporate entrepreneurial process.

SMEs in Sri Lanka have been reported to demonstrate lower levels of innovation and risk-taking behaviour. Owner-managers and entrepreneurs build strong relationships with financial institutions, government authorities and policymakers to limit risk and stimulate innovation, ultimately improving the overall performance of their enterprises. Sri Lankan entrepreneurs and owner-managers of SMEs need to enhance their critical thinking, problem-solving skills, creative thinking and leadership style. To enhance innovativeness and decrease risk-taking behaviour, it is imperative to strengthen soft skills such as interpersonal communication, nonverbal cues, verbal proficiency, leadership styles and behavioural competencies.

Limitations and Future Research

Practical barriers hinder collecting crucial information from business owners, who frequently require additional support when presenting and spreading knowledge. Because of concerns regarding customer confidentiality, owner-managers and managers are reluctant to publish credible performance indicators. As a result, corporate success is measured subjectively, leading to performance appraisal bias. This study is based on respondents' opinions about specific company performance data and facts. Performance measures were subjectively measured and may not accurately reflect actual outcomes. Therefore, future studies could employ objective indices of firm performance, such as accounting performance, market share growth and share price increases.

The second constraint is the small sample size; future studies should attempt to replicate the same findings across SMEs in Sri Lanka by increasing the number of samples. Additional research can concentrate on SME exporters in Sri Lanka. To compete in international markets, SMEs must invest in new ideas, innovations and product development. Another limitation is that this study used a cross-sectional method to obtain data. In subsequent research, eliminating these limitations might be possible using a longitudinal approach or performing in-depth case studies that collect data for a dependent, interdependent and moderate variable at two additional periods.

Future investigators examining Sri Lankan SMEs should integrate EO with personality traits, rational decision-making, competency in structural infrastructure, social capital, network connections, marketing focus, social networks and innovative performance. Researchers from other developing countries, too, can employ the same studies in the future to evaluate the entrepreneurial mindset of business owners and the overall performance of their companies, as well as the transformational and transactional leadership behaviours exhibited by their CEOs.

Acknowledgements

We thank the editors and reviewers whose helpful comments and suggestions have made this chapter publishable. We also want to thank the Team ICMR and the Sabaragamuwa University of Sri Lanka for their full support.

References

Altinay, L., Madanoglu, M., De Vita, G., Arasli, H., & Ekinci, Y. (2016). The interface between organisational learning capability, entrepreneurial orientation, and SME growth. *Journal of Small Business Management*, *54*(3), 871–891.

Antonakis, J., Avolio, B. J., & Sivasubramaniam, N. (2003). Context and leadership: An examination of the nine-factor full-range leadership theory using the multifactor leadership questionnaire. *The Leadership Quarterly*, *14*, 261–295. https://doi.org/10.1016/S1048-9843(03)00030-4 Add

Arham, A. F., Sulaiman, N., Kamarudin, F. H., & Muenjohn, N. (2017). Understanding the links between transformational leadership and entrepreneurial orientation in Malaysian SMEs. In N. Muenjohn & A. McMurray (Eds.), *The Palgrave handbook of leadership in transforming Asia*. Palgrave Macmillan. https://doi.org/10.1057/978-1-137-57940-9_29

Barney, J. (1991). Firm resources and sustained competitive advantage. *Journal of Management*, *17*(1), 99–120. https://doi.org/10.1177/014920639101700108

Bass, B. M., Avolio, B. J., Jung, D. I., & Berson, Y. (2003). Predicting unit performance by assessing transformational and transactional leadership. *Journal of Applied Psychology*, *88*(2), 207–218. https://doi.org/10.1037/0021-9010.88.2.207

Boukamcha, F. (2019). The effect of transformational leadership on corporate entrepreneurship in Tunisian SMEs. *Leadership & Organisation Development Journal*. https://doi.org/10.1108/LODJ-07-2018-0262

Chatterjee, S., & Kumar Kar, A. (2020). Why do small and medium enterprises use social media marketing and what is the impact: Empirical insights from India. *International Journal of Information Management*, *53*, 102103.

Covin, J. G., Green, K. M., & Slevin, D. P. (2006). Strategic process effects on the entrepreneurial orientation–sales growth rate relationship. *Entrepreneurship Theory and Practice*, *30*(1), 57–81. https://doi.org/10.1111/j.1540-6520.2006.00110.x

Covin, J. G., & Miller, D. (2014). International entrepreneurial orientation: Conceptual considerations, research themes, measurement issues, and future research directions. *Entrepreneurship Theory and Practice*, *38*, 11–44. https://doi.org/10.1111/etap.12027

Covin, J. G., & Slevin, D. P. (1989). Strategic management of small firms in hostile and benign environments. *Strategic Management Journal*, *10*(1), 75–87. https://doi.org/10.1002/smj.4250100107

Deligianni, I., Dimitratos, P., Andreas, P., & Aharoni, Y. (2016). Entrepreneurial orientation and international performance: The moderating effect of decision-making rationality. *Journal of Small Business Management*, *54*(2), 462–480. https://doi.org/10.1111/jsbm.12152

Dess, G. G., & Lumpkin, G. T. (2005). The role of entrepreneurial orientation in stimulating effective corporate entrepreneurship. *Academy of Management Executive*, *19*(1), 147–156.

Diabate, A., Sibiri, H., Wang, L., & Yu, L. (2019). Assessing SMEs' sustainable growth through entrepreneurs' ability and entrepreneurial orientation: An insight into SMEs in Côte d'Ivoire. *Sustainability*, *11*(24), 7149. https://doi.org/10.3390/su11247149

Dionne, S. D., Yammarino, F. J., Atwater, L. E., & Spangler, W. D. (2004). Transformational leadership and team performance. *Journal of Organisational Change Management*, *17*(2), 177–193. https://doi.org/10.1108/09534810410530601

Engelen, A., Gupta, V., Strenger, L., & Brettel, M. (2015). Entrepreneurial orientation, firm performance, and the moderating role of transformational leadership behaviours. *Journal of Management*, *41*(4), 1069–1097.

Fairoz, F. M., Hirobumi, T., & Tanaka, Y. (2010). Entrepreneurial orientation and business performance of small and medium scale enterprises of Hambantota District Sri Lanka. *Asian Social Science*, *6*(3), 34–46.

Gunawardana, S. J. (2016). 'To finish, we must finish': Everyday practices of depletion in Sri Lankan export-processing zones. *Globalisations*, *13*(6), 861–875. https://doi.org/10.1080/14747731.2016.1155341

Isichei, E. E., Agbaeze, K. E., & Odiba, M. O. (2020). Entrepreneurial orientation and performance in SMEs: The mediating role of structural infrastructure capability. *International Journal of Emerging Markets*, *15*(6), 1219–1241. https://doi.org/10.1108/IJOEM-08-2019-0671

Klein, G. (2023). Transformational and transactional leadership, organisational support, and environmental competition intensity as antecedents of intrapreneurial behaviours. *European Research on Management and Business Economics*, *29*(2), 100215. https://doi.org/10.1016/j.iedeen.2023.100215

Lumpkin, G. T., & Dess, G. G. (1996). Clarifying the entrepreneurial orientation construct and linking it to performance. *The Academy of Management Review*, *21*(1), 135. http://doi.org/10.2307/258632

Lumpkin, G. T., & Dess, G. G. (2001). Linking two dimensions of entrepreneurial orientation to firm performance: The moderating role of environment and industry life cycle. *Journal of Business Venturing*, *16*, 429–451.

Madushanka, H., & Sachitra, V. (2021). Factors influencing the export engagement of small and medium-sized enterprises in Sri Lanka: Resource-based view. *South Asian Journal of Social Studies and Economics*, *9*(3), 38–49. https://doi.org/10.9734/sajsse/2021/v9i330244

Matzler, K., Schwarz, E., Deutinger, N., & Harms, R. (2012). The relationship between transformational leadership, product innovation, and performance in SMEs. *Journal of Small Business & Entrepreneurship*, *21*(2), 139–151.

Miller, D. (1983). The correlates of entrepreneurship in three types of firms. *Management Science*, *29*(7), 770–791. https://doi.org/10.1287/mnsc.29.7.770

Nguyen, N. P., Nguyen, T. T. H., Nguyen, H., & Flynn, O. (2023). Does transformational leadership influence organisational culture and performance: Empirical evidence from an emerging country. *IIMB Management Review*, *35*(4), 382–392.

Putniņš, T. J., & Sauka, A. (2020). Why does entrepreneurial orientation affect company performance?. *Strategic Entrepreneurship Journal*, *14*(4), 711–735. https://doi.org/10.1002/sej.1325

Rasheed, M. A., Shahzad, K., & Nadeem, S. (2021). Transformational leadership and employee voice for product and process innovation in SMEs. *Innovation & Management Review*, *18*(1), 69–89. https://doi.org/10.1108/INMR-01-2020-0007

Razavi, S. H., & Ab Aziz, K. (2017). The dynamics between entrepreneurial orientation, transformational leadership, and intrapreneurial intention in the Iranian R&D sector. *International Journal of Entrepreneurial Behavior & Research*, *23*(5), 769–792.

Rowold, J. (2005). *Multifactor leadership questionnaire*. Mind Garden.

Soomro, B. A., & Shah, N. (2020). Entrepreneurial orientation and performance in a developing country: Strategic entrepreneurship as a mediator. *Business Strategy and Development*, *3*(4), 567–577. https://doi.org/10.1002/bsd2.122

Wijetunge, W. A. D. S., & Pushpakumari, M. D. (2014). Entrepreneurial orientation and business performance of small and medium scale enterprises of Western Province in Sri Lanka. *Kelaniya Journal of Management*, *2*(2), 51–67. https://doi.org/10.4038/kjm.v2i2.6550

Wiklund, J., & Shepherd, D. (2005). Entrepreneurial orientation and small business performance: A configurational approach. *Journal of Business Venturing*, *20*(1), 71–91. http://doi.org/10.1016/j.jbusvent.2004.01.001

Yang, C.-W. (2008). The relationships among leadership styles, entrepreneurial orientation, and business performance. *Managing Global Transitions*, *6*(3), 257–275.

Chapter 7

Business Continuity Strategies During COVID-19 Pandemic: A Case From a Small and Medium Enterprise (SME)

Abiththa Godage Vishva Maithri[a]
and Kumudu Kushlani Kapiyangoda[b]

[a]University of Moratuwa, Sri Lanka
[b]University of Colombo, Sri Lanka

Abstract

This study explores the strategies implemented by one of the prominent software development companies in Sri Lanka to ensure business continuity during the COVID-19 pandemic. It adopts a qualitative methodology with a case study approach. Interviews were incorporated as the prominent method of data collection. This research adopts a theoretical framework to illustrate the business continuity strategies adopted during the COVID-19 pandemic. The strategies identified in preparation for the crisis included forming a crisis-handling team, spotting and classifying foreseen risks, and incorporating previous experiences as learning points. The incorporation of ISO standards facilitated the development of strategies to respond to the crisis. Opportunities in the software development industry were utilized for business stabilization, operating costs were optimized, and unique strategies were implemented to manage human resources. Routine checklists were prepared, continuous assessments of competitors and the workforce were performed, and risk profiles and ratings were updated to suit the pandemic. The findings from this study could be incorporated by practising managers when devising strategies to ensure business continuity amid a crisis.

Keywords: COVID-19 pandemic; crisis; business continuity strategies; qualitative research; case study; software development company

Shaping Entrepreneurial Marketing, Volume 1, 103–116

doi:10.1108/978-1-83708-852-220251007

Introduction

Scholars have explored how organizations respond to crises differently. Notably, studies have illustrated how organizations have implemented strategies to ensure business continuity in response to diverse crises such as the COVID-19 pandemic (Acciarini et al., 2021; Haryono & Wijaya, 2023; Karlsson & Offord, 2023; Purnomo et al., 2021), financial crises (Barontini & Taglialatela, 2021; Ciasullo et al., 2022), and natural disasters (Lozada-Contreras et al., 2022), among others.

Researchers have explored how organizations ensure business continuity amid financial crises and natural disasters. Accordingly, Lozada-Contreras et al. (2022) highlighted that firms implement customer relationship management resilience strategies when responding to natural disasters and that a comprehensive and adaptive customer relationship management contingency model is adopted to ensure business continuity. Meanwhile, Barontini and Taglialatela (2021) showed that innovative activities resulting in patent applications provide strategic resources helpful to tackle the crisis rather than increase risk. Regarding innovation, Ciasullo et al. (2022) studied over 190 big-data small and medium enterprises (SMEs) in Europe. They found that extensive data analysis capability and co-innovation are positively associated with organizational resilience, which, in turn, facilitates business continuity.

Studies have also investigated how organizations responded and implemented strategies to ensure business continuity during the COVID-19 pandemic. Purnomo et al. (2021) found that the COVID-19 pandemic provided both opportunities and restrictions for small and medium enterprises, which, in turn, significantly interrupted their business models. According to the authors, small and medium enterprises can be especially vulnerable and ensure continuity and growth by allocating resources and appropriate strategies to maximize opportunities and face challenges. Furthermore, Acciarini et al. (2021), in a study conducted on four significant companies operating in Italy, illustrated the short-term actions and long-term strategies planned and carried out by these companies in response to the COVID-19 pandemic. Specifically, the authors highlight the similarities and dissimilarities between the strategic responses and avenues for business development in the future. In addition, Karlsson and Offord (2023) illustrated the impact the pandemic had on higher education institutions (HEIs). This study showed that even though a continuity strategy relevant to the sector already existed, lack of knowledge meant that the strategy was not used immediately. This was costly regarding staff and student well-being, but ultimately, HEIs were adapted by converging on a practical solution that showed inherent resilience. Furthermore, Haryono and Wijaya (2023) demonstrated the strategic framework used by event organizers in Indonesia to navigate the COVID-19 pandemic successfully and found that to survive the COVID-19 pandemic, the event organizers had to incorporate an open communication strategy, adapt according to the changing environmental conditions while taking steps supported by information in managing the crisis. As the study revealed, the event organizers' crisis management strategy consisted of five stages: research on the crisis, formation of a crisis team, planning steps to manage the crisis, implementation of a new work system and adapting to the new system's culture.

In contrast to the above research, our study explores the strategies implemented by one of the leading software development companies in Sri Lanka to ensure business continuity amid the COVID-19 crisis. Past studies on COVID-19 have focused on the impact of the pandemic on businesses (Karia & Saleh, 2021; Mather, 2020). However, there is a lack of studies exploring the strategies companies developed to ensure business continuity during a pandemic. Therefore, our research aims to fill this lacuna. Accordingly, this study aims to identify the strategies that a software development company (to maintain the anonymity of the case firm, we name the company as Software Company Ltd.) developed to ensure business continuity amid the COVID-19 pandemic.

Literature Review

Organizational Strategies

Institutions employ organizational strategies to streamline their operations and achieve organizational goals. Accordingly, studies have explored competitive business strategies (Kaliappen & Hilman, 2017), innovation strategies (Kaliappen & Hilman, 2017) and the implementation of environmentally friendly business strategies (Kemper, 2012), among others. Another stream of studies has explored business continuity strategies among this wide array of strategies.

A business's successful operation depends on continuing its core business activities and supporting services (Morwood, 1998). According to Alsalman (2018), business continuation is a function of management that ensures effective risk responses while securing the shareholders' interests.

Business Continuity Amid COVID-19

Business continuity is the smooth operation of business activities without any interruption. Alsalman (2018) perceives continuity of business activities as a management-related framework developed to ensure that correct responses are provided for risks while securing the shareholders' interest. As illustrated by Morwood (1998), the survival of a business is based on the assurance of the operation of principal business activities and support services. Accordingly, systems need to operate smoothly to secure important assets and to ensure that critical areas of the business are in operation amidst unexpected disruptions in business activities (Matthys, 2010).

Scholars found that business continuity strategies were essential across businesses amid the COVID-19 pandemic (Sawalha, 2020). Due to this crisis, most business entities and institutions across the globe were disturbed for an extended period, causing companies to suffer notable financial and non-financial losses (KPMG, 2020). A range of studies have explored the area of business continuity, focusing on the hospitality industry (Jones & Comfort, 2020), supply chains (Medel et al., 2020), family businesses (Kraus et al., 2020), etc.

Scholars explored how organizations ensured business continuity during the COVID-19 pandemic. Organizations actively change policies and regulations while preparing and changing business continuation plans (Karia & Saleh, 2021), inspired by their learning from past experiences (Gunessee & Subramanian, 2020). Furthermore, focusing on supply chains, scholars identified that cooperating with the distributors and manufacturers, ordering large quantities and maintaining an acceptable credit ratio aided in the smooth functioning of supply chains amid a crisis (Chowdhury et al., 2020).

Scholars also investigated how organizations implemented business continuity strategies during the COVID-19 pandemic. Purnomo et al. (2021) found that small and medium enterprises focused on surviving while ensuring growth by utilizing their available resources. Furthermore, a study by Acciarini et al. (2021) conducted in four major companies operating in Italy in different industries demonstrated the short-term actions and long-term strategies planned and implemented in response to the COVID-19 pandemic. In addition, Karlsson and Offord (2023) illustrated the impact the pandemic had on HEIs and shed light on how HEIs adapted by converging on a practical solution, showing inherent resilience. Furthermore, Haryono and Wijaya (2023) illustrated the event organizers' crisis management strategy, which consists of five stages: researching the crisis, setting up a team to manage the crisis, coming up with steps to manage the crisis, institutionalizing novel work arrangements and adapting to the new system's culture.

Significant leadership and governance challenges were followed by the COVID-19 pandemic (Mather, 2020). Accordingly, leaders are considered the key actors who aid in linking employees with the organization during a crisis (Hinojosa et al., 2020). Thereby, strategies have been developed to facilitate managing staff (Karia & Saleh, 2021) while responding accordingly to ease off the impact of the pandemic on its employees (Gomez et al., 2020), especially in occasions of remote working (Leiva & Clark, 2020). Likewise, scholars have also illuminated that responsive organizations that adapt and change proactively will thrive in the next normal (Mather, 2020). Therefore, these changes in strategies were crucial in responding to the crisis.

Business Continuity Model

Some scholars have developed models to capture business continuity amid COVID-19. Accordingly, studies have incorporated models to illuminate how companies changed their business strategies according to evolving environmental factors, how the crisis created unintended cultural change and how the crisis has made companies embrace digitalization temporarily (Kraus et al., 2020). Furthermore, studies have also encapsulated how cross-sector collaborations have facilitated building resilience amid COVID-19 (Medel et al., 2020). In addition, the study of Finsterwalder and Kuppelwieser (2020) focused on how the well-being of actors across different levels of the service ecosystem is influenced amid the COVID-19 pandemic. On a related note, Fox et al. (2020) incorporated a model to identify how organizations steered by authentic leaders and possess flexible business models were more closely engaged with stakeholders than forms led by less authentic leaders during the COVID-19 pandemic. Likewise, scholars have incorporated models to identify business strategy changes during COVID-19.

Our study leans on the business continuity model initially developed by Castillo (2005). In this model, Castillo (2005) integrated a disaster preparedness model with a business continuity model while identifying elements such as crisis preparedness, crisis response/recovery, stabilization and assessment. In developing this model, the author has illuminated the crisis Boeing aircraft manufacturers faced with cancelling orders after the 9/11 attack. Even though, Castillo (2005) developed a business continuity model, there is less evidence of the strategies organizations could adopt to respond to a crisis. Furthermore, no evidence exists on the business continuity strategies developed amid COVID-19, focusing on software development businesses. Therefore, our research aims to address this lacuna by exploring the business continuity strategies one of the leading software development firms in Sri Lanka (Software Company Ltd.) adopted during the COVID-19 pandemic.

Methodology

Qualitative research aims to explore research questions in-depth in a real institutional context (Lillis, 2008). Taking into consideration the nature of the research question (i.e., what strategies were developed by a software development company to ensure business continuity amid the COVID-19 pandemic), the authors adopted a case study approach as part of a qualitative methodology (Yin, 2009), which would help in obtaining rich and in-depth data on the business continuity strategies adopted by the organization being studied. Subsequently, Software Company Ltd., one of the top five software development companies operating in Sri Lanka, was selected for the case study.

Interviews were conducted to collect data from the field. Accordingly, 10 top-level managerial employees attached to Software Company Ltd. were interviewed: Assistant General Manager, General Manager, Head of Human Resources (HR), Head of Project Management, Head of Software Quality Engineering, Head of Software Development and four executive-level team leaders. These interviews each spanned over an hour. Thematic analysis (Braun & Clarke, 2013) was performed to make the data analysis more systematic and comprehensive. The interview data was transcribed, and the themes and codes related to business strategies and business continuity were identified. The findings section details the themes related to the theoretical framework developed.

Findings

This study explores the business continuity strategies adopted by one of the leading software development companies in Sri Lanka (Software Company Ltd.) amid the COVID-19 crisis, based on the theoretical framework from Castillo (2005).

Accordingly, leaning on this model, we encapsulate the company's business continuity strategies into several steps: preparing for the crisis, responding to the crisis, ensuring business stability and assessing business performance. Fig. 7.1 shows the theoretical framework.

Crisis Preparedness

In preparing for the crisis, the company established a team to manage crises, identified and classified foreseen risks and incorporated prior experiences as learning points in developing business continuity plans. As explained by the General Manager:

> Software Company Ltd. has established an incident management system which includes a local incident management team that reports to the regional incident management team, as well as a vice president, a senior vice president, and a chief transformation officer, respectively.

This incident management system has created global-level traceability. Furthermore, depending on the impact level of the crisis, guidance is provided to handle crises. In addition, Software Company Ltd. has established a system to identify and rate potential risks. As the Assistant General Manager explained:

> We do a risk assessment. We identify the impact of a particular situation and plan and operationalise our responses based on that. So, we assess the severity and impact of the crisis, and we rate the risks as 1 to 5. So, we have a particular guideline which shapes our response depending on the risk level.

In addition, lessons learned from previous experiences are also incorporated when deciding strategies. As the Assistant General Manager explained:

> The learnings from the 2019 April attack were applied in developing strategies to face the COVID-19 pandemic. Similar strategies imposed when closing the operations overnight were repeated when facing the island-wide lockdown due to COVID-19.

Accordingly, as the Assistant General Manager further explained, to continue operations where the office could not be reached, all employees were provided basic facilities (such as laptops and dongles) in advance.

Crisis Response

The ISO 22301 standard aided in developing strategies to ensure business continuity while responding to the crisis. As explained by the General Manager, the

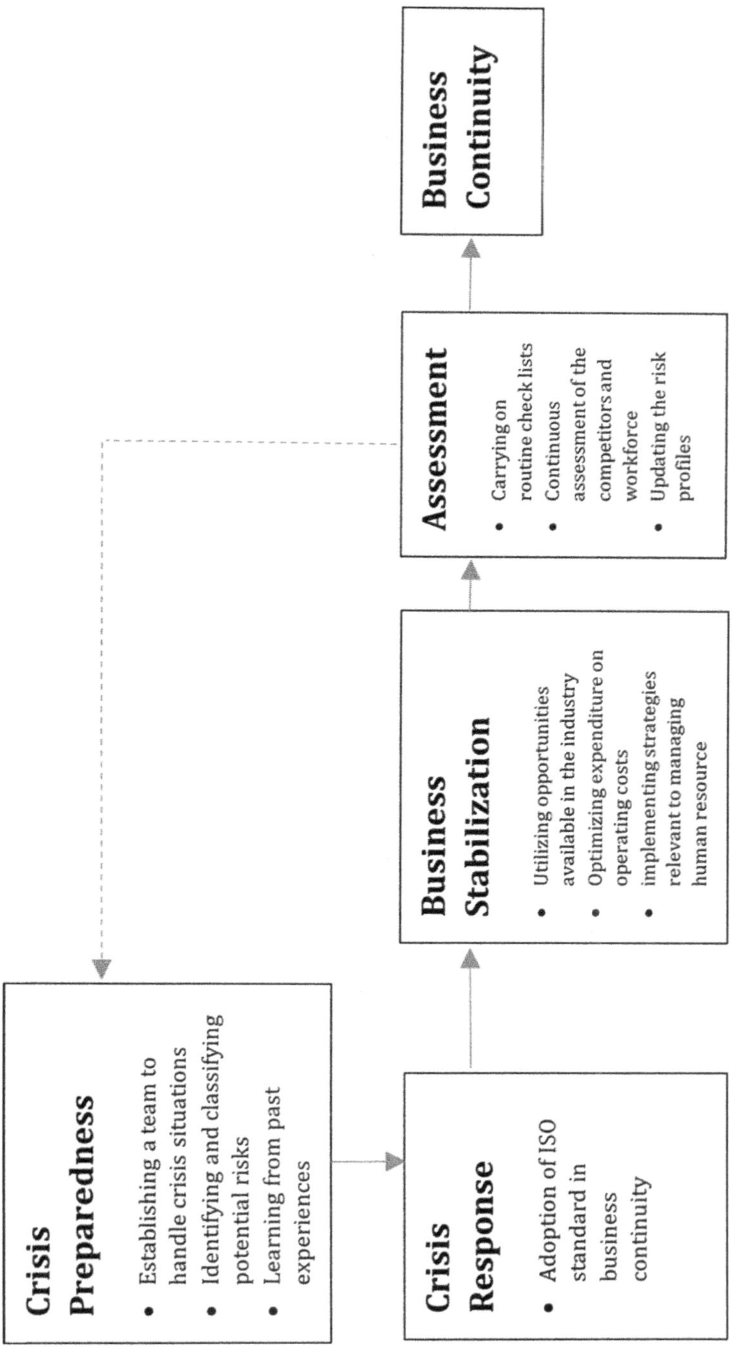

Fig. 7.1. Business Continuity Theoretical Framework. *Source:* Authors' own, based on the literature review.

adaptation of the ISO 22301 guidelines provided a framework for responding to COVID-19:

> ISO 22301 is on business continuity management system. So, under this, we have a set of guidelines that tell us how to document things, who is responsible for certain actions, and who has access to certain things. So, we need to identify the processes, document the actions, test the actions, produce results, and raise awareness. So, once we adhere to these guidelines, we automatically receive a crisis response plan.

The Assistant General Manager further supported these ideas as he explained that these measures helped in responding to crises rather than reacting to a crisis incident:

> I think the key here is responding to a particular incident rather than reacting. Because if you are prepared for a particular situation, you respond because you have all the controls and mechanisms ready. So, these frameworks help us get those things in place. How do we respond in a situation like this? It is more like a drill we have done in advance. Because when the situation happens, we do not need to scratch our heads and spend our time thinking about what to do.

Accordingly, the company has developed mechanisms to facilitate mass communication in a crisis. Furthermore, adopting the ISO standard has enabled the company to maintain documents and rank risks accordingly while mapping how to respond in each foreseeable situation.

Business Stabilization

In stabilizing the business, Software Company Ltd. implemented several strategies, such as utilizing opportunities available in the industry, optimizing operating costs and adopting particular Human Resource Management (HRM) strategies to cope with the challenges imposed by COVID-19. As elucidated by the Head of Software Development, the impact of COVID-19 depended on the type of industry to which the business was attached. Therefore, business continuity strategies would have had to lean on the nature of the industry. As he explained:

> I think the impact is different from industry to industry. If you take the tourism and FMCG industries, they are hard hit. If you look at the IT industry, it is not a hard hit. Since COVID-19, people have seen the opportunity to automate things. So now we seek to maximise our profits from these opportunities which emerged in the market.

In addition to these comments, the Head of Software Quality Engineering explained that strategies should be implemented to optimize operating costs while reducing unnecessary expenses.

As the Head of HR explained, particular strategies were implemented to manage human resources. Accordingly, team management was given top priority. Brainstorming and problem-solving with team members and collaboration among team members played a crucial role in developing trust among them while stabilizing the operations. In this regard, special programs were conducted to ease the way of employees working from home. As explained by the Head of HR:

> We had to reset our minds to work from home, not the office. So, we conducted programs on employee well-being while communicating tips on working remotely and working from home.

Furthermore, team leaders were explicitly trained to manage their teams remotely. Accordingly, people's connectivity issues were addressed. On such occasions, team leaders were educated on going beyond their technical capabilities while bringing a human aspect to the team.

To achieve targets, the top management had to build closer relationships with the project management teams to identify and address field-level issues immediately. The Assistant General Manager explained:

> We were conscious about the productivity matrix. Moreover, of course, managing project deliverables was thought of. So, we started working closer with the project management team to see what spillovers there were. How do we support the teams? These were the key areas that we looked into to minimise the impact on the business and the people contributing to our business objectives.

Accordingly, the plans and profit targets were adjusted depending on the situation.

Assessment

The company has adopted strategies such as conducting routine checks and periodical assessments of employees and competitors while maintaining updated risk profiles. Checklists are prepared to closely monitor the routine work of the employees, which the team leader monitors daily and weekly to ascertain the work in progress.

As the Head of Project Management explained, in a work-from-home situation, this constant monitoring is essential to ensure business continuity:

> In a work-from-home situation, it is important for the team leaders to monitor the employees' activities closely. This close monitoring also enables us to improve the work processes continuously.

Furthermore, continuous assessment of the competitors and workforce is also essential in a pandemic. As elucidated by a team leader:

> Initially, there was much instability within the industry. Moreover, people did not want to move from one job to another. However, many foreign companies now recruit people from Sri Lanka, and they can work from Sri Lanka without leaving the country. Along with this opportunity, people will be moving out. Therefore, it is essential to be vigilant about the trends emerging in the workforce.

In addition, the Assistant General Manager noted the importance of assessing the actions of competitors and new entrants during a pandemic situation:

> Importantly, now we have faced the threat of new entrants and competition imposed by new entrants. Before the pandemic, Company X was our competitor, but now Company Y has also become our competitor with their revamping of systems. So they are new entrants in different forms.

Therefore, the risk profiles were reassessed and updated to manage similar crises in the future.

Discussion

This section discusses the findings from the study. As Matthys (2010) illustrated, systems must operate smoothly to safeguard critical assets and ensure that the business's primary operations operate well during a sudden shock to the business process. Similarly, our study also illustrates that it is essential that the core operating activities of the business, such as software development and managing human resources, function smoothly to ensure business continuity. Similar to the studies of Purnomo et al. (2021), Acciarini et al. (2021), Karlsson and Offord (2023) and Haryono and Wijaya (2023), our study also explored how organizations respond to the COVID-19 crisis. Importantly, our study details how organizations implemented strategies to ensure business continuity in response to the COVID-19 pandemic.

The strategies adopted by Software Company Ltd. were diffused across several business areas, such as human resource management, business operations, risk assessment, etc. (Karasan et al., 2018). Scholars have suggested that business continuity plans developed in crises are often based on experience (Gunessee & Subramanian, 2020). Similarly, our study also explains that the business continuity plans developed to respond to COVID-19 were based on past crises faced by the company (i.e., the April 2019 terrorist attack). Lozada-Contreras et al. (2022) established that firms implement customer relationship management resilience strategies in response to a natural disaster. However, based on one of the leading software-developing companies in Sri Lanka, our study focuses on elucidating how business continuity strategies were used to ensure business continuity amid the COVID-19 pandemic. Regarding innovation, Ciasullo et al. (2022) stated that extensive data analysis capability and co-innovation are positively associated with organizational resilience. Similarly, our study establishes that alternative opportunities should be utilized to ensure business continuity amid the COVID-19 pandemic.

Similar to the study of Purnomo et al. (2021), our study also states that the software development company on which we focused our research also embarked on survival strategies rather than adopting growth strategies while designing new strategies to utilize newly emerging opportunities from the field. At the same time, Acciarini et al. (2021) established that long-term and short-term strategies are incorporated for business continuity. However, our study found that short-term strategies were mainly valuable for surviving a crisis. In line with the findings of Karlsson and Offord (2023), our study also demonstrates that practical strategies unique to particular organizations are implemented as business continuity strategies, especially during a crisis. Furthermore, similar to the findings of Haryono and Wijaya (2023), our study sheds light on how setting up a team and devising plans to manage the crisis act as part of the business continuity strategies at the organization under study. However, our study does not explicitly detail how the organizational culture was changed to ensure business continuity.

As noted by previous scholars, the COVID-19 crisis created noteworthy governance and leadership issues for organizations (Mather, 2020), and institutional leaders help to keep employees connected with the organization during a crisis (Hinojosa et al., 2020; Karia & Saleh, 2021). Similarly, in our study, the leaders attached to Software Company Ltd., were the main actors who worked closely with the employees. Accordingly, they were provided with special training to manage employees remotely. However, as disclosed by the findings, it is evident that these leaders were explicitly trained to go beyond their technical capabilities while bringing a human aspect to the team and reducing the impact of the pandemic on its employees (Gomez et al., 2020).

Conclusions and Implications of the Study

In conclusion, adopting the business continuation model of Castillo (2005), we identified the business continuity strategies implemented by Software Company Ltd., in response to COVID-19. These strategies included forming a crisis-handling team, identifying and classifying foreseen risks, and incorporating previous experiences as learning points. The incorporation of ISO standards facilitated the development of strategies for responding to the crisis. For business stabilization, the opportunities that emerged from the industry were utilized, operating costs were optimized, and unique strategies were implemented to manage human resources. For assessment, routine checklists were prepared, continuous assessments of competitors and the workforce were performed, and risk profiles and ratings were suitably updated.

This study makes several contributions. Very little research has been done on strategies for business continuity during the COVID-19 pandemic in the Sri Lankan software industry. Accordingly, this is one of the first such studies. Furthermore, the strategies identified by this study could also be implemented by managers during other crises.

Future researchers could explore the business continuity strategies adopted by different organizations, such as family businesses, multinational entities, government institutions, etc., during different crises. They could also explore how businesses in different locations adopt business continuity strategies. Furthermore, different theoretical lenses could also be incorporated to identify how business continuity strategies occur in an organization.

There are several limitations to this study. Firstly, the researchers spent only three months collecting data. It would have been better if more time had been spent in the field, enabling more in-depth exploration. In addition, quantitative methods could have been included to identify the business continuity strategies commonly adopted by organizations.

Acknowledgements

We thank the editors and anonymous reviewers whose comments and suggestions made this chapter publishable. We also want to thank Team ICMR and the Sabaragamuwa University of Sri Lanka for their strong support.

References

Acciarini, C., Boccardelli, P., & Vitale, M. (2021). Resilient companies in the time of COVID-19 pandemic: A case study approach. *Journal of Entrepreneurship and Public Policy*, *10*(3), 336–351.

Alsalman, S. (2018). Business continuity management: Definitions, drivers, practices, key processes, and effectiveness. *International Journal of Business and Management Review*, *6*(3), 62–71.

Barontini, R., & Taglialatela, J. (2021). Patents and small business risk: Longitudinal evidence from the global financial crisis. *Journal of Small Business and Enterprise Development*, *29*(2), 279–292.

Braun, V., & Clarke, V. (2013). Teaching thematic analysis: Overcoming challenges and developing strategies for effective learning. *The Psychologist*, *26*(2).

Castillo, C. (2005). Disaster preparedness and business continuity planning at Boeing: An integrated model. *Journal of Facilities Management*, *3*(1), 8–26.

Chowdhury, M. T., Sarkar, A., Saha, P. K., & Anik, R. H. (2020). Enhancing supply resilience in the COVID-19 pandemic: A case study on beauty and personal care retailers. *Modern Supply Chain Research and Applications*, *2*(3), 143–159.

Ciasullo, M. V., Montera, R., & Douglas, A. (2022). Building SMEs' resilience in times of uncertainty: The role of extensive data analytics capability and co-innovation. *Transforming Government: People, Process and Policy*, *16*(2), 203–217.

Finsterwalder, J., & Kuppelwieser, V. G. (2020). Equilibrating resources and challenges during crises: A framework for service ecosystem well-being. *Journal of Service Management*, *31*(6), 1107–1129.

Fox, C., Davis, P., & Baucus, M. (2020). Corporate social responsibility during unprecedented crises: The role of authentic leadership and business model flexibility. *Management Decision*, *58*(10), 2213–2233.

Gomez, S. M., Mendoza, O. E. O., Ramírez, J., & Olivas-Luján, M. R. (2020). Stress and myths related to the COVID-19 pandemic's effects on remote work. *Management Research: The Journal of the Iberoamerican Academy of Management*, *18*(4), 401–420.

Gunessee, S., & Subramanian, N. (2020). Ambiguity and its coping mechanisms in supply chains lessons from the COVID-19 pandemic and natural disasters. *International Journal of Operations & Production Management*, *40*(7/8), 1201–1223.

Haryono, C. G., & Wijaya, C. (2023). The crisis management strategies of Indonesian event organisers in the face of COVID-19. *Journal of Hospitality and Tourism Insights*, *6*(4), 1552–1568.

Hinojosa, A. S., Shaine, M. J. D., & McCauley, K. D. (2020). A strange situation indeed: Fostering leader-follower attachment security during an unprecedented crisis. *Management Decision*, *58*(10), 2099–2115.

Jones, P., & Comfort, D. (2020). The COVID-19 crisis and sustainability in the hospitality industry. *International Journal of Contemporary Hospitality Management*, *32*(10), 3037–3050.

Kaliappen, N., & Hilman, H. (2017). Competitive strategies, market orientation types, and innovation strategies: Finding the strategic fit. *World Journal of Entrepreneurship, Management and Sustainable Development*, *13*(3), 257–261.

Karasan, A., Erdogan, M., & Ilbahar, E. (2018). Prioritisation of production strategies of a manufacturing plant by using an integrated intuitionistic fuzzy AHP & TOPSIS approach. *Journal of Enterprise Information Management*, *31*(4), 510–528.

Karia, N., & Saleh, F. I. M. (2021). The effect of TQM practices on INGOs' staff work-related attitudes. *Benchmarking: An International Journal*. https://doi.org/10.1108/BIJ-02-2021-0080

Karlsson, P. S., & Offord, M. (2023). Higher education during crisis: A case study on organic resilience. *Continuity and Resilience Review*, *5*(2), 185–197. https://doi.org/10.1108/CRR-10-2022-0030

Kemper, A. (2012). Saving the planet: A tale of two strategies (ensuring environmentally-friendly business strategies). *Strategic Direction*, *28*(9). https://doi.org/10.1108/sd.2012.05628iaa.009

KPMG. (2020). Business continuity in a COVID-19 world. https://home.kpmg/xx/en/home/insights/2020/03/business-continuity-in-a-covid-19-world.html. Accessed on June 16, 2020.

Kraus, S., Clauss, T., Breier, M., Gast, J., Zardini, A., & Tiberius, V. (2020). The economics of COVID-19: Initial empirical evidence on how family firms in five European countries cope with the coronavirus crisis. *International Journal of Entrepreneurial Behavior & Research*, *26*(5), 1067–1092.

Leiva, A. M., & Clark, M. E. (2020). COVID-19 considerations for SEC cybersecurity guidance, disclosure, enforcement, and parallel proceedings: Navigating the new normal. *Journal of Investment Compliance*, *21*(2/3), 111–126.

Lillis, A. (2008). Qualitative management accounting research: Rationale, pitfalls, and potential: A comment on Vaivio (2008). *Qualitative Research in Accounting & Management*, *5*(3), 239–246.
Lozada-Contreras, F., Orengo-Serra, K. L., & Sanchez-Jauregui, M. (2022). Adaptive customer relationship management contingency model under disruptive events. *Journal of Advances in Management Research*, *19*(2), 198–219.
Mather, P. (2020). Leadership and governance in a crisis: Some reflections on COVID-19. *Journal of Accounting & Organisational Change*, *16*(4), 579–585.
Matthys, E. A. (2010). *Business continuity management*. Benefolio.
Medel, K., Kousar, R., & Masood, T. (2020). A collaboration–resilience framework for disaster management supply networks: A case study of the Philippines. *Journal of Humanitarian Logistics and Supply Chain Management*, *10*(4), 509–553.
Morwood, G. (1998). Business continuity: Awareness and training programs. *Information Management & Computer Security*, *6*(1), 28–32.
Purnomo, B. R., Adiguna, R., Widodo, W., Suyatna, H., & Nusantoro, B. P. (2021). Entrepreneurial resilience during the Covid-19 pandemic: Navigating survival, continuity and growth. *Journal of Entrepreneurship in Emerging Economies*, *13*(4), 497–524.
Sawalha, I. H. (2020). Business continuity management: Use and approach's effectiveness. *Continuity & Resilience Review*, *2*(2), 81–96.
Yin, R. K. (2009). *Case study research: Design and methods* (4th ed.). Sage.

Chapter 8

Factors Affecting the Performance of the Pickers in 3PL Warehouses in Sri Lanka: A Systematic Review of Literature

Agostheenu Paris Kankanamalage Jinendri Prasadika[a], *Annista Nishanthy Wijayanayake*[b] *and Dona Hiruni Hansinie Niwunhella*[c]

[a]University of Sri Jayewardenepura, Sri Lanka
[b]University of Melbourne, Australia
[c]University of Kelaniya, Sri Lanka

Abstract

This chapter aims to explore the factors that impact the performance of pickers in third-party logistics (3PL) warehouses in Sri Lanka. Warehouses are critical to a supply chain because they store inventories. In Sri Lanka, warehousing is the most outsourced function in the supply chain. In a warehouse, order picking, the most expensive job, is collecting items from storage locations to tally with the order list, and the employee responsible for this is the picker. Therefore, it is necessary to recognize the factors impacting the picker's performance. This research conducted a systematic narrative review, summarizing and analyzing the existing literature on three topics: 3PL providers in Sri Lanka, the selector and order-picking process and employee performance. The factors identified from the literature were categorized into employee-related and order-picking-related factors. Most papers investigating employee performance have focused on motivation, leadership and financial reward. In contrast, the papers that analyzed the order-picking process focused on routing, storage assignment and order batching. It is essential to identify the factors affecting the performance of selectors. The 3PL warehouse managers can focus on those factors when improving picker and warehouse performance.

Shaping Entrepreneurial Marketing, Volume 1, 117–131

Published under exclusive licence by Emerald Publishing Limited
doi:10.1108/978-1-83708-852-220251008

Keywords: Third-party logistics warehouses; picker performance; order picking; warehouse management; productivity

Introduction

Organizations that cater to various aspects of the supply chain process, such as warehousing, distribution, transportation and freight forwarding, as a service to other organizations are known as third-party logistics (3PL) providers. Because the success of logistics performance is crucial to logistics service providers and their customers, 3PL providers have become competitive in the 3PL industry (Richard & Rein, 2004). Given the advantageous geopolitical location of Sri Lanka in the Indian Ocean, there is great potential for the country to develop into an Asian logistical hub. The logistics performance of Sri Lanka ranked 94th in 2018 and 89th in 2014 out of 160 countries (The World Bank, n.d.). Critical dimensions of the Logistics Performance Index (LPI) and their score out of 5.0 are Customs (2.58), Infrastructure (2.49), Logistics Competence (2.42), Timeliness (2.79), Tracking and Tracing (2.79) and International Shipments (2.51).

In 2019, the total 3PL revenue in Sri Lanka was about US$1.1 billion, 6.8% of the total revenue (Armstrong & Associates Inc, n.d.). This implies that Sri Lanka has a poor logistics performance compared to other countries. The logistics performance of Sri Lanka can be further developed if the factors that hinder performance are identified and treated. Warehouses owned by 3PL service providers are popular among businesses. In the Sri Lankan 3PL industry, a few significant local firms dominate the whole industry (De Alwis, 2016). The study also highlights the cost focus, skill gaps, lack of professionalism and low margins as challenges and omnichannel evolution, green logistics, micro-logistics and E-logistics opportunities for Sri Lanka's 3PL sector.

It is said that warehousing is the most outsourced logistical component of businesses in Sri Lanka. Order picking is the collection and delivery of items from storage locations in the warehouse. Out of all the warehouse operations, the order-picking process costs up to 55% (Grosse & Glock, 2013). The picker is the employee in charge of this procedure. The picker must work with material handling equipment along the warehouse aisles to pick items.

Usually, pickers receive a list of goods with quantity to pick from storage. In the past, order picking was of minor importance, but now, businesses have realized the importance of improving the productivity of this process. Because of the high operational costs of the order-picking process, it should be prioritized to lower costs and increase output in the warehouse. At the same time, customers will look for response time, order accuracy and order quality because of the growing popularity of e-commerce and just-in-time production initiatives. Customer satisfaction depends hugely on how well the picker performs the picking of orders. Therefore, the demand for adequately planned order picking has arisen. The order-picking process directly impacts customer satisfaction and requires quick and accurate processing. On the other hand, human resources are a crucial element of any organization. Some warehouses have been automated partially, which can impact the human factors (HF) related to the pickers (Winkelhaus et al., 2021). The order-picking process, however, is predominantly manual – over 80% on average (De Koster et al., 2007). Therefore, the productivity of the order-picking process mainly depends on the picker handling the orders. Various methods can improve the effectiveness of the 3PL warehouses. However, the literature shows that the picker's performance has received less focus. The efficiency of the pickers is one of the key elements in boosting warehouse performance. As order picking is manual, improving the pickers' performance would improve the whole process. Therefore, to optimize the productivity of the warehouse, it is vital to stay focused on picker performance. Performance measures play an essential role in success by allowing performance evaluation and benchmarking the results against similar organizations. To measure performance, it is necessary to identify the factors affecting it beforehand. Previous literature has identified the factors that impact employees separately into general and order-picking processes. This study is focused on enhancing picker performance and thereby determining the factors that have an impact on picker performance.

Methodology

A systematic literature review was performed to examine the factors that impact the performance of pickers in 3PL warehouses in Sri Lanka. Given the need for a comprehensive understanding of this topic, a systematic literature review was chosen as the research method. The following six steps were carried out for the systematic literature review (Jones & Evans, 2000).

(1) Formulating a research question to guide the review.
(2) Establishing criteria for article selection.
(3) Systematically searching for relevant literature and unpublished studies.
(4) Selecting articles that meet the predetermined criteria.
(5) Extracting relevant findings from the selected studies.
(6) Summarizing the best available results.

Review Question

The research question that guided the literature search in this study is: 'What factors impact the performance of the pickers in 3PL warehouses in Sri Lanka?' This research question serves as a guide for identifying and selecting relevant articles.

Criteria for Inclusion of Articles

The inclusion and search criteria for the study were decided, as shown in Table 8.1.

This study established specific criteria to identify relevant publications for the analysis. The search focused on peer-reviewed journal articles, conference papers

Table 8.1. Article Inclusion Criteria.

Characteristics	Inclusion Criteria
Publication type	Peer-reviewed journal articles, conference papers, book chapters
Language(s)	English
Period	From 2000 to 2021
Research design	Conceptual and empirical
Content	Employee performance, 3PL industry in Sri Lanka, order-picking process
Source	Google Scholar, Research Gate, Scopus

Source: Authors' own.

and book chapters. Articles written in English were considered. Regarding publication dates, the literature concerning employee performance was published after 2010, whereas the literature concerning the order-picking process was published after 2000.

The research design of the selected articles could be either conceptual or empirical, as the aim was to explore the factors affecting the performance of the pickers in 3PL warehouses. The content of the studies included in the review addressed matters directly related to the factors that impact 3PL warehouses in Sri Lanka.

Google Scholar, Research Gate and Scopus were the primary sources for the literature search. The inclusion criteria specified in previous review articles supported this decision.

Article Screening Process

The article search process followed a three-step approach: identification, screening and inclusion.

(1) Step 1: During the identification stage, search terms and phrases such as 'third-party logistics providers in Sri Lanka', 'picker and order-picking process', 'employee performance' and relevant keywords were used. A total of 176 articles were shortlisted during this stage. The papers focused on operations other than order picking in a warehouse were excluded.
(2) Step 2: Upon completing the identification stage, a thorough review of the obtained studies was conducted to assess their relevance and adherence to the inclusion criteria. Studies that provided insights into order picking and employee performance were retained for further analysis. During this stage, 102 articles that met the inclusion criteria were identified.
(3) Step 3: An additional search was conducted using the Google Scholar search engine to ensure a comprehensive review. The screening process involved reviewing the titles and abstracts of the obtained studies. Top-tier peer-reviewed journals were prioritized during this step. As a result, 38 articles were deemed relevant for further analysis.

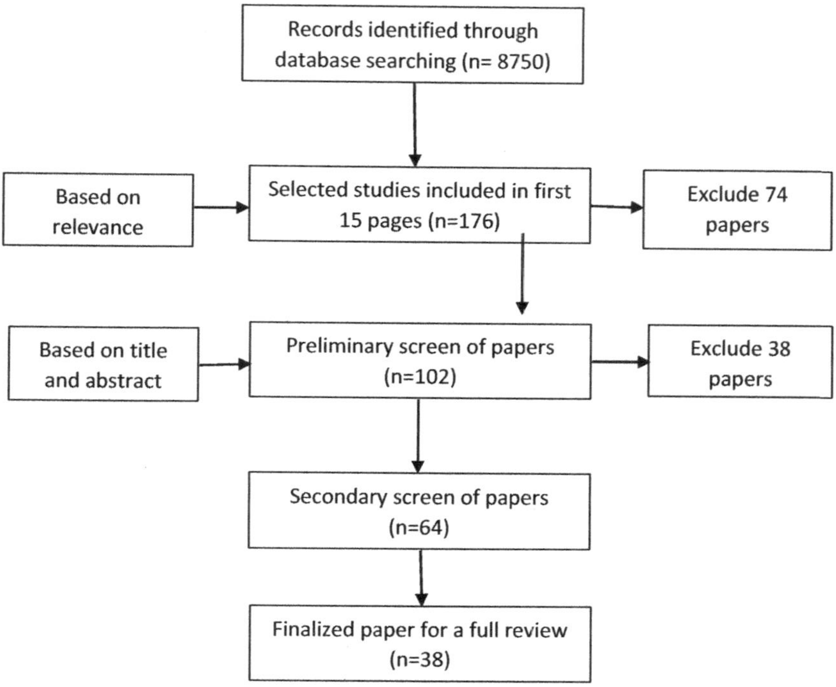

Fig. 8.1. Process of Literature Selection. *Source:* Authors' own.

The summary of the article inclusion criteria and the search process is depicted in Fig. 8.1.

3PL Providers

Malkanthie and Jayamanna (2016) noted, 'The world logistics industry is practising up to 7PL within a short period, Sri Lanka is still grappling with 3PL activities.' The paper analyzed the challenges, constraints and reasons impeding the development of the 3PL industry in Sri Lanka to keep up with the global competition. Further, the study listed major obstacles and future difficulties in the 3PL industry of Sri Lanka. Hettiarachchi and Ranwala (2015) found the variables that influence the urge to outsource 3PL activities and the satisfaction of customers as 'Tangible', 'Image and Trust', 'Empathy and Relationships', 'Reliability and Responsiveness' and 'Assurance'. According to the study, 'the most used 3PL services in Sri Lanka are warehouse operations, distribution, and shipment consolidation'. Among them, the most used 3PL service is the warehouse. The study further states that cost savings, less capital expenditure and the ability to concentrate on core operations in business are reasons for outsourcing logistics services in Sri Lanka (Hettiarachchi & Ranwala, 2015).

Sugathadasa and Rajapaksha (2011) investigated the satisfaction of 3PL users with information technology, supply chain security and green supply chain practices of 3PL providers. Karunarathna et al. (2020) state that a significant critical challenge faced by 3PL firms in Sri Lanka is labour shortages, and the most effective strategy to overcome this challenge is digitalization. According to Fernando and Rajapaksha (2016), 3PL service is not used by medium-sized clothing companies in Sri Lanka as a total quality management (TQM) practice. However, 3PL is essential for large-scale and extra-large-scale clothing enterprises to remain competitive globally. According to Malkanthie and Kelum (2017), the reasons for the forward gap between 3PL service providers and their customers are 'labour problems, lack of facilities, and poor technology usage', while the reasons for the reverse gap are 'poor communication, inaccurate information, inaccurate orders, cultural mismatch and poor coordination'.

Picker and Order-Picking Process

Most studies on order picking have focused mainly on design and control aspects, such as storage allocations, warehouse layout, batching and routing (Chackelson et al., 2013). Picker-to-part systems are primarily used in manual material handling. De Koster (2004) identified two categories of picker-to-parts systems: low-level order picking is when the picker manually selects products while travelling the warehouse aisles, whereas high-level order picking uses a lifting truck or a crane to reach the storage bins. Commonly employed storage policies encompass class-based, random, dedicated and cube-per-order indexes (COIs). According to Tsige (2013), using a random storage assignment technique reduces the distance an order picker must cover. Petersen et al. (2005) investigated methods to enhance order-picking productivity, focusing on slotting and storage techniques. The assignment of storage locations for a specific stock-keeping unit (SKU) necessitates knowledge of the SKU's attributes. The golden zone storage method, which involves storing high-demand SKUs between the picker's waist and shoulders, is highlighted in the research. Compared to alternative storage policies, the golden zone storage assignment technique, according to simulation data, shortens order fulfilment times. Furthermore, the report emphasizes how slotting metrics like turnover, popularity and COI help pickers travel less and complete orders faster (Petersen et al., 2005).

Tompkins et al. (2003) assessed the manual activities involved in the pick-to-parts order-picking system, revealing that travel time significantly contributes to the overall order-picking time. Bartholdi and Hackman (2011) argued that travel adds labour hours without improving the product's value, constituting a non-value-adding element and, hence, a waste. Petersen and Aase (2004) emphasize that travel time increases with the distance covered in the manual order-picking process. The primary goal of warehouse design and optimization is to minimize travel distance, so the layout and routing are crucial. The layout of the picking area is a critical factor in enhancing the productivity of picking systems (Caron et al., 2000). Effective warehouse planning is vital in reducing the time required for order picking. Routing strategies determine the sequence of items on the picklist and play a crucial role in time reduction. Given the time devoted to travel, optimal routing minimizes travel time. According to De Koster et al. (2007) and Tompkins et al. (2003), half of the time taken for order picking is attributed to the time the order picker travels.

Moeller (2011) suggests that line sequence optimization in pick orders is viable for reducing order-picking time and optimizing efficiency. Grosse and Glock (2013) investigated how human learning can affect order picking, observing that pickers' performance improves with an increased number of completed orders, leading to a decrease in the time taken to identify and pick products. Grosse et al. (2015) underline the importance of HF in order picking and order-picking design and planning models.

The investigation conducted by Caron et al. (2000) explains the impact of warehouse layout on the travel distance during order picking. The study reveals that the layout design contributes to more than 60% of the total travel distance. Key parameters influencing the layout design include the frequency of pick stops per tour, the overall length of picking aisles and the configuration of the COI-based ABC curve. Based on this, De Koster et al. (2007) and Heragu (2008) emphasize several critical factors to be taken into consideration when designing warehouse layouts, such as the configuration and shape of cross aisles, number of blocks, length, quantity and width of picking aisles, the elevation of racks, and the strategic placement of input and output points. These considerations are essential in optimizing the efficiency and productivity of the warehouse layout, thereby contributing to the overall effectiveness of the order-picking process. This article implies the importance of understanding warehouse layout design in examining the factors that enhance operational efficiency and streamline the workflow of the order-picking process.

Picker Performance

A picker is an employee who picks items from storage locations in the warehouse. To ensure ongoing success, it is crucial to have a comprehensive understanding of the elements that impact the performance of pickers. Like other employees, pickers significantly contribute to the success or failure of a 3PL warehouse. Therefore, pickers exhibit characteristics similar to those of other employees in general. It is essential to investigate the significant factors that affect an employee's performance while examining the picker's performance. Employee performance is a crucial determinant of their value to the company. Saeed et al. (2016) discovered that HF such as job content, manager's attitude, financial rewards, organizational culture and personal issues affect employee performance. Alawiyah et al. (2017) demonstrated a significant impact of training, leadership style and motivation on the effectiveness of logistics employees. The level of trust between leaders and followers and employees' satisfaction with their work can influence their relationship. Employee motivation is an intrinsic drive that forces individuals to complete tasks related to their work.

According to Wahyono et al. (2020), emotional intelligence positively and substantially impacts employee performance and job motivation. Employees who have high emotional intelligence perform well at work because they can manage pressure and fit in with the surroundings. Employee success is impacted by burnout, workplace stress and motivation (Rosita & Yanuar, 2019). Payments based on performance also help enhance employees' productivity by increasing their motivation. Many researchers have shown that dispersion in compensation might have various effects on employees' work performance. According to Long et al. (2011) and Frye (2004), financial considerations significantly improve employees' performance at work. Also, it said that financial incentives can support workers in achieving better performance levels.

Data Analysis and Findings

Initially, the literature review explored factors influencing employee performance, followed by examining factors affecting the order-picking process. The number of papers considered for the literature review per published year is summarized in the graph below (Fig. 8.2).

Numerous studies have attempted to identify the factors influencing the performance of various types of employees, focusing on HF that impact job performance. Many of these studies (57%) highlight leadership as a critical factor influencing employee performance. Additionally, motivation (36%) and financial rewards (29%) emerged as the second and third most frequently cited factors affecting employee performance. Furthermore, factors such as job content, emotional intelligence, proactivity, adaptability, skill flexibility, commitment, learning, work experience, satisfaction, self-directedness, attitude and work

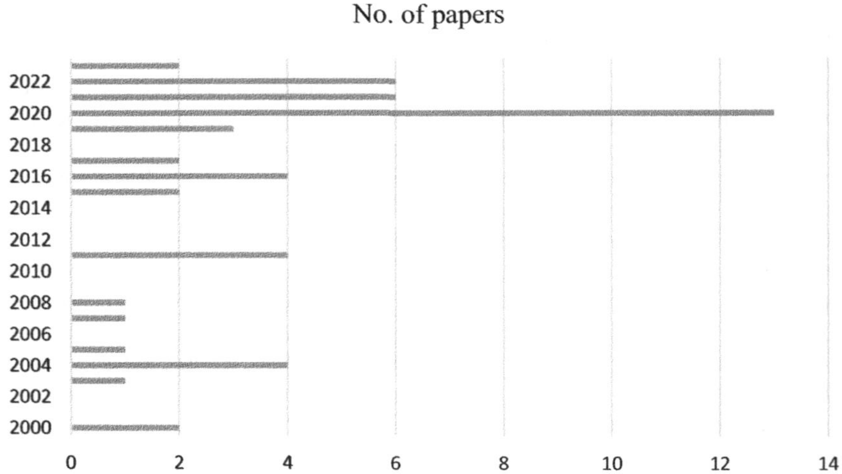

Fig. 8.2. Papers Published Yearly. *Source:* Authors' own.

discipline received comparatively less attention from researchers. To assess the relationship between these factors and employee performance, researchers used methods such as multiple regression analysis. Past studies indicate that the factors influencing performance vary across different industries. Therefore, the benefits of analyzing the factors that affect picker performance are shown in this study. Table 8.2 summarizes the factors affecting employee performance identified through past literature.

In the second category, which identifies the factors affecting the order-picking process, some studies have developed optimization models to improve order-picking efficiency. Most papers (31%) have considered storage assignment, routing and order batching in increasing the performance of the order-picking process. The researchers have given the OP method, line sequence, slotting, learning and job assignment the least attention. Table 8.3 summarizes the factors affecting the order-picking process were identified in past literature.

Conclusion

This paper presented an extensive analysis of the factors influencing the performance of pickers within 3PL warehouses, classifying them into two primary categories: factors that impact employee performance and the nature of the order-picking process. Given the manual nature of order picking, it is vital to separately identify factors affecting employee performance and the order-picking process. Therefore, a thorough examination, dissecting the two categories, was conducted. Most papers that analyzed employee performance have shown that motivation, leadership and financial rewards are the factors with the most focus. In contrast, the papers investigating the order-picking process showed that storage assignment, order batching and routing are the factors with the most focus.

The gap in previous research underscores the necessity of identifying the factors influencing picker performance. This can be addressed by integrating the three categories, picker-related factors, management-related factors and warehouse-related factors, in one research (Prasadika et al., 2022). One limitation of this study is the dearth of literature on picker performance in Sri Lankan 3PL warehouses and other developing countries. When investigating factors impacting picker performance, it is vital to distinguish between internal factors, controllable by pickers and external factors, which are beyond their control.

Future Research

Due to the lack of past literature investigating factors affecting employee performance and the order-picking process simultaneously, it is better to address both areas when focusing on picker performance. For future research, it is highly recommended to place greater emphasis on integrating the three main categories of factors: picker-related factors, such as work experience, physical fitness and training, which are controllable and internal to the picker; management-related factors, such as leadership and organizational culture; and warehouse-related

Table 8.2. Summary of Factors Affecting Employee Performance.

	Arifani and Susanti (2020)	Tuffaha (2020)	Badrianto and Ekhsan (2020)	Wahyono et al. (2020)	Rosita and Yanuar (2019)	Yandi and Havidz (2022)	Iis et al. (2022)	Nguyen et al. (2020)	Anshori et al. (2020)	Martini and Sarmawa (2019)	Sopiah et al. (2020)	Syamsuddin et al. (2021)	Candradewi and Dewi (2019)	Kamar et al. (2020)
Leadership	√			√				√	√					√
Organizational culture		√				√		√		√				
Financial reward	√							√			√	√	√	
Motivation		√			√		√	√			√			
Work experience					√									
Burnout				√	√									
Emotional intelligence				√										
Proactivity														
Satisfaction			√			√								
Working environment			√			√	√	√						
Competence	√	√												
Talent management											√			

Source: Authors' own.

Table 8.3. Summary of Factors Affecting the Order-Picking Process.

	Vanheusden et al. (2020)	**Kovac and Djurdjevic (2020)**	**Setayesh et al. (2022)**	**Žulj et al. (2022)**	**Wang et al. (2020)**	**Leng et al. (2021)**	**Masae et al. (2020)**	**Mirzaei et al. (2021)**	**Kim et al. (2020)**	**Zhang and Gao (2023)**	**Cao et al. (2023)**	**Rasmi et al. (2022)**	**Yang et al. (2020)**
Storage assignment		√			√	√			√			√	
Routing		√					√			√	√	√	
OP method	√	√						√					
Job assignment											√		
Slotting									√				
Order batching	√			√						√	√	√	√
Human factor			√										

Source: Authors' own.

factors, such as storage assignments, order batching, facility safety and working environment, all of which affect the order-picking performance and efficiency. In developing countries like Sri Lanka, manual order-picking methods are still used. Therefore, future researchers can focus on how new technologies can enhance the order-picking process in 3PL warehouses in developing countries. Since most of the research has highlighted the importance of finances on the performance of employees, payment schemes, including hourly payment, piece rate payment or a mix of both, are another area that can be optimized when enhancing picker performance.

Acknowledgements

We thank the editors and anonymous reviewers whose comments and suggestions made this chapter publishable. We also want to thank Team ICMR and the Sabaragamuwa University of Sri Lanka for their strong support.

References

Alawiyah, T., Backhtia, Y., & Daud, I. (2017). Factors that affect the performance of logistics employees at pharmaceutical wholesalers X in Banjarmasin. In *2nd Sari Mulia International Conference on Health and Sciences (SMICHS)* (p. 6). https://doi.org/10.2991/smichs-17.2017.80

Anshori, M. Y., Karya, F. D., Muslihah, N., & Herlambang, T. (2020). Analysis of transformational leadership style for employee performance with job satisfaction as intervening variable. *International Journal of Advanced Science and Technology*, *29*(9), 3967–3973.

Arifani, A. Z. T., & Susanti, A. Y. (2020). Literature review factors affecting employee performance: Competence, compensation, and leadership. *Dinasti International Journal of Economics, Finance & Accounting*, *1*(3), 538–549.

Armstrong and Associates Inc. (n.d.). *Global 3PL market size estimates*. https://www.3plogistics.com/3pl-market-info-resources/3pl-market-information/global-3pl-market-size-estimates/. Accessed on July 08, 2021.

Badrianto, Y., & Ekhsan, M. (2020). Effect of work environment and job satisfaction on employee performance in pt. Nesinak industries. *Journal of Business, Management, & Accounting*, *2*(1), 85–91.

Bartholdi III, J. J., & Hackman, S. T. (2008). *Warehouse and distribution science*. Supply Chain and Logistics Institute, School of Industrial and Systems Engineering, Georgia Institute of Technology.

Candradewi, I., & Dewi, I. G. (2019). Effect of compensation on employee performance towards motivation as a mediation variable. *International Research Journal of Management, IT and Social Sciences*, *6*(5), 134–143.

Cao, Z., Zhou, L., Lin, C., & Zhou, M. (2023). Solving an order batching, picker assignment, batch sequencing, and picker routing problem via information integration. *Journal of Industrial Information Integration*, *31*, 100414. https://doi.org/10.1016/j.jii.2022.100414

Caron, F., Marchet, G., & Perego, A. (2000). Optimal layout in low-level picker-to-part systems. *International Journal of Production Research*, *38*(1), 101–117.

Chackelson, C., Errasti, A., Ciprés, D., & Laho, F. (2013). Evaluating order picking performance trade-offs by configuring main operating strategies in a retail distributor: A design of experiments approach. *International Journal of Production Research*, *51*(20), 6097–9109.

De Alwis, G. (2016). *Emerging opportunities in Sri Lanka's third-party logistics space.* In T. L. Gunaruwan (Ed.), *Proceedings of the 1st International Conference on Research for Transport and Logistics Industry (R4TLI)*, June 3–4, 2016, Colombo, Sri Lanka (pp. 115–117). Sri Lanka Society for Transport and Logistics.

De Koster, R. (2004). How to assess a warehouse operation in a single tour. In M. Lahmar (Ed.), *Facility logistics: Approaches and solutions to next generation challenges* (pp. 39–60). Taylor & Francis Group; Auerbach.

De Koster, R., Le-Duc, T., & Roodbergen, K. J. (2007). Design and control of warehouse order picking: A literature review. *European Journal of Operational Research*, *182*(2), 481–501.

Fernando, H., & Rajapaksha, U. G. (2016). *The impact of 3PL service on total quality management of apparel industry in Sri Lanka.* In *Proceedings in Management, Social Sciences and Humanities. 9th International Research Conference-KDU*, September 8–9, 2016, in Rathmalana, Sri Lanka (pp. 234–243).

Frye, M. B. (2004). Equity-based compensation for employees: Firm performance and determinants. *Journal of Financial Research*, *27*(1), 31–54.

Grosse, E. H., & Glock, C. H. (2013). An experimental investigation of learning effects in order picking systems. *Journal of Manufacturing Technology Management*, 850–872. https://doi.org/10.1108/JMTM-03-2012-0036

Grosse, E. H., Glock, C. H., Jaber, M. Y., & Neumann, W. P. (2015). Incorporating human factors in order picking planning models: Framework and research opportunities. *International Journal of Production Research*, *53*(3), 695–717.

Heragu, S. S. (2008). *Facilities design* (3rd ed.). CRC Press. https://doi.org/10.1201/9781420066272

Hettiarachchi, P., & Ranwala, L. (2015). *Determinants of customer satisfaction in third party logistics outsourcing relationship in Sri Lanka.* In *8th International Research Conference, KDU, Malabe, Sri Lanka*, August 27–28, 2015, in Ratmalana, Sri Lanka (pp. 126–131).

Iis, E. Y., Wahyuddin, W., Thoyib, A., Ilham, R. N., & Sinta, I. (2022). The effect of career development and work environment on employee performance with work motivation as an intervening variable at Aceh's office of agriculture and livestock. *International Journal of Economic, Business, Accounting, Agriculture Management and Sharia Administration (IJEBAS)*, *2*(2), 227–236.

Jones, T., & Evans, D. (2000). Conducting a systematic review. *Australian Critical Care: Official Journal of the Confederation of Australian Critical Care Nurses*, *13*(2), 66–71. https://doi.org/10.1016/s1036-7314(00)70624-2

Kamar, K., Novitasari, D., Asbari, M., Winanti, & Goestjahjanti, F. S. (2020). Enhancing employee performance during the COVID-19 pandemic: The role of readiness for change mentality. *Jurnal Dinamika Manajemen*, *11*(2), 154–166.

Karunarathna, N., Vidanagamachchi, K., & Wickramarachchi, R. (2020). A calibrated model of critical success factors for Industry 4.0 warehousing performance improvement: Insights from multiple case studies. *International Journal of Multidisciplinary Sciences and Advanced Technology*, 100–126.

Kim, J., Méndez, F., & Jimenez, J. (2020). Storage location assignment heuristics based on slot selection and frequent itemset grouping for large distribution centres. *IEEE Access*, *8*, 189025–189035.

Kovac, M., & Djurdjevic, D. (2020). Optimisation of order-picking systems through tactical and operational decision-making. *International Journal of Simulation Modelling*, 89–99. https://doi.org/10.2507/IJSIMM19-1-505

Leng, J., Yan, D., Liu, Q., Zhang, H., Zhao, G., Wei, L., Zhang, D., Yu, A., & Chen, X. (2021). Digital twin-driven joint optimisation of packing and storage assignment in large-scale automated high-rise warehouse product-service system. *International Journal of Computer Integrated Manufacturing*, *34*(7–8), 783–800.

Long, C. P., Bendersky, C., & Morril, C. (2011). Fairness monitoring: Linking managerial controls and fairness judgments in the organisation. *Academy of Management Journal*, *54*(5), 1045–1068.

Malkanthie, M. A., & Jayamanna, J. M. (2016). *Exploration of factors hindering the growth of the 3PL market in Sri Lanka*. In *Academy for Global Business Advancement (AGBA) 13th World Congress,* November 26–28, 2016, in Surakarta (Solo), Central Java, Indonesia.

Malkanthie, M. A., & Kelum, W. G. (2017). *Reverse service quality gap of the 3PL (third-party logistics) market in Sri Lanka*. In *Academy for Global Business Advancement (AGBA), 14th World Congress,* November 23–25, 2017, in Eldoret, Uasin Gishu County, Kenya.

Martini, I. A., & Sarmawa, I. W. (2019). The role of employee work motivation in mediating the work culture towards their performance. *Jurnal Ekonomi dan Bisnis Jagaditha*, *6*(1), 15–21.

Mirzaei, M., Zaerpour, N., & De Koster, R. (2021). The impact of integrated cluster-based storage allocation on parts-to-picker warehouse performance. *Transportation Research Part E: Logistics and Transportation Review*, *146*, 102207.

Moeller, K. (2011). Increasing warehouse order picking performance by sequence. *Procedia Social and Behavioral Sciences*, 177–185.

Nguyen, P. T., Yandi, A., & Mahaputra, M. R. (2020). Factors influencing employee performance are motivation, leadership, environment, culture, organisation, work achievement, competence, and compensation. *Dinasti International Journal of Digital Business Management*, *1*(4), 645–662.

Petersen, C. G., & Aase, G. (2004). A comparison of picking, storage, and routing policies in manual order picking. *International Journal of Production Economics*, 11–19.

Petersen, C. G., Siu, C., & Heise, D. R. (2005). Improving order picking performance utilising slotting and golden zone storage. *International Journal of Operations & Production Management*, *25*(10), 997–1012.

Prasadika, A. P. K. J., Wijayanayake, A., & Niwunhella, D. H. H. (2022). Analysing factors that impact the performance of pickers in third-party logistics warehouses in Sri Lanka. In *International Research Conference on Smart Computing and Systems Engineering (SCSE)*, September 1, 2022, in Colombo, Sri Lanka (pp. 239–245). https://doi.org/10.1109/SCSE56529.2022.9905151

Rasmi, S. A. B., Wang, Y., & Charkhgard, H. (2022). Wave order picking under the mixed-shelves storage strategy: A solution method and advantages. *Computers & Operations Research*, *137*, 105556.

Richard, W., & Rein, J. (2004). Customer perceptions on logistics outsourcing in the European consumer goods industry. *International Journal of Physical Distribution and Logistics Management*, *34*(8), 628–644.

Rosita, & Yanuar, T. (2019). Burnout, work experience, and work motivation affect employee performance, with emotional intelligence as variable moderation. *Journal of Business Studies*, *4*(1), 2443–3837.

Saeed, R., Mussawar, S., Lodhi, R. N., Iqbal, A., Nayab, H. H., & Yaseen, S. (2016). Factors affecting the performance of employees at the workplace in Pakistan's banking sector. *Middle-East Journal of Scientific Research*, *17*(9), 1200–1208.

Setayesh, A., Grosse, E. H., Glock, C. H., & Neumann, W. P. (2022). Determining the source of human-system errors in manual order picking concerning human factors. *International Journal of Production Research*, *60*(20), 6350–6372.

Sopiah, S., Kurniawan, D. T., Nora, E., & Narmaditya, B. S. (2020). Does talent management affect employee performance? The moderating role of work engagement. *The Journal of Asian Finance, Economics and Business*, *7*(7), 335–341.

Sugathadasa, P. T., & Rajapaksha, S. S. (2011). Investigating the relationship between third-party logistics users and providers in the FMCG Industry in Sri Lanka. In *17th ERU research symposium*. Moratuwa.

Syamsuddin, R. A., Pratama, A., Sunarsi, D., Affandi, A., Rifuddin, B., & Mujahidin (2021). The effect of compensation and work discipline on employee performance with work motivation as an intervening variable. *Jurnal Ilmiah Manajemen*, *9*(1), 89–94.

The World Bank. (n.d.). Logistics performance index (LPI). https://lpi.worldbank.org/report. Accessed on June 07, 2021.

Tompkins, J., White, J., Bozer, Y., & Tanchoco, J. (2003). *Facilities planning*. Wiley.

Tsige, M. T. (2013). *Improving order-picking efficiency via storage assignment strategies*. Master's thesis. University of Twente.

Tuffaha, M. (2020). The determinants of employee's performance: A literature review. *Journal of Economics and Management Sciences*, *3*(3).

Vanheusden, S., Van Gils, T., Caris, A., Ramaekers, K., & Braekers, K. (2020). Operational workload balancing in manual order picking. *Computers & Industrial Engineering*, *141*, 106269.

Wahyono, T., Zaman, B., Saifudin, & Hartono, R. (2020). Analysis of factors affecting BRI bank employee performance. *Journal of the Social Sciences*, *48*(3).

Winkelhaus, S., Grosse, E. H., & Morana, S. (2021). Towards a conceptualisation of order picking 4.0. *Computers & Industrial Engineering*, *159*, 107511.

Yandi, A., & Havidz, H. B. H. (2022). Employee performance model: Work engagement through job satisfaction and organisational commitment (A study of human resource management literature study). *Dinasti International Journal of Management Science*, *3*(3), 547–565.

Yang, P., Zhao, Z., & Guo, H. (2020). Order batch-picking optimisation under different storage scenarios for e-commerce warehouses. *Transportation Research Part E: Logistics and Transportation Review*, *136*, 101897.

Zhang, K., & Gao, C. (2023). Improved formulations of the joint order batching and picker routing problem. *International Journal of Production Research*, *61*(21), 7386–7409.

Žulj, I., Salewski, H., Goeke, D., & Schneider, M. (2022). Order batching and batch sequencing in an AMR-assisted picker-to-parts system. *European Journal of Operational Research*, *298*(1), 182–201.

Chapter 9

Do Human Resource Management Practices Ensure Employee Happiness? Unveiling the Moderating Effect of Work–Life Balance

Renusha Mithulan

University of Jaffna, Sri Lanka

Abstract

This chapter systematically investigates the nexus of human resource management (HRM) practices and employee happiness and how work–life balance (WLB) functions as a moderating variable within the context of the travel trade industry in Sri Lanka. In the modern working era, understanding the organizational practices related to human resources and WLB has become imperative, considering every stakeholder's expectations and consideration for holistic well-being. The study employed the hypothetico-deductive method and a survey strategy. The researcher gathered data from 379 participants in the travel trade industry through a structured questionnaire. The study's findings reveal a positive and significant relationship between HRM practices and employee happiness, and WLB significantly moderates the relationship. Academically, it contributes to the existing literature by providing new insights and knowledge. This study also offers a basis for investigating the need for HRM practices to enhance employee happiness in the workplace. Practically, it considers organizations that intend to improve employee happiness, especially the travel trade industry. Further, this study provides a basis for future research and prompts further exploration into the concept of employee happiness in the context of the travel trade industry.

Keywords: Employee happiness; human resource management practices; moderating role; travel trade industry; work–life balance

Shaping Entrepreneurial Marketing, Volume 1, 133–150

Published under exclusive licence by Emerald Publishing Limited
doi:10.1108/978-1-83708-852-220251009

Introduction

Happiness serves as the cornerstone for individual well-being and peaceful survival. It is also an intrinsic motivational factor for individuals to enhance their performance in the organizational context. The term happiness has been broadly examined in recent studies (Al Suwaidi et al., 2020; Behera et al., 2024; Blanchflower & Bryson, 2024; Jaiswal & Gupta, 2024; Smith et al., 2023) across various domains, including philosophy theology, psychology and sociology. Although happiness has captured the attention of philosophers for many years, it remains a relatively new concept in psychology literature (Otken & Gul, 2013).

In recent years, academics have increasingly stressed the significance of enhancing happiness in positive psychology, positioning it as a crucial contributor to people's overall well-being (Park et al., 2009, as cited in Otken & Gul, 2013; Smith et al., 2023). This heightened interest is evident in recent research that delves into the multifaceted aspects of employee happiness (Bani-Melhem et al., 2020; Tambyah et al., 2024). Happy employees exhibit positive behaviours that lead to better organizational performance (Chia & Chu, 2016; Fisher, 2010), elevated positive mood, wellness and attitude (Bani-Melhem et al., 2020), improved productivity (Rivera et al., 2024), increased commitment and enhanced work engagement (Field & Buitendach, 2011). Conversely, unhappy employees can be detrimental to organizations, resulting in reduced productivity (Fereidouni et al., 2013; Vestal, 2015), increased illness (Kimball & Nink, 2006), heightened turnover costs (Gregory, 2011) and increased absenteeism and presenteeism that cause managers and business leaders to face difficulties in retaining the talent workforce (Renusha, 2022b).

As cited by Kimball and Nink in 2006, a report from the Conference Board in 2005 indicated a growing dissatisfaction among employees with their jobs. Furthermore, the entire human race grappled with the challenges presented by the COVID-19 crisis (Bailey & Breslin, 2021; Singh & Mishra, 2020), prompting organizations to adapt to the new situation by incorporating work-from-home strategies. Despite being employed as a strategy, this shift had detrimental effects on parenting, marital harmony, work–family balance (WLB) and social support for many employees (Chung et al., 2020), impacting overall employee happiness.

Though happiness matters for every individual, it should last for a more extended period. Some academics believe that companies that can maintain long-term workplace happiness could enhance and sustain productivity (Jaiswal & Gupta, 2024; Wesarat et al., 2014). Consequently, they must comprehend the employee-related factors to enhance workplace happiness. Nowadays, employees expect respect, equal treatment, safety, recognition (Chron Contributor, 2020; Climek et al., 2024), career advancement and job enrichment from the organization. These are usually done through the organizations' human resource management (HRM) practices. If employees facilitate these functions, they feel contentment, thus leading to employee happiness. However, there is a dearth of research exploring the linkage between HRM and happiness globally (Opatha & Uresha, 2020), and no study has yet examined WLB as a moderating variable in the HRM practices and employee happiness linkage in the Sri Lankan context.

Therefore, this study seeks to fill the empirical and contextual gaps by examining how employee WLB influences HRM practices and employee happiness linkage within Sri Lanka's travel trade industries.

To systematically discuss the research problem and the gaps identified in the existing literature, the research questions of this study were formulated in the following manner:

RQ1. What is the relationship between HRM practices and employee happiness?
RQ2. Does employee WLB moderate the relationship between HRM practices and employee happiness?

The following research objectives were formulated to align with these research questions:

RO1. To investigate the relationship between HRM practices and employee happiness.
RO2. To examine how employees' WLB moderates the relationship between HRM practices and employee happiness.

Literature Review

Employee Happiness

Happiness is an integral part of organizations that plays a momentous role in fostering a positive work environment (Dahiya & Rangnekar, 2018). It is defined by Opatha (2019b, p. 235) as encompassing both 'a feeling of pleasure, satisfaction, or becoming pleased' and 'a sense of pleasure, and a profound sense of a life well-lived.' A happier work environment is an imperative element in organizations since it functions as a motivational factor, encouraging individuals to actively engage in the allocated duties and responsibilities in their organizations (Adnyana & Veronica, 2023; Al Suwaidi et al., 2020; Ausat et al., 2024; Singha, 2024).

Further, the existing literature distinguishes between hedonic and eudaimonic happiness, the two primary types of happiness (Kashdan et al., 2008; Opatha & Uresha, 2020). Hedonic happiness concerns an individual's feelings about their life (Ryan & Deci, 2001). Such hedonic happiness can be further classified into two types: affective hedonic happiness, which prioritizes pleasure over suffering, and cognitive hedonic happiness, which denotes overall life satisfaction (Lomas & VanderWeele, 2023; Opatha, 2019a, 2019b). On the other hand, eudaimonic happiness emphasizes complete alignment with one's potential (Ryan & Deci, 2001). Therefore, recognizing happiness is critical in the organizational context and highlights its multifaceted nature and profound impact on employee performance. Therefore, the researcher aimed to explore the interconnection between HRM practices, WLB and employee happiness.

Human Resource Management (HRM) Practices

HRM is a crucial area in the organization that deals with human capital (Mithulan & Opatha, 2023). Several authors have defined the HRM concept: 'HRM is the efficient and effective utilisation of human resources to achieve goals of an organisation' (Opatha, 2009, p. 7); 'Human resource management is the process of acquiring, training, appraising, and compensating employees, and of attending to their labour relations, health and safety, and fairness concerns' (Dessler, 2013, p. 4). 'Job design, job analysis, human resource planning, recruitment, selection, hiring, induction, performance evaluation, training and development, career management, pay management, welfare management, management of incentives, employee movements, health and safety management, discipline management, grievance handling, and labour relations' are the 18 HRM functions identified by Opatha (2009, p. 12) which have been classified into three: acquire, develop and retain (De Silva et al., 2016). Opatha (2019b, p. 28) stated, 'HRM is divided into five main areas: employment planning, staffing, human resource development, rewards management, and employee and labour relations.' Moreover, the holistic nature of HRM can be further classified into acquiring, developing, retaining, motivating and other vital areas (Opatha, 2019b).

Such HRM functions positively impact organizational performance, social well-being (Bailey & Breslin, 2021), employee attitude (Renusha, 2022a), commitment (Pimenta et al., 2024), retention (Pham et al., 2023), engagement (Jose et al., 2024), loyalty (Renusha, 2022b), satisfaction (Alolayyan et al., 2023) and happiness (Opatha & Uresha, 2020). Hence, it is crucial to consider the nexus between HRM practices and employee happiness for organizational success.

Work–Life Balance

WLB has become a prominent concept in the contemporary work environment. People are more attentive to balancing their work and personal lives (Lockwood, 2003) because both men and women in the family work in today's world. Several authors defined WLB as follows: 'It is a condition when there are no conflicts or interferences between work and family/private life roles' (Frone, 2003, p. 145). 'It is defined as the individual's ability to meet their work and family commitments, as well as other non-work responsibilities and activities' (Delecta, 2011, p. 187). WLB has undoubtedly become a significant priority for individuals seeking a high quality of life (Soomro et al., 2018), enjoying life, and staying healthy and prosperous (Adnan-Bataineh, 2019). Moreover, WLB increases an organization's and its employees' overall performance beyond individual well-being. To this end, the researcher argues that exploring the nexus of HRM practices, WLB and employee happiness is imperative.

Theoretical Framework

The researcher employed theories, logical assumptions and existing literature to establish connections between the three variables. HRM practices have been treated as independent because they directly impact the dependent variable, employee happiness. WLB is the moderating variable in the HRM practices and employee happiness linkage. Accordingly, the current study investigates these variables within the theoretical framework illustrated in Fig. 9.1.

Fig. 9.1 illustrates a schematic representation of the nomological network. The general systems theory (GST) was employed to determine the causal relationships between the three variables, outlining how outcomes may emerge through 'inputs, processing, and outputs' (Pouvreau, 2014). This study includes HRM practices as input within the GST framework. WLB acts as the process that accelerates the conversion of inputs into the preferred output, while employee happiness represents the intended output. Furthermore, as proposed in the research hypotheses, the social exchange theory clarifies the HRM practices and employee happiness linkage.

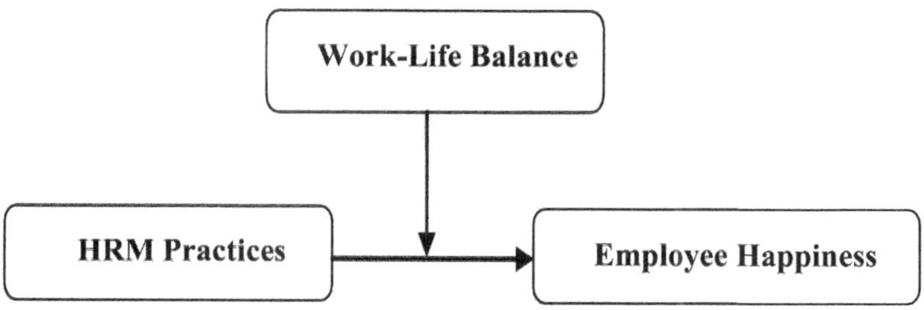

Fig. 9.1. Nomological Network of Employee Happiness.
Source: Author's own.

Hypothesis Development

HRM Practices and Employee Happiness

It can be argued that HRM practices result in employee happiness, based on the literature that is currently accessible. If an organization maintains good HRM practices, its employees show their commitment (Pimenta et al., 2024), engagement (Jose et al., 2024) and job satisfaction (Cherif, 2020). Moreover, such HRM practices have been positively associated with better organizational performance (Bailey & Breslin, 2021; Barmby et al., 2012; Silla et al., 2010). Additionally, it fosters a positive working environment, prompting employees to exhibit a positive attitude (Renusha, 2022a), thereby contributing to happiness at work. Therefore, the author asserts that employee happiness results from an organization's HRM practices.

Furthermore, the social exchange theory can substantiate that providing sufficient training and development, proper evaluation and feedback on performance, and rewards can motivate employees to perform better at work (Opatha & Uresha, 2020). Thus, HRM practices enhance and ensure employee happiness. This theoretical and logical perspective resulted in the development of the first hypothesis of this research, as stated below.

H1. HRM practices and employee happiness have a positive and significant relationship.

Moderating Role of WLB

According to the current literature, it is conceivable to hypothesize that good organizational HRM practices would increase employee happiness. Nevertheless, such a postulated link is invalid for employees who do not balance work and life but may be true for individuals who maintain a healthy WLB. Organizations often prioritize the implementation of effective HRM practices to enhance employee happiness. However, this goal can only be achieved if employees have WLB. Therefore, every organization should focus on employee WLB to create a strong relationship between HRM practices and employee happiness. Hence, employee WLB moderates the HRM practices and employee happiness linkage. With this argument and explanation, the researcher formulated a second hypothesis as follows:

H2. WLB significantly moderates the HRM practices and employee happiness linkage.

Methodology

Study Design

This explanatory study aimed to discover the nexus of independent (HRM practices) and dependent (employee happiness) variables within the nomological network. Consequently, a correlational study design was employed. The focus was on employees in the travel trade sector in Sri Lanka, as they directly interact with customers, making employee happiness a significant factor. The analysis focused on this set of employees to examine their organizations' HRM practices and overall happiness.

Due to scheduling limitations, the research adopted a cross-sectional time frame. The study population was not precisely defined since numerous travel trade industries operate in Sri Lanka. Using convenient sampling, 384 employees were chosen, and surveys were distributed to them. Responses were received from 379 participants, resulting in a 98% response rate, which meets the acceptable standards per Saunders et al. (2009).

Measures and Instruments

Since there are three variables: HRM practices, employee happiness and WLB, the author developed three instruments. Based on existing literature, the variables were adequately defined and measured through multi-item interval scales. HRM practices were evaluated across five dimensions: 'employment planning, staffing, human resource development, rewards management, and employee and labour relations' (Opatha & Uresha, 2020). WLB was assessed through three dimensions: 'work interference with personal life, personal life interference with work, and work/personal life enhancement.' Employee happiness was measured in terms of hedonic and eudaimonic happiness. All items about these aspects were measured through a five-point Likert scale.

Validity and Reliability

Content validity was ensured with proper conceptualization and operationalization. Furthermore, the questionnaire items for each element were adopted from existing literature (Opatha & Uresha, 2020), ensuring the face and content validity of the three instruments. Exploratory factor analysis (EFA) was utilized to assess the construct validity of the instruments. The suitability of the items for principal component analysis was established using the Kaiser–Meyer–Olkin (KMO) index. The KMO values for the three instruments were all above 0.5 (HRM practices – 0.837, WLB – 0.788 and employee happiness – 0.834), in addition to Bartlett's sphericity test, demonstrating a solid correlation between the items and verifying that the sample size was sufficient for factor analysis.

The reliability of the measurements was evaluated by calculating Cronbach's coefficient alpha. All three variables' scores were more than 0.70, indicating that the questionnaire's items consistently measured the same construct (Spector, 1992). Cronbach's alpha values for HRM practices (0.942), WLB (0.895) and employee happiness (0.844) varied from 0.844 to 0.942. Since all three dimensions were sufficiently reliable, they were retained (Nunnally & Bernstein, 1994). Three instruments, totalling 47 items, were included in the questionnaire to represent the variables being studied.

The researcher employed the Statistical Package for Social Sciences (SPSS) to analyze the collected data. Common problems like missing values and outliers were dealt with during data gathering (Schlomer et al., 2010). No outliers or missing values were found during data purification. The first hypothesis was tested using the Pearson Product-Moment Correlation Technique, which examined the relationship between variables. The second hypothesis was investigated using hierarchical multiple regression analysis, which looked at the moderating role of WLB in the HRM practices and employee happiness linkage.

Data Analysis and Results

The final data included 379 valid responses. Of these respondents, 227 were male and 152 were female. A substantial number of participants had a bachelor's

Table 9.1. Demographic Information.

Parameter	Frequency (n = 379)	%
Gender		
Male	227	59.9
Female	152	40.1
Age		
21–29	137	36.1
30–39	171	45.1
40–49	71	18.7
Above 50	00	0.0
Education		
Advanced level	88	23.2
Diploma	65	17.2
Professional course	57	15.0
Bachelors' degree	143	37.7
Masters' degree	26	06.9
Work experience		
Less than one year	83	21.9
2–5 years	120	31.7
6–10 years	80	21.1
More than 10 years	96	25.3

Source: Author's own.

degree as their educational qualification. Additionally, the majority had two to five years of work experience in their current organization, comprising 37.7% and 31.7%, respectively. Table 9.1 illustrates the demographic information gathered from the participants.

Further, Table 9.2 illustrates the values of the correlation coefficients of all variables of this study.

Hypothesis Testing

The study proposed two hypotheses; the expected relationships are summarized in Table 9.3. The + sign denotes a positive relationship between variables.

This research developed two hypotheses. The results of the correlation analysis used to evaluate Hypothesis 1 (H1) are shown in Table 9.4.

As per the above table, the correlation analysis indicates a significant correlation ($p < 0.01$) between HRM practices and employee happiness. Consequently,

Table 9.2. Correlation Coefficients.

	Age	Gender	Education	Experience	HRM Practices	WLB	Happiness
Age	1						
Gender	−0.228**	1					
Education	−0.531**	−0.035	1				
Experience	0.593**	0.021	−0.407**	1			
HRM practices	−0.014	−0.265**	0.012	−0.092	1		
WLB	−0.088	0.177**	0.036	−0.139**	0.265**	1	
Happiness	−0.030	−0.110*	0.083	−0.049	0.558**	0.257**	1

Source: Author's own.

Note: **Significant at 0.01 (2-tailed), *Significant at 0.05 (2-tailed).

Table 9.3. Hypothesized Relationships.

No	Relationship	Hypotheses
01	HRM practices and employee happiness linkage	H1(+)
02	HRM practices and employee happiness linkage through the moderation of WLB	H2

Source: Author's own.

Table 9.4. Pearson Correlation Coefficient (Testing H1).

Variables	Testing	Values
HRM practices and employee happiness	Pearson correlation coefficients	0.558**
	Significance	0.000
	Number	379

Source: Author's own.

Note: **Significant at 0.01.

the correlation analysis supports accepting the first hypothesis (H1) developed in the study. Therefore, it is proposed that the relationship between these two variables is positive and significant.

Furthermore, according to the second hypothesis, WLB significantly moderates the nexus of HRM practices and employee happiness. A moderator variable modifies the intensity of the independent and dependent variable linkage (Baron & Kenny, 1986). This study used the Baron and Kenny technique for moderation analysis, which consists of three steps (Frazier et al., 2004).

The initial step (Path a) reveals how the predictor variable (HRM practices) impacts the outcome variable (employee happiness). The second step (Path b) illustrates how the moderator variable (WLB) affects the outcome variable (employee happiness). Finally, the third step (Path c) demonstrates how the product of the predictor and moderator variables influences the outcome variable.

The moderation model depicted in Fig. 9.2 illustrates the causal association between three variables: HRM practices (predictor), WLB (moderator) and the interaction between HRM practices and WLB (predictor × moderator) and their combined effect on the outcome variable (employee happiness). Bissonnette et al. (1990) suggest that the hierarchical multiple regression analysis evaluates the moderating effect while preserving the natural character of continuous variables and minimizing errors (Type I and Type II) in finding moderator effects.

The hierarchical multiple regression analysis results, illustrated in Table 9.5, reveal that the effect is statistically significant (p-value = 0.004, below 0.01).

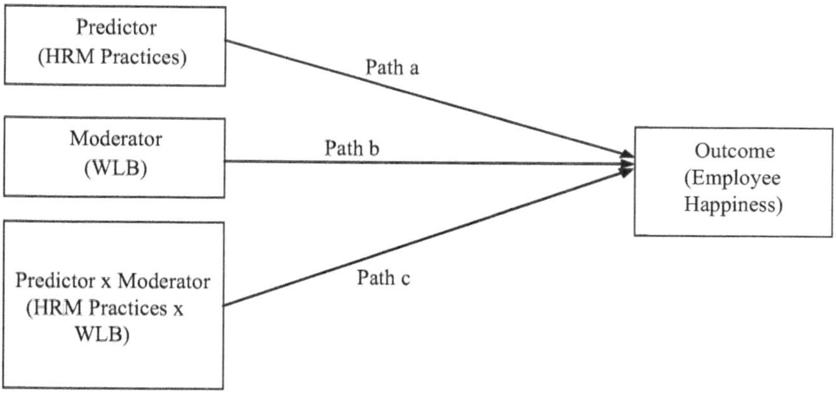

Fig. 9.2. Model of the Moderation. *Source:* Author's own, based on the literature review.

Table 9.5. Hierarchical Multiple Regression for the Testing of Moderation.

Step	Path	Interaction	Coefficient	Significant
1	a	HRM practices × Employee happiness	0.558	0.000
2	b	WLB × Employee happiness	0.257	0.002
3	c	HRM practices × WLB × Employee happiness	0.432	0.004

Source: Author's own.

Baron and Kenny, in 1986, stated that the moderator variable is supported when the product of the predictor and the moderator (Path c) is statistically significant. Therefore, the second hypothesis (H2) was accepted. The moderating effect has been depicted in Fig. 9.3. The graph illustrates the interaction effect of the moderating variable. Determining the mean values of the moderating variable plotted at high, moderate and low (±1 SD) clarifies the slopes, illustrating how the variables in this study interacted. Moreover, the results confirm that HRM practices significantly impact happiness when WLB is high. Conversely, the nexus of HRM practices and employee happiness is weakened when WLB is low rather than high.

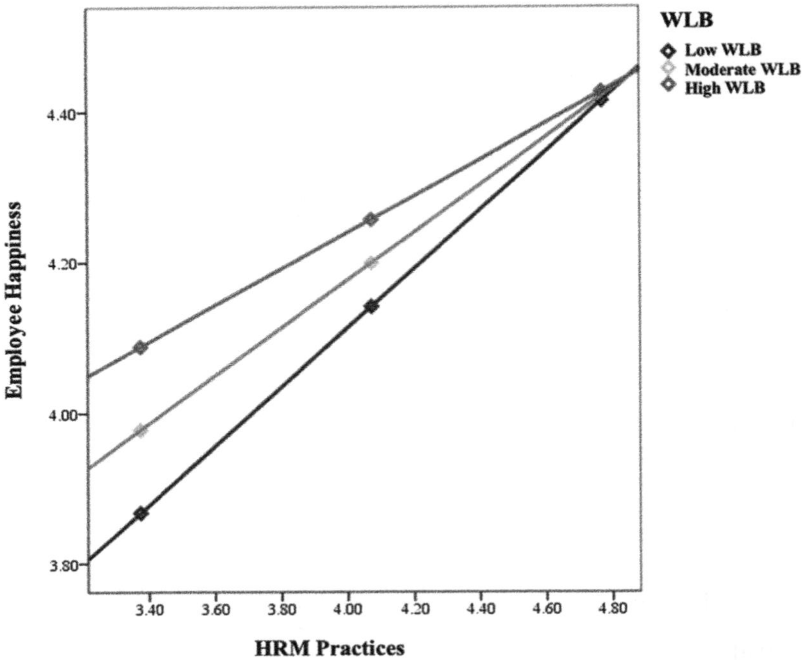

Fig. 9.3. The Moderating Effect of WLB. *Source:* Author's own.

Results From Hypothesis Testing

Please refer Table 9.6 for the results from hypothesis testing.

Table 9.6 Hypothesis Testing.

No	Hypotheses of the Study	Coefficient Values	Result
1	HRM practices and employee happiness	0.558 (p = 0.000)	Supported
2	The moderating effect of WLB on HRM practices and employee happiness linkage	0.451 (p = 0.004)	Supported

Source: Author's own.

Discussion

The conceptual framework of this study was generated by combining theories, empirical evidence from scholars and the author's reasoning. Two hypotheses were then formulated and tested among employees in the Travel Trade industries in Sri Lanka.

The main objective of this study was to test the nexus of HRM practices and employee happiness in the workplace. Statistical research has shown a significant positive correlation between HRM practices and employee happiness. Such findings align with existing literature, including studies by Opatha and Uresha (2020) and Guerci et al. (2022), which reached similar conclusions. Consequently, this study underscores the importance of HRM practices in organizations to increase employee happiness in the workplace.

The second objective was to examine WLB's moderating influence on the nexus of HRM practices and employee happiness. The analysis confirmed that WLB significantly moderates this relationship. Therefore, managers in the workplace should create, manage and maintain a work environment that fosters happiness, as Gavin and Mason (2004) and Rego and Cunha (2008) emphasize. Such happiness can be achieved by implementing strategies to improve employee WLB, such as flexible work schedules, a greater focus on employee well-being than working hours, review of employee workloads, regular monitoring of employee attitude, conducting employee surveys regarding their WLB and adequate counselling. Furthermore, the researcher argues that achieving sustainable employee happiness relies on effective HRM practices and favourable WLB. Hence, the study highlights the importance of organizations and individuals proactively implementing measures supporting their employees' WLB, ultimately improving their happiness.

Conclusion and Implications of the Study

Employee happiness is crucial to every individual and organization since it creates a pleasant, collaborative and effective work environment. Individuals devote most of their valuable time to their work life. Therefore, the work they engage in should give them contentment. To this end, happy employees perform at a higher level, which helps to improve overall organizational performance (Chia & Chu, 2016; Fisher, 2010). Therefore, managers must look after their industry to maximize employee happiness right from the initial stages of employment, notably through effective HRM practices. This explanation stands out as a noteworthy insight of this study.

Further, top-level managers must ensure that their employees balance their families and organizations well, which is the crucial part that affects employee happiness in the workplace. Therefore, organizations should ensure that their employees maintain a healthy WLB. This study also validates the measures for assessing the effect of WLB on the nexus of HRM practices and employee happiness, providing a foundation for future research in this area. Additionally, working professionals and managers can gain a better understanding of the significance of HRM practices and WLB in enhancing employee happiness. Beyond its theoretical contributions, this study highlights, for HR managers and other professionals, the critical role HRM practices and WLB play in fostering employee happiness within organizations.

Limitations and Future Directions for the Study

This study only focused on the travel trade employees in the Sri Lankan context. Hence, the research is limited to one industry (travel trade) and one country (Sri Lanka). This context may have limited the scope for generalizability of the study. To increase the broader applicability of the results, the author suggests that future studies should include a variety of organizational settings. Furthermore, this research was limited to one dependent, moderator and independent variable. It is recommended that future researchers identify and consider more independent variables, mediating variables and control variables in this research area beyond those selected for this study. By incorporating other variables, the study could lead to a better understanding of the concepts, especially other factors influencing employee happiness. Further, the author recommends that future researchers conduct longitudinal and comparative studies across industries, organizational sizes and multiple cultures.

Acknowledgements

I thank the editors and anonymous reviewers whose comments and suggestions made this chapter publishable. I also want to thank Team ICMR and the Sabaragamuwa University of Sri Lanka for their strong support.

References

Adnan-Bataineh, K. (2019). Impact of work-life balance, happiness at work, on employee performance. *International Business Research*, *12*(2), 99–112.

Adnyana, I. M., & Veronica, E. (2023). How a company's physical work environment, leadership style, and employee motivation affect job satisfaction and performance. *Jurnal Manajemen Bisnis*, *10*(2), 479–489.

Al Suwaidi, E. Y. M., Akmal, S., & Alshami, S. A. (2020). A conceptual framework of happiness at the workplace in promoting employee happiness in a public organisation. *International Journal of Advanced Science and Technology*, *29*(9), 6151–6159.

Alolayyan, M. N., Almomani, R. Z. Q., Al-Qudah, S. H., Al-Hawary, S. I. S., Mohammad, A. A. S., Al-aware, K. M., Ababneh, R. I., Alshurideh, M. T., & Mohammad, A. I. (2023). Electronic HR practices are a critical factor in employee satisfaction in private hospitals in Jordan. In M. Alshurideh, B. H. Al Kurdi, R. Masa'deh, H. M. Alzoubi, & S. Salloum (Eds.), *The effect of information technology on business and marketing intelligence systems* (pp. 1009–1025). Springer International Publishing.

Ausat, A. M. A., Shafiq, M. A., Wafik, D., & López, N. A. S. (2024). The role of transformational leadership in improving employee psychological wellbeing: A review. *Apollo: Journal of Tourism and Business*, *2*(1), 148–157.

Bailey, K., & Breslin, D. (2021). The COVID-19 pandemic: What can we learn from past research in organisations and management? *International Journal of Management Reviews*, *23*(1), 3–6.

Bani-Melhem, S., Al-Hawari, M. A., & Quratulain, S. (2020). Leader-member exchange and frontline employees' innovative behaviours: The roles of employee happiness and service climate. *International Journal of Productivity and Performance Management*, *71*(2), 540–557. https://doi.org/10.1108/IJPPM-03-2020-0092

Barmby, T., Bryson, A., & Eberth, B. (2012). Human capital, matching, and job satisfaction. *Economics Letters*, *117*, 548–551. https://doi.org/10.1016/j.econlet.2012.07.026

Baron, R. M., & Kenny, D. A. (1986). The moderator-mediator variable distinction in social psychological research: Conceptual, strategic, and statistical considerations. *Journal of Personality and Social Psychology*, *51*(6), 1173.

Behera, D. K., Rahut, D. B., Padmaja, M., & Dash, A. K. (2024). Socioeconomic determinants of happiness: Empirical evidence from developed and developing countries. *Journal of Behavioral and Experimental Economics*, 102187. https://doi.org/10.1016/j.socec.2024.102187

Bissonnette, V., Ickes, W., Bernstein, I., & Knowles, E. (1990). Personality moderating variables: A warning about the statistical artefact and a comparison of analytic techniques. *Journal of Personality*, *58*(3), 567–587.

Blanchflower, D. G., & Bryson, A. (2024). The female happiness paradox. *Journal of Population Economics*, *37*(1), 1–27.

Cherif, F. (2020). The role of human resource management practices and employee job satisfaction in predicting organisational commitment in the Saudi Arabian banking sector. *International Journal of Sociology and Social Policy*, *40*(7/8), 529–541.

Chia, Y. M., & Chu, M. J. (2016). Moderating effects of presenteeism on the stress-happiness relationship of hotel employees: A note. *International Journal of Hospitality Management*, *55*, 52–56.

Chron Contributor. (2020). What should workers expect from their employers? *Chron. Com*. https://work.chron.com/should-workers-expect-employers-12394.html

Chung, S. K. G., Chan, X. W., Lanier, P., & Wong, P. (2020). Associations between work-family balance, parenting stress, and marital conflicts during the COVID-19 pandemic in Singapore. *Journal of Child and Family Studies*, *32*(1), 132–144. https://doi.org/10.1007/s10826-022-02490-z

Climek, M., Henry, R., & Jeong, S. (2024). Integrative literature review on employee turnover antecedents across different generations: Commonalities and uniqueness. *European Journal of Training and Development*, *48*(1/2), 112–132.

Dahiya, R., & Rangnekar, S. (2018). Employee happiness is a valuable tool for driving organisations. In A. Kumar, M. Yadav, S. Rangnekar, & S. K. Trivedi (Eds.), *Harnessing human capital analytics for competitive advantage* (pp. 24–54). IGI Global.

De Silva, V. A., Opatha, H. H. D. N. P., & Gamage, A. S. (2016). Towards extending the ethical dimension of human resource management. https://doi.org/10.5539/ibr.v9n10p151

Delecta, P. (2011). Work-life balance. *International Journal of Current Research*, *3*(4), 186–189.

Dessler, G. (2013). *Fundamentals of human resource management*. Pearson.

Fereidouni, H. G., Najdi, Y., & Amiri, R. E. (2013). Do governance factors matter for happiness in the MENA region? *International Journal of Social Economics*, *40*(12), 1028–1040. https://doi.org/10.1108/IJSE-11-2012-0208

Field, L. K., & Buitendach, J. H. (2011). Happiness, work engagement and organisational commitment of support staff at a tertiary education institution in South Africa. *SA Journal of Industrial Psychology*, *37*(1), 01–10.

Fisher, C. D. (2010). Happiness at work. *International Journal of Management Reviews*, *12*(4), 384–412.

Frazier, P. A., Tix, A. P., & Barron, K. E. (2004). Testing moderator and mediator effects in counselling psychology research. *Journal of Counseling Psychology*, *51*(1), 115.

Frone, M. R. (2003). Work-family balance. In J. C. Quick & L. E. Tetrick (Eds.), *Handbook of occupational health psychology* (pp. 143–162). American Psychological Association. https://doi.org/10.1037/10474-007

Gavin, J. H., & Mason, R. O. (2004). The virtuous organisation: The value of happiness in the workplace. *Organisational Dynamics*, *33*(4), 379–392. https://doi.org/10.1016/j.orgdyn.2004.09.005

Gregory, K. (2011). The importance of employee satisfaction. *The Journal of Business & Information Management Division*, 29–37.

Guerci, M., Hauff, S., & Gilardi, S. (2022). High-performance work practices and their associations with health, happiness, and relational well-being: Are there any tradeoffs? *The International Journal of Human Resource Management*, *33*(2), 329–359.

Jaiswal, R., & Gupta, S. (2024). Money talks, happiness walks: Dissecting the secrets of global bliss with machine learning. *Journal of Chinese Economic and Business Studies*, *22*(1), 111–158.

Jose, G., Nimmi, P. N., & Kuriakose, V. (2024). HRM practices and employee engagement: Role of personal resources—A study among nurses. *International Journal of Productivity and Performance Management*, *73*(1), 1–17.

Kashdan, T. B., Biswas-Diener, R., & King, L. A. (2008). Reconsidering happiness: The costs of distinguishing between Hedonics and Eudaimonia. *The Journal of Positive Psychology*, *3*(4), 219–233.

Kimball, L. S., & Nink, C. E. (2006). How to improve employee motivation, commitment, productivity, well-being, and safety. *Corrections Today*, *68*(3), 66.

Lockwood, N. R. (2003). *Work/life balance. Challenges and solutions*. SHRM Research.

Lomas, T., & VanderWeele, T. J. (2023). Toward an expanded taxonomy of happiness: A conceptual analysis of 16 distinct forms of mental wellbeing. *Journal of Humanistic Psychology*. https://doi.org/10.1177/00221678231155512

Mithulan, R., & Opatha, H. H. D. N. P. (2023). The moderating effect of personal character and the mediating effect of organisational citizenship behaviour on the ethical orientation of HRM-ethical behaviour linkage. *Sri Lankan Journal of Human Resource Management*, *13*(1), 1–26.

Nunnally, J. C., & Bernstein, I. H. (1994). *The theory of measurement error* (3rd ed.). McGraw-Hill Inc.

Opatha, H. H. D. N. P. (2009). *Human resource management, personnel.* Author Publication.

Opatha, H. H. D. N. P. (2019a). A study of bachelor's degrees in human resource management in three Sri Lankan leading state universities. *Universal Journal of Educational Research, 7*(11), 2361–2371. https://doi.org/10.13189/ujer.2019.071114

Opatha, H. H. D. N. P. (2019b). *Sustainable human resource management.* University of Sri Jayewardenepura.

Opatha, H. H. D. P. J., & Uresha, K. I. (2020). HRM and its impact on employee happiness: An empirical study on Sri Lankan employees. *Asian Journal of Social Sciences and Management Studies, 7*(2), 114–123.

Otken, A. B., & Gul, S. E. (2013). The relationship between work-life balance and happiness from the perspectives of generation X and Y. *Humanities and Social Sciences Review, 2*(4), 45–53.

Pham, N. T., Tuan, T. H., Le, T. D., Nguyen, P. N. D., Usman, M., & Ferreira, G. T. C. (2023). Socially responsible human resources management and employee retention: The roles of shared value, relationship satisfaction, and servant leadership. *Journal of Cleaner Production*, 137704. https://doi.org/10.1016/j.jclepro.2023.137704

Pimenta, S., Duarte, A. P., & Simões, E. (2024). How socially responsible human resource management fosters work engagement: The role of perceived organisational support and affective organisational commitment. *Social Responsibility Journal, 20*(2), 326–343.

Pouvreau, D. (2014). On the history of Ludwig von Bertalanffy's "general systemology" and its relationship to cybernetics-part II: Contexts and developments of the systemological hermeneutics instigated by von Bertalanffy. *International Journal of General Systems, 43*(2), 172–245.

Rego, A., & Cunha, M. P. (2008). Authentizotic climates and employee happiness: Pathways to individual performance? *Journal of Business Research, 61*, 739–752.

Renusha, M. (2022a). Green orientation of human resource management and green attitude of employees: Moderation effect of personal character. *Kelaniya Journal of Human Resource Management, 17*(2), 103–115. https://doi.org/10.4038/kjhrm.v17i2.113

Renusha, M. (2022b). Are employees loyal to you? Examining the moderating effect of organisational justice on HRM practices and employee loyalty linkage. *Journal of Business Studies, 9*(1), 17–30. https://doi.org/10.4038/jbs.v9i1.83

Rivera, A. R., Gálvez-Mozo, A., & Tirado-Serrano, F. (2024). The imperative of happiness in positive psychology: Towards a psychopolitics of wellbeing. *New Ideas in Psychology, 72*, 101058.

Ryan, R. M., & Deci, E. L. (2001). On happiness and human potentials: A review of research on hedonic and eudaimonic well-being. *Annual Review of Psychology, 52*(1), 141–166.

Saunders, M., Lewis, P., & Thornhill, A. (2009). *Research methods for business students.* Pearson.

Schlomer, G. L., Bauman, S., & Card, N. A. (2010). Best practices for missing data management in counselling psychology. *Journal of Counseling Psychology, 57*(1), 1.

Silla, I., Gracia, F. J., Mañas, M. A., & Peiró, J. M. (2010). Job insecurity and employees' attitudes: The moderating role of fairness. *International Journal of Manpower, 31*(4), 449–465.

Singh, P., & Mishra, S. (2020). Ensuring employee safety and happiness in times of COVID-19 crisis. *SGVU International Journal of Economics and Management*, *8*(2), 1–16.

Singha, S. (2024). Nurturing positive organisational climates to enhance work success: A positive psychology approach. In E. Baykal (Eds.), *Fostering organisational sustainability with positive psychology* (pp. 84–107). IGI Global.

Smith, B. W., deCruz-Dixon, N., Erickson, K., Guzman, A., Phan, A., & Schodt, K. (2023). The effects of an online positive psychology course on happiness, health, and well-being. *Journal of Happiness Studies*, *24*(3), 1145–1167.

Soomro, A. A., Breitenecker, R. J., & Shah, S. A. M. (2018). Relation of work-life balance, work-family conflict, and family-work conflict with the employee performance-moderating role of job satisfaction. *South Asian Journal of Business Studies*, *7*(1), 129–146.

Spector, P. E. (1992). *Summated rating scale construction*. Sage.

Tambyah, S. K., Tan, S. J., & Lun, Y. W. (2024). *Happiness and wellbeing in Singapore: Beyond economic prosperity* (p. 194). Taylor & Francis.

Vestal, K. (2015). Unhappy employees: A challenge for leaders. *Nurse Leader*, *13*(5), 12–13.

Wesarat, P. O., Sharif, M. Y., & Abdul Majid, A. H. (2014). A conceptual framework of happiness at the workplace. *Asian Social Science*, *11*(2), 78–88.

Chapter 10

Implications of Job Hopping on Employees: A Case Study From the Sri Lankan Software Development Industry

Sivananthan Nishanthi[a] *and Kumudu Kushlani Kapiyangoda*[b]

[a]University of Moratuwa, Sri Lanka
[b]University of Colombo, Sri Lanka

Abstract

This study aims to explore the implications of job hopping for employees attached to the software development industry in Sri Lanka and to observe whether job hopping meets employee expectations. Adopting a qualitative methodology and a case study approach, this study incorporates the Tonnquist's model to identify the gap between job hoppers' expectations and reality. In the software industry, job seekers experience a salary increase as they change jobs, even though they have to work long hours without breaks or holidays. In addition, job hoppers also face issues such as job security, insurance and medical claims and healthy relationships with managers and their peers. Job hopping helps workers ascend the career ladder quickly while dealing with issues of less power in making decisions. Furthermore, the autonomy of newly recruited employees might be limited, which could restrict their career growth. It is also apparent that employees consider the benefits and drawbacks of job hopping before changing. However, difficulties could arise if these implications are not carefully evaluated to meet job hoppers' needs. The findings from this research would facilitate employees making informed decisions before changing jobs.

Keywords: Job hopping; employee implications; software development industry; case study; Tonnquist's model

Shaping Entrepreneurial Marketing, Volume 1, 151–163

doi:10.1108/978-1-83708-852-220251010

Introduction

Job hopping involves workers willingly changing employers every few years (Larasati & Aryanto, 2020). It has recently been considered a significant issue faced by several organizations. However, Ghiselli (1974) identified this issue around 40 years ago, and he named this problem 'hobo syndrome'. He asserted that the tendency to move from one occupation to the next is based on a periodic itch, leading employees to change their jobs without rational intentions (Steenackers & Guerry, 2016). Scholars have explored different aspects of job hopping, such as reasons for employees hopping from one job to another (Bansal, 2014; Larasati & Aryanto, 2020; Leidner & Smith, 2013; Ramkumar et al., 2016; Rani & Samuel, 2019), the organizational impact of job hopping (Larasati & Aryanto, 2020; Hou et al., 2016; Saleem & Qamar, 2017; Steenackers & Guerry, 2016) and the effects of job hopping on employees (Hou et al., 2016; Larasati & Aryanto, 2020). More recent research has focused on the relationships between person–organization fit, learning opportunities, self-directedness, career attitude and job hopping (Siew et al., 2023); how influence from the workplace leads to the behaviour of job hopping (Nguyen & Le, 2022); the effects of job switching behaviour (Lanke & Nath, 2023); the impact of human resource (HR) practices on employee retention, job satisfaction, work experience and job hopping focusing on the apparel industry (Kalia et al., 2023); and how the gap between the productivity of a multinational enterprise and that of its competitor controls the utilization of expatriate managers in its subsidiaries located in foreign countries with a particular focus on job-hopping behaviour of local middle-level managers (Lee et al., 2023).

Observations from the above studies highlighted that past researchers have mainly explored the implications of job hopping on employers and organizations. However, there is minimal research on the implications of job hopping on employees incorporating a systematic theoretical framework. Therefore, our study aims to address this gap in research by adopting the Tonnquist's model while utilizing a qualitative methodology with a case study approach. Accordingly, the objectives of this study are to:

- Identify the implications of job hopping on employees in the Sri Lankan software development industry.
- Analyze whether job hopping fulfils the expectations of employees.

Literature Review

Reasons for Job Hopping

Yuen and Thai (2015) identified a job hopper as an employee who serves for less than one year at their current job. Furthermore, the average number of years an employee (job hopper) would serve an institution is three years (Dharmawansha & Thennakoon, 2014). Our study defines an employee as a job hopper based on the above two definitions. According to past literature, the following were identified as the primary reasons for job hopping: feelings of not being esteemed, low salary, lack of training, loss of trust in seniors (Bansal, 2014), inadequate challenge in the current job (Ramkumar et al., 2016), absence of work–life balance (Larasati & Aryanto, 2020), less appealing organizational environment (Leidner & Smith, 2013), lack of attachment to the organization (Acharya et al., 2021; Rani & Samuel, 2019), changes in career values (Giraud et al., 2019), lack of rapport between employees and their immediate superiors (Bryant & Allen, 2013), etc. In addition, a recent study found that person–organization fit and self-directedness in career attitude correlate significantly with job hopping among Generation Y employees. However, as highlighted by these authors, there is no significant relationship between learning opportunities and job hopping (Siew et al., 2023). Furthermore, on a related note, a study by Nguyen and Le (2022) revealed that motivation to leave an organization leads to job hopping, which might not enhance a career. In addition, as Lanke and Nath (2023) observed, job switching is viewed positively and negatively. As this study showed, employees' job-switching or job-hopping behaviour could be influenced by social and economic-related factors or the need to have fun. This study sheds light on how a new employee (a fresh job hopper) might influence the communities of practice. Kalia et al. (2023) revealed that compensation and performance appraisal have the highest impact on job satisfaction, followed by employee work participation and retention. This research identified that job satisfaction significantly mediates between HR practices like compensation, performance appraisal and employee retention. In the case of job-hopping behaviour, the study observed that employee work participation leads to job satisfaction in loyal employees. Similarly, job satisfaction leads to employee retention (Kalia et al., 2023).

Organizational Impact of Job Hopping

Job hopping seriously impacts organizations (Lanke & Nath, 2023). When an employee leaves the company, it needs to find a replacement, which may raise specific administration and recruitment-related costs. Furthermore, employers lose tacit knowledge and expertise of the employees when they leave the organization. Higher employee turnover in a company could hurt the remaining employees' attitudes (Steenackers & Guerry, 2016). Larasati and Aryanto (2020) demonstrated that when employees leave an organization, the responsibilities of the remaining employees expand, impacting their productivity. Organizational performance is also affected until the newly joined staff members familiarize themselves with the obligations that must be accomplished (Saleem & Qamar, 2017). Job hopping can influence employees' trust in a business's advancement as it gives space for new opportunities. Also, it paves the way for organizational growth by acquiring new skills (Hou et al., 2016). In addition, a recent study by Lee et al. (2023), incorporating a case study of a multinational enterprise and adopting a formal framework, illustrated that managers from other countries are less prone to job hopping than local managers. As the authors illustrate, this job hopping creates a gap between the productivity of a multinational enterprise and that of its competitors.

Effects of Job Hopping on Employees

Job hopping results in both positive and negative consequences for employees. A positive effect of job hopping is that through working in different organizations, employees can obtain a variety of experiences. Accordingly, by selecting more appropriate employment opportunities occasionally, an employee can maximize benefits (Larasati & Aryanto, 2020). Furthermore, job hopping helps to find a perfect job fit for an employee. However, job hopping also causes negative consequences. Often, superiors might fear recruiting job hoppers as much effort is required to build relationships with new teammates (Hou et al., 2016). In addition, certain employers might be reluctant to recruit job hoppers who frequently change their jobs as they perceive that the training costs incurred on such employees might be wasted if they change their employment within a short tenure.

The above studies demonstrate that past researchers have mainly explored the implications of job hopping on employers and companies. However, less research has been done to explore the implications of job hopping on employees incorporating a systematic theoretical framework. Accordingly, our research aims to fill this gap by adopting the Tonnquist's model while incorporating a qualitative methodology with a case study approach.

Theoretical Framework

Maslow's Hierarchy of Needs and the Tonnquist's Model

An employee needs to be motivated to carry on with their duties. This motivation can be influenced by the employee's expectations of their job. When one need is satisfied, another need is given priority. The priority of the needs depends on the individual. Encapsulating these ideas, A. H. Maslow developed a theory in his book, *A Theory of Human Motivation*, identified as Maslow's Hierarchy of Needs (1943). This theory contributed to humanistic psychology and the management of motivation, which could also be related to retention practices. Since retention and job-hopping are two related subjects, we incorporate this theory into this study. As defined by Maslow (1943), there are five basic needs: physiological, safety, social, esteem and self-actualization.

Tonnquist (2016) developed a model based on Maslow's hierarchy of needs that could be incorporated into management to motivate and retain staff by associating intrinsic and extrinsic motivational factors ranging from the lowest to the highest level. The Tonnquist's model indicates the different stages of motivation of an employee. Lassausaie and Lotte (2018) used this model in the real estate industry to connect retention strategies with Maslow's hierarchy of needs. Accordingly, the Tonnquist's model was adopted for this research to highlight the implications for job hoppers in the software industry.

Methodology

According to Merriam (2009), researchers interested in qualitative research are keen on understanding the meaning individuals have built of a particular phenomenon. Since this study focuses on the implications of job hopping, a qualitative methodology was identified as more appropriate to capture individuals' job-related past experiences. Therefore, a qualitative methodology case study was incorporated to facilitate obtaining rich and in-depth data related to this research topic.

According to Yuen and Thai (2015), a job hopper serves an organization for less than one year. Furthermore, the average number of years an employee (job hopper) would remain in an organization is three years (Dharmawansha & Thennakoon, 2014). This study defines an employee as a job hopper based on the above two definitions. Accordingly, participants who switched jobs once a year and from one job to another within three years were selected for the study. Participants were chosen using snowball sampling (Bryman & Bell, 2011). With the outbreak of the COVID-19 pandemic, online interviews were conducted with the help of Skype and Zoom. Table 10.1 illustrates the sample profile. Each interview was conducted for more than 45 minutes. After conducting the interviews, the data were transcribed. Thematic analysis identified by Braun and Clarke (2013) was incorporated into data analysis. Accordingly, the themes and codes related to the Tonnquist's model were identified and elaborated in the findings.

Table 10.1 Details of Interviewees.

Designation	**Number of Interviewees**
Software engineer (SE), senior software engineer (SSE), tech lead (TL)	08
Quality assurance engineer (QA), senior quality assurance engineer (SQA)	05
Business analyst (BA)	05
Managers	04

Source: Authors' own.

Findings

Implications of Job Hopping on Employees in Light of Tonnquist's Model

Phase 01: Wages, Working Hours, Breaks, Vacation

Almost all interviewees explained that their job-hopping decision was mainly based on the salary hike offered by the new employer. However, most participants agreed they tend to work more hours immediately after job hopping as they require more time to obtain product knowledge and cope with the technology change. One of the SSEs explained:

> With changing technologies, we may also face some problems. Maybe you have to learn from scratch, and no one can guide you. So you will feel workload plus stress until you settle with that technology. I felt going right down my learning curve.

It is accepted that the working hours in the IT industry are higher, and employees are agreed to work long hours when there are critical issues or if there are any project deployment dues. One senior QA explained this scenario:

> In the IT industry, working hours are normally higher than in other fields. So, we cannot expect a work-life balance like in other industries. When there is a critical situation, employees are expected to work. However, if this happens continuously, employees tend to move on.

Furthermore, as the interviewees expressed, there was a lack of breaks and opportunities to go on vacation soon after job hopping. However, interviewees expressed that job hopping helped them reach higher salary scales quickly.

Phase 02: Workplace Characteristics, Job Security, Insurance

Job hoppers consider the culture of the workplace and the opportunity to balance work–life when deciding to change their jobs. According to a female SSE:

> If I do not match the organisation's culture, I will seek new opportunities. I am keen on relaxation and the opportunity to balance work and life. If these requirements are not fulfilled, I will change my job.

Job hoppers also seek to join reputed companies as their experience working in them makes them preferred candidates in other organizations. One of the SSEs expressed:

> Some outside people might not know about my details, but they might know about the company I worked for. So they trust my company, and because I am an employee of that particular company, they trust me, too. That means I can value my working company and get advantages from that.

Interviewees expressed that despite the above advantages of job hopping, they suffered from loss of gratuity, insurance and medical benefits from their previous employment. According to a BA:

> Even though there are perks of job hopping, such as an immediate increase in financial benefits, sometimes there is a risk of losing gratuity, insurance, and medical benefits from the previous employment. So, if an employee is retained in the existing employment, he/she could benefit from the retained gratuity, insurance, and medical benefits.

Furthermore, job security is impacted until the new employment is confirmed. A manager explained:

> Also, in case of a crisis, especially during the COVID-19 pandemic, the newly joined employees in their probation period faced a high tendency of losing their jobs. On such occasions, remaining in the previous job is better because it brings stability rather than hopping from one job to another.

Accordingly, it was identified that workplace characteristics, job security and insurance benefits have implications for job hopping.

Phase 03: Manager–Employee Relationship, Group Belongingness

Employees need to build good relationships with their teammates and superiors. However, soon after hopping jobs, most interviewees face problems developing good relationships with their subordinates and superiors. As one of the PMs explained:

> Soon after changing jobs, I faced problems interacting with my subordinates at the new workplace. Some of them were nice to me, but some were not. Sometimes, these ambiguities create frustration and make me think my previous workplace is better. Positive group belongingness matters a lot when performing my duties.

Adding to this point, another PM explained that he faced problems from an employee in the new workplace who possessed many years of experience:

> I faced a problem with one of the employees who has not been granted the promotion he has been waiting for. I heard that I had been recruited for that position. Therefore, I continuously faced difficulty in managing that particular person. So, those kinds of people might try to create problems for newcomers. Also, sometimes they tend to do some activities by by-passing us.

Furthermore, a BA explained that soon after changing jobs, he had to work under demanding supervisors who were reluctant to provide proper guidance, which created a lot of stress and anxiety. As he explained:

> While working in my previous job, I had the opportunity to work under colleagues like supervisors. I won their trust over time, and they treated me as one of them. However, as I changed my job, the new supervisors and I kept a distance and maintained a formal relationship initially. I hope this relationship will ease out soon as time goes by.

Accordingly, it was identified that the manager–employee relationship and group belongingness are affected by job hopping.

Phase 04: Responsibility and Authority, Title, Promotion, Special Privileges

Most employees agreed that they can quickly climb the career ladder through job hopping. Job hopping, according to them, aids in overcoming organizational cultural barriers and internal politics. One QA said:

> In my company, I am also now a QA Engineer, so if I want a senior QA designation, I must stay here for more than five years to get it. That is their culture. However, if I move to an entirely new organisation, I can quickly overcome this barrier and climb the career ladder.

However, one BA mentioned that while higher designations are offered to newly recruited personnel, the company is reluctant to give them more responsibility and higher privileges immediately. Moreover, the newly recruited job hopper might encounter high stress and low self-esteem on such occasions.

Phase 05: Freedom With Responsibility, Possibility of Development, Stimulating Work

One reason for job hopping is employees being bored when engaged in the same task for an extended period. By hopping jobs, they can eliminate this boredom and find exciting or challenging tasks. One SSE expressed:

> I was working with one technology for more than one year. After some time, it is frustrating to do the same thing again and again. I wanted variety, more responsibility, and more challenges in my job. This is the reason I changed my job.

Even though job hoppers enjoy challenging work initially, some face career development problems and have reduced freedom to carry on their tasks soon after hopping from one job to another. However, as they explained, this problem eases once the organization develops its trust in them. As illustrated in the Tonnquist's model, it was identified that job hopping has positive and negative implications for the workers attached to the Sri Lankan software development industry.

Furthermore, the study examined whether job hopping fulfils the employees' expectations. None of the participants said they had experienced more negative experiences following the job hopping. Therefore, it is apparent that employees made sure of both the positive and negative implications of changing jobs by allocating considerable time to thoroughly investigate the company they wished to join. One SSE mentioned:

> Nowadays, we have several ways to investigate a company. Such as through the internet and close friends. We can understand whether this place suits us or fulfils our expectations.

It is evident that employees carefully evaluate the merits and demerits of job hopping before changing jobs. Thus, they often make decisions that fulfil their expectations. However, job hoppers might face difficulties after changing jobs if these merits and demerits are not carefully evaluated to match their needs.

Discussion

According to Jinadasa and Wickramasinghe (2005), person–job fit is closely related to employee turnover. Sometimes, employees join an organization to get a job, but if dissatisfied, they could eventually benefit by job hopping. Therefore, job hopping aids an employee in finding a perfect job that fits them. Furthermore, Siew et al. (2023) found that person–organization fit and career attitude correlate significantly with job hopping of Gen Y employees. In line with these ideas, our study, based on the Sri Lankan software development industry, demonstrated that person–organization fit is a crucial factor that triggers job hopping. However, contrary to the above study, we demonstrated a clear relationship between job-hopping behaviour and learning opportunities in the software development industry of Sri Lanka.

Naresh and Rathnam (2015) mentioned that fewer growth opportunities, expectations of increased salary and less challenging work are some of the reasons for the rise of job hopping in the software industry. On a related note, similar ideas were expressed by Kalia et al. (2023), which were corroborated by the reasons for job hopping revealed by respondents of our study. Furthermore, Nguyen and Le (2022) revealed that motivation to escape from the current workplace leads to job hopping, which might not lead to career advancement. Lanke and Nath (2023) showed that switching between jobs is perceived positively and negatively. As this study demonstrates, switching jobs could be intensified by social and economic factors and the need for fun. However, our study found that the mentality of escaping the workplace or seeking fun does not necessarily trigger job hopping. However, we found that certain socioeconomic factors, such as salary hikes and a craving for responsibility, authority and titles, could trigger job hopping.

Studies by Larasati and Aryanto (2020) and Ramkumar et al. (2016) revealed negative implications of job hopping, including a lack of job security during crises and the fear among job hoppers of potential problems in building relationships with new teammates. Our study confirms similar negative implications job seekers face in Sri Lanka's software development industry.

Similar to Saleem and Qamar (2017), our study found that new employees need time to adapt and become ready to take on new job responsibilities. Importantly, we found that sometimes, the fewer responsibilities given in the initial stages might create stress and tension for the newly recruited employee. Studies by Naresh and Rathnam (2015) and Sambrani and Hemalatha (2016) found that job hoppers often have to compromise with flexi-time arrangements, work-from-home facilities and office transport as soon as they change their jobs. Our study also revealed that job hoppers must compromise with free time and work–life balance and leave facilities due to job hopping.

A study by Hou et al. (2016) illustrates that job hopping is an advantage as fresh blood can bring in new ideas, which are more helpful for improving the organization. The participants of our study also expressed similar thoughts. However, our study found that newly joined employees lack tacit knowledge. If a person joins as a leader, they may face difficulties mentoring their team and managing the stakeholders (Bryant & Allen, 2013). While Lee et al. (2023) found that job hopping of middle-level managers creates productivity issues, our study does not explicitly illuminate such findings.

Conclusion and Contributions

This research explored the implications of job hopping for employees attached to the Sri Lankan software development industry, which is faced with the aid of the Tonnquist's model. In the software industry, job hoppers benefit from a salary increase and a job change. However, with this hike in salary, they often have to work long hours without a break or holiday. In addition, job hoppers also face issues such as job security, obtaining insurance and medical claims, and maintaining healthy relationships with managers and their peers. Job hopping helps workers reach the career ladder quickly while dealing with issues of being allocated less power to make decisions soon after accepting the new appointment.

In addition, even though job seekers initially feel their job is challenging, sometimes the responsibility and power provided to them to carry on with their duties at the initial stage might be limited. Job hopping fulfils most of the expectations of employees because, at present, job hoppers allocate considerable time and effort to evaluate the positives and negatives of switching jobs before making a decision. However, if these positives and negatives are not carefully evaluated to match employee needs, they might suffer after deciding on job hopping.

This study provides several theoretical and practical contributions. Regarding theoretical contributions, it is one of the first studies to observe job-hopping behaviour in light of the Tonnquist's model. This study links the job-hopping behaviour-related literature with literature related to the Tonnquist's model. Practically, the findings from this study will help employees make suitable decisions when job hopping. Furthermore, HR managers could capitalize on the research findings when designing employee retention strategies.

Several directions for future research emerge from this study. Accordingly, future researchers could explore the implications of job hopping for the employees of other industries, such as higher education, education, healthcare, etc., in Sri Lanka while exploring whether job hopping meets their expectations. In addition, this study could be applied to job hoppers in different industries in other countries to observe the implications of job hopping and if job hopping meets employee expectations. Furthermore, future researchers could explore how job-hopping affects employers in several other industries. In addition, future researchers could follow a quantitative approach and survey method to explore the consequences for job-hopping employees.

This research has certain limitations. The data collection for this study took place over six months. However, deep insights could have been extracted if this study had lasted longer. Furthermore, since this study focuses on the Sri Lankan software industry, more insights might have been gained if the number of interviewees had been increased.

Acknowledgements

We thank the editors and anonymous reviewers whose comments and suggestions made this chapter publishable. We also want to thank Team ICMR and the Sabaragamuwa University of Sri Lanka for their support.

References

Acharya, P., Garcia-Tapial, J., & Jena, L. K. (2021). Millennial turnover intentions: How can B-schools make a difference? *Development and Learning in Organisations*, *35*(6), 44–47.

Bansal, G. (2014). Job hopping – Issues and challenges in a dynamic environment: An empirical study. *Gian Jyoti E-Journal*, *4*(2), 7–17.

Braun, V., & Clarke, V. (2013). *Successful qualitative research: A practical guide for beginners*. SAGE Publications.

Bryant, P., & Allen, D. (2013). Compensation, benefits, and employee turnover HR strategies for retaining top talent. *Compensation & Benefits Review*, *45*, 171–175.

Bryman, A., & Bell, E. (2011). *Business research methods*. Oxford University Press Inc.

Dharmawansha, P., & Thennakoon, D. (2014). An exploratory study on job hopping in Sri Lanka: A study on generation 'Y' employees. In *IRCMF 2014: 9th International Research Conference on Management and Finance* at Colombo, Sri Lanka. https://www.researchgate.net/publication/309409129_An_Exploratory_Study_on_Job_Hopping_in_Sri_Lanka_A_Study_on_Generation_'Y'_Employees

Ghiselli, E. E. (1974). Some perspectives for industrial psychology. *American Psychologist*, *29*(2), 80–87.

Giraud, L., Bernard, A., & Trinchera, L. (2019). Early career values and individual factors of objective career success: The case of the French business graduates. *Career Development International*, *24*(4), 350–382.

Hou, Y., Zhu, H., & Wei, L. (2016). The analysis of the effect of job-hopping from the angle of ethics. In *2015 3rd International Conference on Education, Management, Arts, Economics and Social Science*. https://doi.org/10.2991/icemaess-15.2016.108

Jinadasa, L., & Wickramasinghe, V. (2005). IT industry labour turnover: The reality. In *Proceedings of the 10th international conference on Sri Lanka studies*. University of Kelaniya.

Kalia, P., Singla, M., & Kaushal, R. (2023). Human resource management practices and employee retention in the Indian textile industry. *International Journal of Productivity and Performance Management*, *73*(11), 96–121.

Lanke, P., & Nath, P. (2023). Job switching and communities of practice: Mapping facilitators and dampeners to life cycle. *VINE Journal of Information and Knowledge Management Systems*, *53*(3), 414–429.

Larasati, A., & Aryanto, D. (2020). Job-Hopping and the determinant factors. In *5th ASEAN conference on psychology, counselling, and humanities (ACPCH 2019)* (pp. 54–56). Atlantis Press.

Lassausaie, C., & Lotte, K. (2018). Employees' need at work: A case study of employee retention at a real estate firm. https://www.diva-portal.org/smash/record.jsf?pid=diva2%3A1249352&dswid=8120. Accessed on August 02, 2020.

Lee, S., Whang, U., Nahm, S., & Oh, C. H. (2023). Productivity gap and expatriate utilisation. *Multinational Business Review*, *31*(2), 266–289.

Leidner, S., & Smith, S. M. (2013). 'Keeping potential job-hoppers' feet on the ground: Well-trained workers stay loyal to their employer. *Human Resource Management International Digest*, *21*(1), 31–33.

Maslow, A. H. (1943). A theory of human motivation. *Psychological Review*, *50*(40), 370–396.

Merriam, S. (2009). *Qualitative research: A guide to design and implementation*. Jossey-Bass.

Naresh, B., & Rathnam, B. V. (2015). Job hopping in software industry concerning select software companies: A study. *International Journal of Recent Research Aspects*, *2*(1), 38–45.

Nguyen, H. P., & Le, H. N. (2022). Determinants of job-hopping behaviour: The case of the information technology sector. *International Journal of Law and Management*, *64*(3), 308–320.

Ramkumar, A., Kumar, A., Satish Kumar, V., Hazarika, S., Radhika, S., & Shravanthi, V. K. (2016). A study on the factors affecting the job-hopping behaviour of its employees. *International Education & Research Journal*, *2*(6), 97–99.

Rani, N., & Samuel, A. A. (2019). Generational differences in the relationship between prosocial identity fit and affective commitment. *International Journal of Organisation Theory & Behavior*, *22*(3), 259–277.

Saleem, S., & Qamar, B. (2017). Investigating the antecedents of turnover intentions and job hopping behaviour: An empirical study of universities in Pakistan. *South Asian Journal of Business Studies*, *6*(2), 161–176.

Sambrani, S., & Hemalatha, G. (2016). Job hopping of women in the information technology industry. *Anveshana's International Journal of Research in Regional Studies, Law, Social Sciences, Journalism and Management Practices*, *1*(8), 98–100.

Siew, J. F., Wong, S. C., & Lim, C. S. (2023). Should I go or should I stay: Job hopping in Malaysia's small, medium enterprise (SME) service sectors. *European Journal of Training and Development*, *47*(1/2), 105–122.

Steenackers, K., & Guerry, M. A. (2016). Determinants of job-hopping: An empirical study in Belgium. *International Journal of Manpower*, *37*(3), 494–510.

Tonnquist, B. (2016). *Project management: A guide to the theory and practice of project methodology and agile methods* (3rd ed.). Sanoma Utbildning.

Yuen, K. F., & Thai, V. V. (2015). Service quality and customer satisfaction in liner shipping. *International Journal of Quality and Service Sciences*, *7*(2/3), 170–183.

Chapter 11

The Causes and Effects of Work–Life Conflict in Copreneurial Couples in South Asia

Mohit Yadav[a], *Ashutosh Pandey*[b] *and Xuan-Hoa Nghiem*[c]

[a]O.P. Jindal Global University, India
[b]FORE School of Management, India
[c]International School, Vietnam National University, Vietnam

Abstract

This study explores the work–life conflict experienced by South Asian copreneurial couples, examining the interplay between long working hours, cultural expectations, gender roles and blurred work–life boundaries. Employing a qualitative research design, this study utilized in-depth interviews with entrepreneurship, psychology and sociology experts to understand the complexities of work–life conflict faced by South Asian copreneurial couples. The findings reveal that South Asian copreneurial couples grapple with a multifaceted work–life conflict influenced by long working hours, traditional gender roles and the blurred lines between work and personal life. These factors significantly impact the couples' well-being and business performance. The study underscores the need for targeted interventions, such as flexible work arrangements, mental health support and gender equality initiatives, to address the specific challenges faced by South Asian copreneurial couples.

Keywords: Work–life conflict; copreneurial couples; South Asia; entrepreneurship; gender roles; cultural factors; work–life balance

Introduction

Enterprise cultures are present in every part of the world, and people want to establish a business based on passion and innovation. This trend is not an

Shaping Entrepreneurial Marketing, Volume 1, 165–177

doi:10.1108/978-1-83708-852-220251011

exception in South Asia, a region that has witnessed a rise in the launch of start-up enterprises (Ummiroh et al., 2022). Nevertheless, it is true that entrepreneurship is not easy and fun, especially the tricky aspect of work–life balance. This issue remains even more pressing when both spouses/partners are involved in embarking on business.

The field of innovation is gradually shifting and changing; one aspect peculiar to today's society is that an increasing number of businessmen and women are forming partnerships with their spouses or partners. This trend can be attributed to several factors. In most instances, the people who form the business through marriage share some goals and objectives, usually coupled with measurably similar values. When they are on the same page, they can optimize each other; where one lacks, the other is strong, and they feel like a team. This way, both partners may bring complementary strengths to the table, enabling them to address most business issues. Thus, one partner is likely more proficient in financial management, whereas the second might be a marketing or product development specialist.

The start-up work structure is conducive to this type of specialization since couples can design their work schedules to fit their lifestyles. They can appreciate and discuss the requirements of entrepreneurship and provide encouragement during specific business periods (Jennings et al., 2013). Nevertheless, the South Asian setting complicates the phenomenon of copreneurial couples. Culture and emphasis on family, essential to life in the region, may influence work and life experiences.

In most societies, the man is expected to be the breadwinner, while the woman is expected to cook, clean and care for the children (Jennings et al., 2013). In a copreneurial setting, this may lead to a situation where the woman is faced with the dilemma of working with the business and at home, thus leading to work-to-family conflict. The population of South Asia tends to be educated. It strongly focuses on extended families, which can pressure couples to work for the family's benefit rather than build up their businesses. Managing expectations with the heaviness of a start-up is always an enormous pressure. This is because culture encourages collectivism, which overlaps the boundaries between the workplace and other vital areas of life. Telecommuting and co-working arrangements provide limited cues regarding when an employee is 'clocked on' or 'clocked off', hence, the line between work and personal time becomes 'blurred'. This threatens entrepreneurs' success since they depend significantly on their networks to deliver services. Work interfering with personal life and vice versa defines work–life conflict. For copreneurial couples in South Asia, this conflict can manifest in several ways. It exposes people to long working hours to succeed in a competitive market, thus causing them to have less time for their relatives and leisure activities. This can potentially affect one's health, either physically or mentally. This uncertainty is the primary reason most people involved in start-ups face much stress; financial instability is rhythmic. Stress arising from financial issues tends to affect relations and decisions in the business organization.

Entrepreneurship is an ongoing process without a precise end date, and with all the uncertainties and pressures of work–life balance, people feel stressed and burned out. This can be expressed as feelings of emotional fatigue, lack of enthusiasm and often a dip in productivity at work. Less attention is given to private time because of the working hours, and such issues may lead to adverse effects such as strained relations between couples. Inter-role conflict may cost the couple's relational well-being since it may cause emotional loss.

Understanding the causes and effects of work–life conflict in South Asian copreneurial couples is crucial for several reasons. The results from the research can help create interventions and programs that would fit the needs of such couples (Michael-Tsabari et al., 2020). It may involve giving seminars in areas related to personal organization, interpersonal skills, and time and workload management in a way acceptable to the particular culture. One of the outcomes of such studies is the formulation of policies that can assist copreneurial couples. This can range from advertising for fee flexibility to subsidizing childcare. Coping can also increase knowledge about the difficulties of copreneurial couples in South Asia. This can lead to continued discussion on how the duo manages their working hours and work stress and develops a standard workable solution. This research can add to the existing literature by focusing on work–life conflict and the entrepreneurial context, especially in South Asia. Thus, it can create a basis for future investigations to understand possible strategies and treatments for this condition.

Therefore, the dogged spirit of copreneurial couples in South Asia discussed in this paper is truly a dynamic force in the region. Nevertheless, such couples experience comparable difficulties regarding work–life balance because of the culture and the nature of start-ups. This paper explores work conflict to dissect the conflict among these couples to establish the causes and impacts.

Literature Review

Scholars and professionals have conducted numerous investigations to establish the reality of work–life conflict and have found various negative impacts. Research findings show a positive association between work and family conflict and poor results, as highlighted in, for example, Qiu and Freel (2020). As for the peculiarities of attaining work–life balance, it is noteworthy that entrepreneurs, especially those who decide to launch their businesses, appear to have the most stringent work–life balance issues among the population. Crucial research by scholars such as Maziriri et al. (2022) shows that entrepreneurship is primarily characterized by long working hours, financial stress and impulsive decision-making, factors that significantly cause work–life conflicts. These studies describe a rather grim picture of the eagerness to succeed at any given cost in entrepreneurial ventures, which becomes a significant pitfall in an individual's health.

The existing literature provides ample knowledge on the general conflict between work and family life in entrepreneurial careers; however, there is still much to uncover when focusing on copreneurial couples. Literature on working couples, both partners full-time employees, can be considered helpful in understanding the challenges they face. According to a study by Kim and Kim (2018), significant issues in such couples include balancing family chores, children's needs and divergent working hours. Studies also demonstrate that a dual career can be an endless battle between working in two career fields while trying to create a balance. However, research on living and working together is scarce, and most of the data published in the present study area has been derived from Western countries. Scanty attempts have been made to investigate the problem of copreneurial couples in South Asia.

Therefore, to appreciate the totality of the work–life conflict that characterizes copreneurial couples from the South Asian region, it might be necessary to discuss the various cultural factors that pertain to the region. Even though some cultural aspects of work–life balance are discussed in the literature, there is a lack of research on the impact of South Asian culture, specifically on copreneurial couples. Research by scholars like Kim and Kim (2018) working on traditional gender roles depicts that South Asian society is a patriarchal society where women are majorly assigned household duties. This can prove particularly disadvantageous to a copreneurial couple. It becomes subjugative because the woman has to bear the traditional roles of a wife and mother and, at the same time, be an active worker in the business she intends to start. This additional responsibility can often cause conflict with other roles and possibly result in negative emotions such as feeling overwhelmed and resentful.

Moreover, the focus on collectivism and an extended family familiar with South Asian culture, as observed by Languilaire (2019) and Kim and Choi (2017), pose a challenge for a couple beginning an enterprise. Interpersonal relationships and organizational responsibilities often intermingle in these cultures, lacking definitively identifiable work–life balance.

When the partners work from home or rent a small office, which is quite typical for start-ups, it becomes challenging to establish boundaries between work and family time. Constant availability and cultural expectations to be available for the family lead to work intruding into personal time even if one wants to draw a clear line between work and home time, resulting in poor work–life balance.

Besides the general theories related to dual-career couples and cultural constraints, it is helpful to investigate the literature focusing on entrepreneurship in South Asia. For instance, Languilaire's (2019) study explores difficulties faced in operating South Asia–based business people as sources of capital, administrative frameworks and competition are difficult to overcome. The above research shall help establish the context for the current study as it describes the extra burdens affecting copreneurial couples in the South Asian region. The desire to be promoted in such a competitive market, accompanied by the different perceptions of work and family life balance, makes it difficult for these couples.

The literature on work–family conflict and entrepreneurship forms a background that aids in defining conflicts faced by copreneurial couples within South Asia. Nevertheless, certain aspects of this interaction have not been investigated before, and there is no research dedicated to culture's contribution to the given interaction in the context of the region. Therefore, this study proposes narrowing this gap by examining the sources and consequences of work-to-family and family-to-work interference among South Asian copreneurial couples. Thus, this study aims to build upon this current body of literature by exploring work–life conflict on behalf of these entrepreneurs and within the context of Asian culture, gender roles and the other obstacles entrepreneurs face in South Asia.

Methodology

The present study has incorporated a qualitative research strategy based on interviews with selected experts to analyze the drivers of work-to-family conflict among South Asian copreneurial couples. This strategy enables a close examination of the participants' experiences and perspectives, which cannot be achieved with questionnaires and surveys (Dewasiri et al., 2018).

Selection of Experts

It is also important to note that we intentionally invited a group of experts to willingly agree to a semi-structured interview. These experts were selected to integrate people with varied experience and as much knowledge as possible into the team. Ideal candidates included:

- Podiatrists, business consultants or advisors who target co-parental couples in the South Asian market (Rai, 2014). The participants' interviews can help identify the implications of these factors and understand the peculiarities of the couples' experience in handling their commercial ventures and personal affairs.
- Those who have worked with successful people and couples with issues of work–life interface. The wealth of their experience would have revealed the psychological effects of work–family conflict on couples from the South Asian region, with a focus on ecopreneurs.
- Professionals such as social scientists or scholars who have researched entrepreneurship, gender relations or opportunities for work–life balance within the South Asian context. The interviews and data have been appropriately framed and understood using the participants' knowledge of the cultural panorama.

Using snowball sampling, the research targeted a relatively delimited group of experts, meaning that the participants have either held a position as an academic or worked professionally within the cultural sector. Furthermore, the number of women who participated in the study was significantly lower than that of men, and all participants were from South Asia. However, the research covers different regions and years of experience within this region.

Interview Protocol

A guide for conducting semi-structured interviews was designed to systematize the questions while keeping them open-ended to permit digging deeper into apparent issues related to the study's themes. The questions developed for the guide are exploratory to obtain detailed accounts and reflections from the specialists.

Potential themes explored could include:

- This study aims to identify the issues affecting work–family balance among entrepreneurial couples from the South Asian region.
- Examining how culture and gender affect the work life of these couples. The effect of work–life imbalance on the physical and psychological health of the couple and the business.
- Intervention measures that might assist South Asian copreneurial couples to attain a better work–life balance.

The interview questions were pre-tested through a pilot interview before the actual interviews to verify the effectiveness of the interview guide in gathering abundant information.

Data Collection and Analysis

The interviews were conducted face-to-face or online, depending on the participants' wishes. Participants were informed of the research purpose and processes, and their consent to record the interviews was obtained to enhance the capturing of the conversation.

After the interviews, the data collected was transcribed word by word, omitting minor truncations. Thematic analysis was used to analyze the transcribed data. This type of method entails categorizing and coding common themes in the interviews. The research aimed to include different themes into a systematic coding process and subsequent analysis of the connections between these themes to arrive at a construction of the phenomenon under study, namely, work–life conflict for South Asian copreneurial couples.

By employing this type of qualitative research in expert interviews, the study focuses on the phenomena associated with South Asian copreneurial couples' daily working life experiences and the nature of work–life conflict within this cultural framework.

Findings

Based on the information gathered from the expert interviews, this section presents the identified themes that shed light on the work–life conflict among South Asian commercial couples. The interview findings will be elaborated on and exemplified for each theme to show how it manifests in practice.

Theme 1: The Entangled Web of Long Hours and Cultural Expectations

- *Long hours and relentless pursuit:* All participants mentioned the lengthy working hours that come with being an entrepreneur as a significant source of conflict with family. Starting from the following quotes: 'They are always working; there are no business hours.' A business consultant points out that entrepreneurial couples are devoted to struggling and achieving their business goals.
- *Balancing family obligations:* This is made worse because of the cultural value that predominates in South Asia – the family. A therapist observed, 'There is always the expectation to put the family first, but running a business requires one's attention at all times.' Therefore, there is always that pull in two directions, contributing to work interference with family.

Theme 2: Navigating Gender Roles in a Start-Up Setting

- *Double burden for women:* Experts noted that gender roles have more adverse effects on women than men. One social scientist noted, 'This arrangement gives the women the additional burden of cleaning, cooking, and raising children besides working in the business; thus, a stressful condition hampers achieving a work–life balance.'
- *Redefining roles and responsibilities:* Some specialists are concerned about the signs that can lead to positive change. A business consultant remarks, 'In startups, more couples are. . .discussing and redefining roles, which can ease some work–life conflicts for women.'

Theme 3: Blurred Boundaries and the Constant 'On' Mode

- *Working from home:* Flexibility can be an advantage and a constraint. One of the Malaysian participants mentioned that most home-based start-ups are in South Asia. As a psychologist mentioned, flexibility can be considered to be negative: 'When working from home, one is never really working, never really idle; the lines between work and personal life are often barely visible since one is making a definite use of time in order to devote time to a relationship.'
- *Pressure to be available:* Other sources of pressure that business executives highlighted included the cultural imperative to always be 'on'. A social scientist disclosed, 'There is a culture to display professionalism, and this leads to an expectation that couples must be dedicated and hardworking, so they end up "on" constantly, which is a thwart to work–life balance.'

Theme 4: Implications of Work–Life Conflict

- *Burnout and emotional strain:* The experts asserted that the anticipated adverse effects of work interference were evident in couples' relationships. A therapist highlighted that couples were emotionally stressed due to the pressure of work and long hours, so much so that their relationships may also not be exempt.
- *Impact on business performance:* The specialists noted some adverse impacts on the business undertaking (Singh et al., 2023). One business consultant commented: 'If the two individuals that form the couple deal with the work–family conflict, the efficiency in decision-making, the creativity, and the productivity of the business will also be influenced.'

This section only offers a basic framework, or at least the direct impression given to the reader. Based on specific interview data, readers can further expand on each theme by including the following:

- *Additional interview quotes:* Meanwhile, more specific details about each interview should be provided to support the points appropriately made.
- *Contrasting viewpoints:* Implicitly, if there were dissimilarities in the views of the experts, they should be explained in the course of the scientific work, citing possible causes of such differences.
- *Real-life examples:* Some interviews may be helpful for fictionalized anecdotes or real examples with concealed identities, which can give a more precise and exciting representation of the discussed themes.

Through further exploration of the themes outlined in the study, an understanding of the issues that challenge the South Asian copreneurial couples' work–family balance is well illustrated. Such considerations help build the foundation for the discussion section, in which the solutions to the problem addressed in this study are proposed.

Discussion

The research questions from the expert interviews bring out the multifaceted dilemma of South Asian copreneurial couples in work–life interference. The issues affecting these couples include long working hours, culture and expectations about one's performance, gender role issues, and the lack of clear division between work and family time (Jefferson, 2023). However, it does not stop here in the discussion. By reviewing the results and integrating the findings with the existing literature, it is possible to discuss the possible interventions and recommendations for South Asian copreneurial couples to improve work–life balance.

Managers interviewed as part of this study, and some prior studies on entrepreneurship highlighted the time management issue (e.g. Aladejebi, 2020). Thus, couples can be trained to prioritize tasks, divide duties and goals between the partners, and establish an exclusive time for other spheres of life within helpful workshops or coaching programs.

One learns that computers are excellent at times and, at other times, dreadful, but one must understand that by proper use and management, their power can be harnessed and made to work for one's benefit (Sardeshmukh & Smith, 2024). Computer and software support services, project management solutions and communication applications can improve cooperation and allow the couple to achieve professional results regardless of time.

Some of the issues the professionals stressed included communication with extended families. It is recommended that couples talk about their work schedules and justify why they should set time apart from work. Couples could get the necessary support from their families by promoting knowledge and possibly sharing some of the responsibilities.

Okello (2018) stressed the aspect of equity in workload distribution. Starting with the copreneurial couples of South Asian descent, the study established that gender roles can be up for discussion and redefinition. This could entail chores like cleaning, cooking and taking care of the children, as well as specific tasks that relate to the production or growth of the company that each partner could handle best (Ahuruele et al., 2024).

Gender equality policies, as well as social programs and activities in South Asian societies, mean that such couples can be provided with a favourable atmosphere (Helmle et al., 2011). Periodic awareness campaigns and workshops could prepare couples to overcome the barriers of traditional male and female roles and divide responsibilities in business and at home.

Although home-based businesses have many advantages, the specialists noted that a designated work area should exist. Physical separation from the workplace can assist the couple in psychologically detaching from work.

Conclusion

It can be concluded that ambition, resourcefulness and cultural values infuse entrepreneurial spirit and enable it to thrive in South Asia. In the journey to success, copreneurial couples' lives are entirely expressions of work–life conflict (Peregrino-Dartey, 2018). The long working hours, cultural pressures and blurred boundaries between work and personal life may create quite a complex tapestry of challenges. However, this research journey tells a more profound truth about resilience and transformation.

In this sense, the expert interviews helped uncover the complexity of the red flags raised by the work–life conflict skewed towards South Asian copreneurial couples. The unpacking of the themes of round-the-clock work demands, gendered roles and 'on' mode creates a rich and almost cinematic representation of the experiences of such couples. The research does not stop with pointing out those challenges; instead, it proffers a way of navigating through this labyrinth – a tapestry woven with solutions and strategies.

With good time management, acceptance of technology and open communication with family, such couples can gain complete control over their time. Defining clear and concise gender roles within the start-up and society, promoting gender equality and creating a demarcation line between work and personal life can pave the way for a balanced partnership. Moreover, mental health awareness programs, couples support networks and formulating coping strategies may also contribute to the mitigation of the cascading effects resulting from work–life conflict.

The research identifies its limitations. Some surveys should have balanced the use of expert interviews and in-depth case studies based on first-person intervention directly by the couples themselves. Secondly, the research setting in South Asia demands more research in other cultural environments to validate whether the same themes are applicable.

In conclusion, this study of South Asian copreneurial couples defies the concept of sheer entrepreneurialism. It turns into a tale of the humanness of spirit with its ability to adapt, innovate and navigate challenges. Through the measures mentioned in this research, these couples can achieve more than a better work–life balance; they can reinvent the definition of success in the pages composing their lives. Their journey will inspire entrepreneurs trying to come up worldwide since success is not only about building a business but about having a life alongside.

Implications

This discussion on work–life conflict faced by South Asian co-operative couples is relevant beyond the boundaries of current research. It provides a starting point for possible resolution. The results have significant implications for ecopreneurs, the business world, society and the theoretical understanding of work–life balance in a cultural context.

Managerial Implications

- *Entrepreneurial training programs:* Business incubators and entrepreneur training for potential entrepreneurs should include workshops on time management, communication skills and strategies for achieving work–life balance (Arasti et al., 2021). This will equip couples with tools that may help them keep the business running while maintaining their personal lives.
- *Flexible work arrangements:* Business support organizations could lobby for better provision of flexible work, such as co-working spaces incorporating childcare facilities into work arrangements or part-time work for spouses. Such arrangements may work for copreneurial couples based on the particular nature of their businesses.
- *Mental health and wellness resources:* Organizations should collaborate with mental health professionals to conduct workshops and offer related resources on managing stress and emotional health for entrepreneurs and their families.

Social Implications

- *Gender-equal opportunities:* The study suggests that social and educational schemes should promote gender-equal opportunities among South Asian societies. Only by redesigning the stereotypical roles that women play in societies, enabling them to participate in businesses actively, and that too with equal responsibility in households, can couples' partnership be balanced in a copreneurial dimension.
- *Shifting cultural attitudes:* Free, open discussions on work–life balance and the significance of mental health will go a long way in shifting cultural attitudes in South Asian societies. When society understands that success is vital to well-being, copreneurial couples can benefit from their support.
- *Role models and mentorship:* There is a need to promote the success stories of entrepreneurial couples of South Asian descent who demonstrate work–life balance and are effective role models for people who would like to engage in solopreneurship. Shaping mentorship programs that link established entrepreneurial couples to those just starting their entrepreneurial journey can bode well for guidance.

Theoretical Implications

- *Expanding the work–life balance discourse:* The study adds value to the growing discussion on work–life balance by introducing new cultural threads from South Asia. It argues that cultural predispositions, like gender roles and extended family structures, should be considered for work–life conflict studies in different places.
- *The interplay of gender and culture:* The findings about work–life experiences reveal a complicated interconnection between gender and culture. This suggests that future research on work–life balance must probe more into how these factors interact in specific cultural contexts. The implications discussed in this study should be recognized, and a supportive system should be created with the participation of stakeholders from all relevant sectors.
- *Entrepreneurship and well-being:* This paper developed a question on the classical understanding of a 'lone-wolf' entrepreneur and highlighted that loneliness can be a primary factor in sustainable entrepreneurial success. It paves the ground for continuous research to identify the relationship between work–life balance and entrepreneurial outcomes.

This recognition may allow stakeholders in different sectors to create a supportive ecosystem for the South. It can be a study that promises possibilities and hope for positive changes, from equipping couples with practical tools to undergirding a cultural shift towards well-being. The path towards healthier work–life experiences for South Asian copreneurial couples is not an individual effort but a collective journey that will have systemic effects, influencing business, society and the future of entrepreneurship.

Limitations and Future Research Directions

Though rich in insights, there are some limitations to the research. Relying on interviews with experts brings rich qualitative data but restricts the generalizability of its findings to a broader population of South Asian copreneurial couples. Secondly, the present study focused only on the South Asian region and has limited applicability to other cultural contexts. Further studies could establish if the findings are universal across regions. Another limitation is the lack of direct data from participants through surveys or even case studies, thus severely limiting the examination of the lived experiences of these couples.

Future studies could consider including a larger, more diverse sample of South Asian copreneurial couples. Mixed-method research – pairing quantitative and qualitative methods – can provide a more comprehensive understanding of the phenomenon. Longitudinal studies may trace the development of work–life conflict over time and assess the efficacy of various interventions. Comparative studies across different South Asian countries will also contribute to including cultural and experiential nuances related to work–life issues. Addressing these limitations and extending future research will add nuance and richness to existing knowledge about work–life conflict among South Asian copreneurial couples.

Acknowledgements

We are indebted to the editors and anonymous reviewers for their invaluable suggestions and comments in developing this chapter to a publishable level.

References

Ahuruele, W. A., Okereke, E. J., & Ofoegbu, W. C. (2024). Work-life balance initiatives and employee performance of deposit money banks in Rivers State, Nigeria. *Asian Journal of Economics, Finance and Management*, *6*(1), 273–287.

Aladejebi, O. (2020). Copreneurs: The impact of spousal relationships on business success in Nigeria. *Archives of Business Research*, *8*(2), 65–78.

Arasti, Z., Sadeghi, L., & Saeedian, M. (2021). Women in copreneurial businesses in the socio-cultural context of Iran. In U. Guelich, A. Bullough, T. S. Manolova, & L. Schjoedt (Eds.), *Women's entrepreneurship and culture* (pp. 196–226). Edward Elgar Publishing.

Dewasiri, N. J., Weerakoon, Y. K. B., & Azeez, A. A. (2018). Mixed methods in finance research. *International Journal of Qualitative Methods*, *17*(1), 1–13. https://doi.org/10.1177/1609406918801730

Helmle, J. R., Seibold, D. R., & Afifi, T. D. (2011). Work and family in copreneurial family businesses extending and integrating communication research. *Annals of the International Communication Association*, *35*(1), 51–91.

Jefferson, S. A. (2023). *Entrepreneurial mental well-being: Strategies for positive business outcomes*. Doctoral dissertation. Walden University.

Jennings, J. E., Breitkreuz, R. S., & James, A. E. (2013). When family members are also business owners: Is entrepreneurship suitable for families? *Family Relations*, *62*(3), 472–489.

Kim, S. J., & Choi, S. Y. (2017). Family embeddedness and gendered professional entrepreneurship: Evidence from the self-employment of female lawyers in the US. In V. Ratten, V. Ramadani, L.-P. Dana, R. D. Hisrich, & J. J. Ferreira (Eds.), *Gender and family entrepreneurship* (pp. 82–105). Routledge.

Kim, J. J., & Kim, S. J. (2018). Women's leadership in family business organisations. *Korean Women in Leadership*, 141–158.

Languilaire, J. C. E. (2019). Entrepreneurial life-puzzle and wellbeing: The case of Swedish women entrepreneurs. In M.-T. Lepeley, K. Kuschel, N. Beutell, N. Pouw, & E. L. Eijdenberg (Eds.), *The wellbeing of women in entrepreneurship* (pp. 261–279). Routledge.

Maziriri, E. T., Nyagadza, B., Maramura, T. C., & Mapuranga, M. (2022). "Like mom and dad": Using narrative analysis to understand how couplepreneurs stimulate their kids' entrepreneurial mindset. *Journal of Entrepreneurship in Emerging Economies*, *16*(3), 784–811.

Michael-Tsabari, N., Houshmand, M., Strike, V. M., & Efrat Treister, D. (2020). Uncovering implicit assumptions: Reviewing the work-family interface in the family business and offering opportunities for future research. *Family Business Review*, *33*(1), 64–89.

Okello, I. (2018). *Gender dynamics between intimate-partner business owners. A case study of ecopreneur and solo entrepreneur spouses in Uganda*. Doctoral dissertation. Dalhousie University.

Peregrino-Dartey, E. (2018). *Copreneurs' coping strategies for work-family conflict*. Doctoral dissertation. Walden University.

Qiu, H., & Freel, M. (2020). Managing family-related conflicts in family businesses: A review and research agenda. *Family Business Review*, *33*(1), 90–113.

Rai, R. (2014). Role conflict and in pursuit of balance: A study on dual career couple. *South Asian Journal of Marketing & Management Research*, *4*(10), 36–46.

Sardeshmukh, S., & Smith, R. M. (2024). Entrepreneurship and gender in tourism. In R. Hallak & C. Lee (Eds.), *Handbook of tourism entrepreneurship* (pp. 120–130). Edward Elgar Publishing.

Singh, R., Aggarwal, S., & Sahni, S. (2023). A systematic literature review of work-life balance using the ADO model. *FIIB Business Review*, *12*(3), 243–258.

Ummiroh, I. R., Schwab, A., & Dhewanto, W. (2022). Women social entrepreneurs in a Muslim society: How to manage patriarchy and spouses. *Social Enterprise Journal*, *18*(4), 660–690.

Chapter 12

Employee Branding and SME Growth in India: Towards a US$5 Trillion Economy

Ajit Kumar Sarangi, Arun Kaushal and Pawan Kumar

Lovely Professional University, India

Abstract

This research examines how employee branding (EBR) strategies impact the growth of small and medium enterprises (SMEs) in the Indian economy, targeting the nation's objective of reaching a US$5 trillion economy. This study analyzes the strategic importance of EBR to identify the main factors that drive growth and economic expansion in SMEs. This study utilized a qualitative approach to collect in-depth insights from SME leaders and human resources (HR) professionals through semi-structured interviews. The research participants were chosen using purposive sampling to ensure representation from various sectors within the SME domain. This study comprehensively examines EBR practices and their relationship with organizational growth. The initial findings highlight the importance of EBR for encouraging SME growth and emphasize the significance of fostering a positive workplace culture and implementing strategies to retain and engage talent. Participants asserted that effective EBR improves organizational performance and aids in recruiting and retaining highly skilled individuals, thereby assisting in the SME growth trajectory. The study results emphasize the significance of EBR and its consequences for Indian SMEs that want to contribute substantially to India's economic development.

Keywords: Employee branding; EBR; SME; small and medium-sized enterprises; talent management; India; economy

Introduction

India is poised at a critical juncture in its growth trajectory. It is prepared to transition into the next phase of advancement with the ambitious goal of

Shaping Entrepreneurial Marketing, Volume 1, 179–193

Published under exclusive licence by Emerald Publishing Limited
doi:10.1108/978-1-83708-852-220251013

achieving a US$5 trillion economy. This vision aligns with national and international agendas, positioning India to capitalize on substantial opportunities. Understanding the significance of employee branding and its impact on small and medium enterprises (SMEs) is crucial as the country prepares for this important journey.

India's goal of achieving a US$5 trillion economy relies heavily on the robust growth of its SMEs. With over 63 million units, SMEs account for nearly 30% of the GDP and create millions of jobs, making them essential to the Indian economy. Their sustainable growth path is encountering challenges such as intense competition, talent recruitment and employee branding (EBR). This study explores the significant impact of EBR on driving SME growth and the potential to contribute to India's goal of achieving a $5 trillion economy.

SMEs play a crucial role in stimulating economic development, substantially contributing to the GDP and generating many employment possibilities. (Kapoor & Gupta, 2022; Siddiqui & Ilyas, 2020). However, in an intensely competitive atmosphere, the capacity to attract and retain talent is essential for SMEs (Kumar & Kaur, 2019). Employee branding is a powerful tool that gives SMEs a strategic advantage in talent competition.

EBR, defined as 'the deliberate and strategic management of an organization's reputation as an employer' (Lievens & Van den Broeck, 2013), transcends mere recruitment and focuses on constructing an attractive and differentiated organizational identity. Further, Hatch and Brief (2004) describe a strong link between EBR and organizational performance. EBR is crucial in attracting and retaining highly skilled employees, promoting employee involvement and improving the brand's reputation (Berthon et al., 2006; Rowley, 2008).

This study explores how EBR can empower Indian SMEs to achieve the goal of a US$5 trillion economy. It seeks to address the following essential inquiries:

- How can EBR strategies be tailored to suit the specific requirements and limitations of Indian SMEs?
- What are the essential components of a successful employee brand for SMEs in India?
- Does EBR significantly affect different aspects of SME growth, like talent acquisition, employee engagement and financial performance?

Literature Review

EBR entails internalizing the desired brand image and being driven to portray it to consumers and other organization members (Miles & Mangold, 2004). Moreover, Dabirian et al. (2019) emphasized that EBR is a strategic approach that aims to influence the attitudes and viewpoints of employees, prospective employees and other relevant participants regarding a particular organization.

EBR entails creating and advocating a positive and consistent image of an organization's workforce, both internally and externally. EBR aligns workers' attitudes, behaviours and values with the organization's vision, purpose and culture, motivating them to act as brand ambassadors. EBR can bolster the organization's reputation, allure and retain talent and enhance business performance (Kucherov & Zavyalova, 2016; Saini et al., 2022; Theurer et al., 2018).

EBR is essential for the progress and success of SMEs in India. When SMEs prioritize developing a robust brand image within their workforce, employee engagement, loyalty and productivity increase, contributing to the overall expansion and prosperity of the business. Through establishing a favourable EBR, SMEs can effectively draw in and maintain highly skilled employees who share the same values and objectives as the company. This can result in a more motivated and dedicated workforce, resulting in enhanced performance and higher levels of customer satisfaction (Odoom, 2016).

SMEs are a vital component of the Indian economy, substantially contributing to its GDP, employment creation and industrial production. Their contribution to fostering economic growth, promoting innovation and facilitating social development is unquestionable (World Bank, 2019). SMEs are India's primary sources of employment, supporting the livelihoods of millions of individuals, especially in rural and semi-urban regions. Their labour-intensive characteristics facilitate the absorption of the growing workforce, decreasing poverty and improving social conditions. In addition, SMEs have notable flexibility and durability, frequently being the initial entities to react to shifts in the market and developing prospects. Notwithstanding their noteworthy contributions, SMEs in India encounter various obstacles that impede their progress and advancement. These factors encompass a scarcity of skilled labour, limited access to financial resources, inadequate infrastructure and other similar challenges (World Bank, 2021).

Popular Theories of EBR

Brand signalling theory suggests that when an organization communicates brand signals to its employees, such as quality, credibility and consistency, it can influence how they view the brand promise and their role in maintaining it. Brand signals can be communicated through internal communication, training, leadership and rewards. Brand signalling can enhance employees' understanding of the brand, thus impacting their behaviour, performance and outcomes (Karanges et al., 2018).

The Brand Equity Theory, which refers to the higher value of a product or service due to its brand name, is expanded upon by the brand equity theory, which incorporates employer branding as a theory component. Further, Keller (1993) explained that brand equity is defined as the differential effect of different levels of brand understanding on consumers' responses to marketing initiatives. It is the value that a brand delivers to a product or service that other brands do not. Awareness of the brand, strong associations, perceived quality and loyalty to the brand are all essential components. Consistent branding, product quality, customer satisfaction, effective communication and crisis management are essential to brand equity. When referring to the improved value that a firm achieves due to creating and maintaining a powerful and positive employer brand via constant efforts, the term 'employer brand equity' is used. As a result, it is feasible to ascertain how staff members and other stakeholders perceive the company in terms of its role as an employer. Employer brand awareness, employer brand associations, employer brand loyalty and employer brand image are the four primary characteristics that can be considered when analyzing the equity of an employer's brand. It has been demonstrated by Theurer et al. (2018) that the development of employee brand equity can lead to improvements in an organization's performance, as well as its reputation and competitiveness.

The *Value Proposition Theory* suggests that an organization can develop and convey a distinct and persuasive employee value proposition (EVP) to its current and potential employees. The EVP is based on employees' work value preferences, which can differ depending on time and culture. A clearly defined and appealing EVP can impact employee attraction, engagement, retention and advocacy. The EVP refers to the equilibrium between the benefits and contributions that an employee provides to the organization in return for their contribution. Further, Sengupta et al. (2015) and Pattnaik and Mishra (2016) describe EVP as an employee's assessment of the many values provided by the organization, including cultural, work-related, inspirational, developmental, environmental and economic value. EVP is critical to employee engagement, motivation and productivity (Smola et al., 2023). Furthermore, the relationship between EVP dimensions, employee commitment and organizational citizenship behaviours, highlighting the importance of EVP in influencing employee behaviours within organizations. Multiple work environment factors affect employee motivation about value propositions, including external and internal aspects that influence how employees connect with value propositions (Liewendahl & Heinonen, 2020). EVP elements substantially impact employee productivity, loyalty and dedication to employers (Dzhulai, 2023). These components influence a company's ability to fulfil promises to its employees and shape subsequent organizational communication (Dzhulai, 2023). Further, Suomi et al. (2019) describe essential parts of EBR, including organizational culture, rewards, working environment, training, human resources (HR) practices, reputation and values, communication and physical surroundings. Bell et al. (2017) explain that employees' attachment to a brand can transform them into enthusiastic experts who actively disseminate up-to-date brand information to others.

Employee brand ambassadorship has been acknowledged as an influential factor in EBR, emphasizing employee well-being within the workplace (Sakka & Ahammad, 2020). In addition, employee advocacy, which stems from using social media and spreading information through word of mouth, raises awareness and enhances the reputation of organizations (Sonne et al., 2019). Helm et al. (2016) found that the relationship between workers' self-concept, brand identification and brand pride substantially impacts brand citizenship behaviours. This discovery significantly impacts internal branding and human resource management (HRM) initiatives. Dechawatanapaisal (2019) found in his study that EBR helps enhance brand citizenship behaviour and brand loyalty. Further, Prince (2003) describes that the characteristics that are associated with a person's positive attitude towards an organization include the following: the desire to promote the organization to one's friends, the feeling of pride that comes from discussing one's affiliation with the organization, the perception that the organization is the most outstanding alternative for work, and the demonstration of concern for the organization's future. Gronroos (1996) defines employee brand ambassadors as employees who have the highest level of enthusiasm in actively promoting a company's brand and values. They function as authentic delegates, exercising sway over stakeholders both inside and externally to the organization. Organizations may enhance employer branding, attract highly skilled individuals and foster consumer loyalty by employing employee advocacy. An effective ambassador program enables employees to share their positive experiences with the firm, contributing to a strong company culture and reputation. Delivering customer feedback, recruiting skilled workers and advocating for the organization's principles are all crucial responsibilities. Table 12.1 describes the various aspects of EBR.

Table 12.1. Various Aspects of Employee Engagement.

Various Aspects of Employee Branding	Source
Enthusiasm to promote an organisation to friends, experiencing a sense of pride in sharing one's affiliation with the organisation, perceiving the organisation as the most superior choice for employment, and demonstrating concern for the organisation's future.	Prince (2003)
The study examined the correlation between workers' self-concept, brand identification, and brand pride. It found that these elements significantly influence brand citizenship behaviours, which contribute to improving internal branding and human resource management strategies.	Helm et al. (2016)
EBR enhances brand equity with external stakeholders by implementing internal brand management strategies. This entails using brand-focused human resource management, internal communication about the brand, and	Barros-Arrieta and García-Cali (2021); Punjaisri and Wilson (2017)

(Continued)

Table 12.1. *(Continued)*

Various Aspects of Employee Branding	Source
brand management to accomplish targeted brand results among staff members. In this context, some goals include brand awareness, acknowledgement, dedication, commitment, and behaviours demonstrating good citizenship.	
Employee brand ambassadorship is recognised as a significant factor in employee branding, particularly in enhancing employee well-being in the workplace.	Sakka and Ahammad (2020)

Source: Authors' own.

Research Methodology

This research aims to develop a theoretical framework for EBR in SMEs that can be implemented for the present and future workforce. Our research question is: How can EBR strategies be customized to meet the specific needs and constraints of Indian SMEs based on their real-life experiences in the workplace? What are the critical elements of a thriving employee brand for SMEs in India? Does EBR significantly impact various aspects of SME growth, such as talent acquisition, employee engagement and financial performance? This qualitative research aims to conduct a detailed investigation of a specific phenomenon rather than generalizing about a larger population (Creswell, 2002; Dewasiri et al., 2018). While creating this qualitative survey design, the researchers used techniques to enhance their grasp of the phenomenon by working with participants to find patterns and achieve a deeper appreciation of the study.

This study included professional employees who hold leadership positions in various segments of SMEs in India. Conducting a deliberate selection process to identify potential candidates with at least two years of experience in the SME industry enabled the researcher to gather valuable and relevant data related to the phenomenon under investigation (Creswell, 2007). Ten participants were chosen for the interviews. The profiles of the interviewees are provided in Table 12.2.

Data was collected using interviews with semi-structured questions and a relevant literature review. The employer established the upper limit for interviews, specifying that each interview should last 20 to 30 minutes. The semi-structured questions were derived from the literature analysis and the chosen definition of EBR. The concentrated session expedited the process of validating the concept. In the session, attendees actively participated in an engaging discussion that began

Table 12.2. Participant Profile.

Participant	Participant Profile	Year of Experience in SME
P1	Chief Executive officer	6
P2	Chief People Officer	4
P3	Chief Marketing Officer	8
P4	Head Learning and development	3
P5	Head Employee Engagement	2
P6	Head Business	5
P7	Head Customer Experience	7
P8	Head Finance	4
P9	Customer Service Manager	8
P10	Head Operations	9

Source: Authors' own.

with partially planned questions and encouraged free-flowing replies to promote conversation and narrative.

The interview guidelines were derived from the study methodology and literature review. After preliminary testing of the questions, modifications were made before conducting research on-site at an organization's premises. This study aimed to promote self-awareness and flexibility throughout the interaction to encourage the collaborative creation of knowledge between the researchers and the participants. Respondents were provided with information on the present state of our study and the particular subject being studied. The primary inquiries were: (a) What are the various determinants that impact EBR? (b) What are the results or consequences of EBR? (c) What is your perspective on the influence of EBR on small and SMEs in India?

The interviews were conducted via online platforms such as Zoom and MS Teams. After obtaining participants' explicit permission, they were recorded and transcribed using the Amazon Transcribe service.

Data Analysis and Conceptualization of the Model

As stated by Creswell (2002), it is necessary to transcribe data to identify critical themes after gathering data through interviews. The key themes of the interviews were derived through the following process. (1) Utilize the Amazon Transcribe Tool to convert the data into written form and (2) perform a focused data analysis to thoroughly comprehend the results and interviews, which will aid in developing conceptual categories. Below are the key themes that emerged for drivers and outcomes of EBR (see Table 12.3):

Table 12.3. Drivers and Outcomes of Employee Branding.

Drivers of Employee Branding	The Outcome of Employee Branding
Employee communication is vital in creating the brand image (Barros-Arrieta & García-Cali, 2021; Karanges et al., 2018; Suomi et al., 2019; P1, P5, P7, P10)	Strong communication, rewards and recognition, training and development exercises, and a positive work environment strongly influence EBR, resulting in an excellent impact. Advocacy, loyalty, and organisational growth (Karanges et al., 2018; Suomi et al., 2021; P1, P5, P7, P8, P10)
Rewards and recognition are critical components in driving employee branding, which helps in communicating and signalling the right brand strategies and has a direct impact on employee branding and engagement (Punjaisri & Wilson, 2017; Suomi et al., 2019; P4 et al., P7, P8)	Brand advocacy, such as positive word of mouth, plays an important role. When employees are engaged, and employee branding is strong, organisations often experience high brand advocacy and brand ambassadorship (Sakka & Ahammad, 2020; Sonne et al., 2021; P4, P6, P8, P9, P10)
Training and development play a vital role in building a brand and creating a brand identity for employees (Pattnaik & Mishra, 2016; Suomi et al., 2019; P2, P3, P6, P9)	Strong employee branding and brand advocacy help enhance employee brand loyalty. Higher employee branding means higher brand loyalty (Bell et al., 2017; Dechawatanapaisal, 2019; P1, P5, P9, P10)
The work environment is a crucial element of employee branding; a positive environment helps to create a strong employee brand, which in turn helps in increasing brand loyalty among employees (Pattnaik & Misra, 2016; Suomi et al., 2019; P1, P3, P6, P7)	Employee branding has a strong relationship with organisational growth and employee productivity. Employee branding leads to higher employee engagement; hence it helps to bring ownership and organisational growth (P1, P2, P4, P5–P8, P10)

Source: Authors' own.

Employee communication is vital to building an employee brand and creating a positive image. Further, Participant 1 suggested that 'we communicate continuously with employees on various aspects of the organisation with the employee be it organisation update, change announcement, any celebration, etc. all this communication are proactive due to which have been able to reduce the grievance by 80%, and this has resulted directly in the employee NPS. We have programs such as a quarterly open house with the CEO, leaders connect, E-newsletter, weekly digest snippet of last week's happening, and next week's plan.' Participant 7 stated, 'In our organisation, we have created various forums where we constantly communicate to employees; there are forums like employee connect, hot lie to leaders, and a bot-based system where we share and listen to our employee's program such as likeminded group, knowledge sharing session and interactive platform for query and grievance redressal are prevalent amongst employees. This has helped us create sustainable channels to create bonding with employees, which has further helped us enhance positive word of mouth from our employees.'

Participant 4 shared that 'the reward is the key for employer branding. We have created a reward and recognition framework that cuts across all levels of employees, which is transparent, timely, and instant. The Reward and Recognition platform has helped them achieve better NPS and performance for employees.' 'Recognition is one of the things that create confidence and trust amongst the employees; our recognition program is parameterised to bring transparency, we recognise performance, behaviour and living values of the company, it has helped us to drive the right behaviours against employees and enhance retention and performance growth for the employees which in turn help us achieve new height for the organisation' (Participant 5). Further, Participant 6 explained that 'we have instilled the recognition culture in our organization and this is the strength area for us, we have been scoring very high in our recognition program in various employee and employer survey. Because of our reward and recognition program, we can retain talent in our organisation.'

Further, Participant 9 explained, 'Training is the key to employee and organisation success; we have a structured training program which enables us to enhance the skills of our existing employees, which has a strong ROI of productivity. Also, the development program helped us to groom our employees to take on new roles internally. Last year, we placed 53% of employees in the next role. Also, we have seen a reduction in attrition by 11%.' Participant 7 stated, 'We have created a learning academy in our organisation with a clear target of at least 70% of employees learning new skills for the future; through this initiative, we have seen 82% employees learning new skills and 12% enhancement in performance.' Further, Participant 10 describes, 'Training and developing is a key to organisation success and employee success, it instils the caring, growth, and learning culture in the organisation. With proper training and development initiatives, we have been able to show the career trajectory of individuals through various programs we do under training, such as on-the-job training, experiential learning, Virtual reality-based learning, game-based learning, e-learning, LMS, assessment centres and development centres, etc. Our learning and developmental programs are based on performance and potential, further aligned with organisational values and EVP. We are seeing positive word of mouth and advocacy amongst the employees. With learning interventions, we can see the positive impact on employees and in the job market.' 'Training is essential for all to expand their potential, growth, and readiness for future jobs; at our organisation, we not only provide training interventions for our employees but also various training interventions are provided for the candidates also. We provide training, such as preparation for interviews and assessments, about the organisation and its growth plan to the candidates. Also, post-selection, we allocate buddies to provide various training, such as role, system and procedure, policies, etc., to the candidates. It helps in increasing attractiveness, and we have seen lower dropouts. Also, in various social media and review platforms, we have seen our scores increase before and after the implementation of the practices' (Participant 5).

The work environment is crucial to nurturing talent. A positive work environment helps cultivate a positive branding image and a culture of growth in the organization. Participant 3 explained, 'We have various programs like open-door culture, knowledge sharing, transparent goals aligned with functional and organisational growth, skip-level meetings to discuss various topics, wellbeing programs, and family programs. All this helped us instil a positive brand image and brand advocacy amongst employees; this has further helped us enhance employee loyalty.' Participant 9 further described, 'Care is the key to our success in attracting and retaining talent. To build the care culture in our organisation, we have touched upon and designed various programs for various employment categories, such as candidates, employees, and alumni. We have designed various programs for each of the categories; for the candidate, we have Guru, an Interactive bot, proactive feedback mechanism, emotional well-being session before an interview, etc. where, whereas for employees, we have programs like well-being (physical, emotional and financial,), tied up with organisations like Isha Yoga to provide a program like inner engineering, Townhall, employee connect, Live chat with leaders, Manager one on one, continuous feedback, policies such as Prevention on Sexual Harassment, Workplace harassment, conflict of interest, etc. also during the top time such as flood, cyclone, and pandemic we are the front runner to help our employees and family with providing services such as food supplies, medical supplies, hospitalisation, etc.'

Based on the identified constructs, the authors propose a conceptual framework, as stated in Fig. 12.1.

Fig. 12.1. Model Employee Branding Element and Outcome.
Source: Author's own.

Discussion

In examining research from a HR perspective, theory development significantly impacts practices, particularly in terms of how findings can contribute to enhancing brand loyalty and organizational growth. This study significantly contributes to SMEs in India by examining how EBR positively affects employee loyalty and organizational growth. The study references the works of Dechawatanapaisal (2019), Suomi et al. (2019), and Karanges et al. (2018). In order to give priority to organizational culture, incentives, working environment, training, HR practices, reputation, values, communication, and physical environment, organizations that focus on EBR need to take additional measures (Suomi et al., 2019).

Further, Participant 10 stated, 'We communicate and over-communicate to build culture and ingrain the organisation's values, which help us cultivate a positive brand image amongst the employees.' According to Participant 1, 'Our organisation works on various levels of communication for our employees regularly. We use communication methods like change announcements, mailers, leaders connect, and peers connect. Further, communication helps us create a strong brand image amongst employees and leads to strong employee branding and employee advocacy.' Participant 3 further explained, 'Our organisation values play an important role in defining our strategy; the five values, i.e., confidence, innovation, trust, nurturing, and proactiveness, have been defined based on various parameters. Our customer and employee value proposition (EVP) are linked to each value. We further emphasize our internal and external communication based on values and EVP. We use various communication methods such as town hall, mailers, Bot communication, Applications for Candidates and employees, buddy programs, Gen-AI-based employee handbooks, and VR-based connections with leaders to engage our employees and candidates.' 'Communication is the centre of employer branding at our organisation; we frequently communicate with candidates (selected, rejected, dropped, etc.) to provide information about the company and gather feedback to enhance our process and attractiveness. For employees, we do not use an individual approach based on skills, competency, and performance; for example, top performers get direct access to the leaders through a direct line, whereas buddies get assigned to new joiners and low performers to handhold them and show them the paths. We use communication tools like AI-based feedback collection, Applications for policies and procedures, Applications to ask questions and get answers from experts within the company, intranet, and WhatsApp for all new announcements' (Participant 8).

'In our organisation, we have a working population of 3000+ employees in both white and blue collar; creating a strong brand image and strong employee brand is very important for us. We take various initiatives like recognising the right behaviours, timely communication, training, and development to inculcate our organisation's culture. It helps us create the right brand identity amongst employees, which has helped us create loyalty. Further, we have seen organisational growth with positive employee branding and advocacy' (Participant 5).

Participant 10 stated that 'recognition plays an important role in attracting and retaining talent; we have recognition and reward programs for candidates and employees. We recognise candidates who accept offers and complete formalities on time with trophies and cash awards. In contrast, we recognise them on time and before joining with a joining bonus and certificate from the CEO's desk. The reward and recognition program is closely tied to employees' performance and behaviours. We recognise top performers periodically, i.e., monthly, quarterly, and annually. Whereas there are various instant recognitions for living the values of the organisation, helping others, and going the extra mile to serve the company and customer.' *Participant 6 emphasizes that* 'intrinsic rewards such as recognition, praise, career advancement, and challenging opportunities help us to motivate our high potential employees. We show growth path to the external world, i.e., our candidate, using the success stories of our employees. In contrast, we use extrinsic rewards for our employees and new joiners to make them better performers. We provide monetary rewards, foreign tours with family, team outlining to exotic locations, etc., which motivate employees. We have a few awards, such as Naya Josh for exceptionally performing new joiners.' According to Participant 8, timely, transparent and instant recognition helps to enhance the brand image, 'programs in our company, such as do more win more, various performance contest such as Lakshya for the sales team is a highly profound program, where not only employees talk about it but also this is a highlight in the job market. With the Do More Win More program, employees can earn 200% of their salary CTC, a selling point for us in the market. In contrast, the Lakshya program provides various opportunities to choose from, such as foreign trips, learning in foreign universities, etc. These two programs are highly transparent, and people know what they must do to achieve it. Also, it is instant, and each high performer gets visibility from the senior leaders. Our employees discuss the program on various review platforms and social media (Linkedin, Facebook, Instagram, etc.). As an organisation for us, the benefits are threefold: 1. We can create high performers, 2. Retain top talents, and 3. Attract the right talent.'

According to Pattnaik and Misra (2016), a positive work environment helps create strong EBR, which in turn helps enhance employee loyalty. Participant 7 explained, 'Our organisation believes in creating a healthy working environment. We do it through cross-collaboration projects, team outings, CSR activity, and various outbound training programs. We consistently get higher scores in all employee surveys, resulting in higher NPS, advocacy, and productivity.'

Implications for Practice

In recent years, EBR has gained popularity. Multiple studies have examined the subject from various perspectives, and there is growing consensus on its significance in fostering employee loyalty (Barros-Arrieta & García-Cali, 2021; Punjaisri & Wilson, 2017). Nevertheless, data or studies regarding the influence of EBR are scarce.

This work offers a unique and valuable addition to the discipline of EBR for SMEs in India, which is crucial for India's path towards achieving a US$5 trillion economy (Kapoor & Gupta, 2022; Siddiqui & Ilyas, 2020). The findings indicate that specific influential factors of EBR can enable SMEs to improve EBR efforts and foster employee loyalty. Employees with a positive brand image command higher loyalty and productivity (Bell et al., 2017; Dechawatanapaisal, 2019).

Limitation and Future Scope of Work

This research is not meant to be generalized to other institutions or nations. Due to its fundamental attributes, the study's geographical range and time limits are restricted, including a maximum interview length of 20–30 minutes. The study's results are based on the premise that the volunteer participants provided profound and authentic views on the phenomenon.

This study examined the perspectives of experienced SME leaders on the drivers of EBR. The authors recommend the following for further investigation on EBR: (a) the implementation of EBR in SMEs while considering different levels of employees, (b) analyzing the variations in EBR factors between SMEs and other sectors and (c) conducting a mixed-method study to compare EBR factors.

Conclusion

The study suggests EBR is essential for expanding small and medium-sized firms (SMEs). Various elements influencing EBR are employee advocacy, loyalty and organizational growth. Every organization wants loyal and productive employees who can help in organizational growth. Regarding the semi-structured interviews, it has been seen that there is a strong association between EBR, advocacy, loyalty and organizational performance. Also, Participant 2 stated that *strong EBR helps foster employee loyalty, which further helped us create a wow customer experience.* Hence, all SMEs should focus on strengthening EBR efforts.

Acknowledgement

We are genuinely grateful to the editors and anonymous reviewers for their valuable suggestions and comments, helping turn this chapter into one that would publish.

References

Barros-Arrieta, D., & García-Cali, E. (2021). Internal branding: Conceptualisation from a literature review and opportunities for future research. *Journal of Brand Management*, *28*(2), 133–151.

Bell, S. J., Auh, S., & Eisingerich, A. B. (2017). Unravelling the customer education paradox: When and how should firms educate their customers? *Journal of Service Research*, *20*(3), 306–321.

Berthon, P., Ewing, M., & Napoli, G. (2006). Aligning employee recruitment and retention strategies with corporate brands. *Journal of Business Research*, *59*(2), 181–191.

Creswell, J. W. (2002). *Educational research: Planning, conducting, and evaluating quantitative and qualitative research*. Sage.

Creswell, J. W. (2007). *Qualitative inquiry & research design: Choosing among five approaches* (2nd ed.). Sage.

Dabirian, A., Zarei, M. M., & Farashahi, Z. (2019). The effect of employee branding on employer branding and organisational performance: A meta-analysis. *Journal of Business Research*, *139*, 155–165.

Dechawatanapaisal, D. (2019). Internal branding and employees' brand outcomes: Do generational differences and organisational tenure matter? *Industrial and Commercial Training*, *51*(4), 209–227. https://doi.org/10.1108/ICT-10-2018-0089

Dewasiri, N. J., Weerakoon, B., & Azeez, A. A. (2018). Mixed methods in finance research. *International Journal of Qualitative Methods*, *17*(1), 1–13. https://doi.org/10.1177/1609406918801730Y. K.

Dzhulai, M. (2023). Adaptation of the employer brand of a Ukrainian company in the EU market during the full-scale Russian-Ukrainian war. *Scientific Bulletin of Mukachevo State University. Series "Economics"*, *10*(1), 9–18.

Grönroos, C. (1996). Relationship marketing: Strategic and tactical implications. *Management Decision*, *34*(3), 5–14.

Hatch, M. J., & Brief, A. P. (2004). The importance of making sense of acquisition: A brand sensemaking perspective. *The Academy of Management Review*, *29*(3), 363–380.

Helm, S., Renk, U., & Mishra, A. (2016). Exploring the impact of employees' self-concept, brand identification, and brand pride on brand citizenship behaviours. *European Journal of Marketing*, *50*(1/2), 58–77.

Kapoor, S., & Gupta, S. (2022). Role of MSMEs in the growth of the Indian economy. *International Journal of Research and Analytical Reviews*, *9*(1), 212–221.

Karanges, E., Johnston, K., Lings, I., & Beatson, A. (2018). Brand signalling: An antecedent of employee brand understanding. *Journal of Brand Management*, *25*(3), 235–249.

Keller, K. L. (1993). Conceptualizing, measuring, and managing customer-based brand equity. *Journal of Marketing*, *57*(1), 1–22.

Kucherov, D., & Zavyalova, E. (2016). Employer branding practices in Russian companies. *Journal of Business and Industrial Marketing*, *31*(4), 485–495.

Kumar, A. S., & Kaur, S. (2019). Talent management practices in small and medium enterprises (SMEs): A case study of selected Indian SMEs. *International Journal of Business and Management Research*, *11*(1), 175–184.

Lievens, A., & Van den Broeck, H. (2013). Employer branding: Theoretical and practical implications. *European Journal of Marketing*, *47*(11/12), 1751–1770.

Liewendahl, H. E., & Heinonen, K. (2020). Frontline employees' motivation to align with value propositions. *Journal of Business & Industrial Marketing*, *35*(3), 420–436.

Miles, S. T., & Mangold, G. W. (2004). A conceptualisation of the employee branding process. *Journal of Services Marketing*, *18*(6), 675–686.

Odoom, R. (2016). Brand-building efforts in high and low-performing small and medium-sized enterprises (SMEs). *Development*, *23*, 1229–1246.

Pattnaik, S. K., & Misra, R. K. (2016). Employer value proposition: A conceptual framework and scale development for Indian information technology professionals. *International Journal of Human Capital and Information Technology Professionals (IJHCITP)*, *7*(4), 15–32.

Prince, J. B. (2003). Career opportunity and organisational attachment in a blue-collar unionised environment. *Journal of Vocational Behavior*, *63*(1), 136–150.

Punjaisri, K., & Wilson, A. (2017). The role of internal branding in the delivery of employee brand promise. *Journal of Brand Management*, *24*(1), 41–58.

Rowley, C. (2008). Employer branding: More than just a slogan? *International Journal of Human Resource Management*, *19*(7), 1021–1030.

Saini, G. K., Lievens, F., & Srivastava, M. (2022). Employer and internal branding research: A bibliometric analysis of 25 years. *Journal of Product & Brand Management*, *31*(8), 1196–1221.

Sakka, G., & Ahammad, M. F. (2020). Unpacking the relationship between employee brand ambassadorship and employee social media usage through employee well-being in the workplace: A theoretical contribution. *Journal of Business Research*, *119*, 354–363.

Sengupta, A., Bamel, U., & Singh, P. (2015). Value proposition framework: Implications for employer branding. *Decision*, *42*(3), 307–323.

Siddiqui, T., & Ilyas, M. Z. (2020). The role of micro, small, and medium enterprises (MSMEs) in promoting economic growth and employment creation in Pakistan. *Journal of Entrepreneurship and Innovation*, *1*(2), 133–148.

Smola, L., Kondur, O., Yaroslav, M., Orhiiets, O., Bazyliak, N., & Lipentsev, A. (2023). Image as an educational component of personnel policy in public management bodies: Humanitarian aspect. *Journal of Interdisciplinary Research*, *13*(2), 122–129.

Sonne, H., Guerreiro, J., & Wohlschlegel, B. (2019). Increasing awareness and reputation of Merck s.a. Portugal through employee advocacy. *Developments in Marketing Science: Proceedings of the Academy of Marketing Science*, 619–633.

Suomi, K., Saraniemi, S., Vähätalo, M., Kallio, T. J., & Tevameri, T. (2019). Employee engagement and internal branding: Two sides of the same coin? *Corporate Reputation Review*, *24*, 48–63.

Theurer, C. P., Tumasjan, A., Welpe, I. M., & Lievens, F. (2018). Employer branding: A brand equity-based literature review and research agenda. *International Journal of Management Reviews*, *20*(1), 155–179.

World Bank. (2019). *Small and medium enterprises in India: Challenges and opportunities*. World Bank Group.

World Bank. (2021). *India's SMEs at a crossroads: Policies for recovery and resilience*. World Bank Group.

Chapter 13

How Can Social Media Support Improve the Sustainability Practices of Sri Lankan Small and Medium Enterprises (SMEs)?

Vidana Gamage Pavani Lakshika
and Batuwan Thudawa Kankanamge Chathuranga

University of Sri Jayewardenepura, Sri Lanka

Abstract

This chapter investigates how social media can support improving sustainability practices in Sri Lankan small and medium enterprises (SMEs). This chapter employs the systematic literature review (SLR) methodology. The researcher used keywords to explore the articles from recognized databases for the literature review. Accordingly, 40 articles from different databases were used for the analysis. This chapter explores seven critical themes for social media support of sustainability practices in Sri Lankan SMEs: sustainable supply chain management, sustainability communication, building sustainable relationships through social media-driven customer relationship management (CRM), crowdsourcing ideas and solutions, marketing and brand building and enhancing operations performance. This SLR significantly contributes to understanding how social media can enhance sustainable practices in SMEs. It effectively bridges the knowledge gap at the intersection of social media and sustainability within SMEs. The key findings from this chapter offer significant insights for SMEs, scholars, practitioners and policymakers, aiding better decisions on using social media to foster a sustainable future. To the best of the authors' knowledge, this research represents a substantial contribution to the existing literature on leveraging social media to enhance sustainability practices within Sri Lankan SMEs.

Keywords: Social media; SME; Sri Lanka; sustainability; social media support

Shaping Entrepreneurial Marketing, Volume 1, 195–207

Published under exclusive licence by Emerald Publishing Limited
doi:10.1108/978-1-83708-852-220251014

Introduction

In the modern era of industrial and technological advancement, small and medium enterprises (SMEs) have been instrumental in achieving the economic sustainable development goals (SDGs). These goals include 'promoting inclusive and sustainable economic growth, employment and decent work for all' (SDG 8) and 'promoting sustainable industrialization and fostering innovation' (SDG 9). Therefore, harnessing emerging technologies to transform SMEs – which represent 90% of global firms, employ 50% of the global workforce and contribute substantially to economic development in emerging markets – plays a pivotal role in catalyzing the achievement of the SDGs (World Bank, 2018).

SMEs are pivotal for any economy due to the value they add to their country (Tian et al., 2021). These SMEs are essential, particularly for developing countries (Arshad et al., 2020). Sri Lanka, a developing country, has many SMEs and accounts for over one million. According to the SME policy framework for development in Sri Lanka, SMEs are categorized as businesses employing fewer than 300 individuals and generating annual revenues not surpassing LKR750 million.

SMEs are essential for economic growth, generating employment opportunities, exports and innovation activities, particularly in emerging nations (Arshad et al., 2020; Gherghina et al., 2020). Therefore, SMEs' performance is essential for a developing country's economy (Tian et al., 2021). Technology provides many benefits for business organizations, and the firms that effectively utilize the multiple technical advancements of today can reap multiple advantages. Despite its significance, SMEs frequently encounter obstacles in integrating and leveraging digital technologies, especially social media, limiting their ability to expand and compete (Horváth & Szabó, 2019). Platforms like Facebook, Instagram, WhatsApp and Twitter have the potential to narrow the digital divide by equipping SMEs with the tools to enhance customer engagement and streamline business operations (Abed et al., 2015; Kang & Park, 2018). Social media is pivotal for fostering innovation and advancing sustainable, inclusive industrialization among SMEs (Jiménez et al., 2021).

Digital technologies are getting easier to access and are more reasonably priced for SMEs. Digitalization offers SMEs numerous advantages, including heightened production and efficiency, improved product and service quality, data-driven decision-making capabilities, enhanced flexibility, accelerated time to market and bolstered sustainability efforts (Chen et al., 2022; Linder, 2019). Thus, it is clear that SMEs can perform far better when they use social media (Fang et al., 2021); it is an essential channel of growth for SMEs (Solomon et al., 2023).

While social media has influenced SMEs, only a few have adopted and successfully leveraged this pivotal tool (Abed, 2020; Ahmad et al., 2019). Kaplan and Haenlein (2010) contend that SMEs can leverage social media platforms to engage with stakeholders to remain competitive and sustainable (Ali Abbasi et al., 2022). Earlier research considered social media a crucial element for SMEs operating in highly competitive global markets, leading to substantial benefits (Chatterjee & Kar, 2020). In this regard, it has been noted that a relatively small proportion of SMEs have embraced and leveraged social media to improve business performance, foster stronger customer relationships, obtain a competitive edge and increase sales – all of which are critical to the long-term viability of SMEs (Amoah et al., 2021; Brink, 2017; Jibril et al., 2019; Jin & Hurd, 2018).

Therefore, adopting social media practices can improve SMEs' sustainability performance. However, there is a gap in understanding how these practices support Sri Lankan SMEs. This chapter, therefore, focuses on undertaking a systematic literature review (SLR) to understand how social media can improve sustainability practices in Sri Lankan SMEs.

Methodology

SLR endeavours to comprehensively identify and synthesize pertinent research through structured, transparent and reproducible methods throughout each process stage (Mohamed Shaffril et al., 2021). This approach allows for a holistic understanding of the phenomenon under study (Dewasiri et al., 2022, 2023; Jayawardena & Dewasiri, 2023). Accordingly, an SLR was employed as the methodology of this study to scrutinize the literature produced in the last 10 years on the utilization of social media by SMEs and ways to improve sustainable practices.

The study unfolds across three distinct phases: Literature Identification (Phase 1), Data Extraction (Phase 2) and Data Analysis, Synthesis and Interpretation (Phase 3). During the literature identification phase, a systematic search was conducted to locate full-text articles written exclusively in English. Articles were selected based on specified keywords from Table 13.1 in either title, abstract or keywords.

Table 13.1. Keywords.

Keywords
'Social Media' OR 'Social Networking Sites' OR 'Online Engagement Platforms' OR 'Social Networking' OR 'Audience Participation' OR 'Social Media Engagement'
AND
'Sustainable Practices' OR 'Environmental Sustainability' OR 'Corporate Sustainability' OR 'Green Business Practices' OR 'Sustainable Development Goals' OR 'SDGs' OR 'Sustainability Communication' OR 'Performance' OR 'Green Marketing' OR 'Sustainability Reporting' OR 'Eco-Friendly Branding' OR 'Long-Term Growth' OR 'Sustain*'
AND
'Small And Medium-Sized Enterprises' OR 'SME' OR 'Small Businesses' OR 'Medium-Sized Businesses' OR 'Entrepreneurial Ventures' OR 'Startups' OR 'Family-Owned Businesses'

Source: Authors' own.

During Phase 2, the researchers conducted a manual review of the titles and abstracts of the selected articles as part of the screening process. This process excluded articles deemed irrelevant to the research topic and duplicate publications, resulting in the selection of 40 articles from four databases: Elsevier Science Direct (n = 11), Taylor and Francis (n = 10), Springer (n = 10) and Emerald Insight (n = 9) for the final analysis.

In the final phase, a qualitative analysis explored the selected 40 articles to uncover critical themes. The focus was on understanding how social media improves sustainability practices among SMEs. Each article underwent a thorough examination to determine its discussion on the role of social media in sustainability efforts. The resulting seven main themes reveal how social media supports SMEs in improving their sustainability practices.

Findings

This SLR comprehensively analyzes how social media can enhance sustainable practices in SMEs in Sri Lanka. By thoroughly examining a wide range of scholarly literature, the study identified and revealed several mechanisms through which social media engagement fosters sustainability in SMEs. The analysis revealed seven core themes: sustainable supply chain management, sustainability communication, waste reduction, building sustainable relationships through social media–driven customer relationship management (CRM), crowdsourcing ideas and solutions, marketing and brand building, and enhancing operational performance. These themes collectively highlight the role of social media as a strategic instrument for promoting sustainability and providing valuable insights for practitioners, policymakers and scholars interested in developing sustainable practices in Sri Lanka's SMEs.

Sustainable Supply Chain Management

Examining dynamic changes within businesses and sectors is a relatively recent area represented by sustainable supply chain capabilities (Beske et al., 2014). When businesses compete in a market, supply chain skills are a vital tactic utilized to control expenses and enhance financial performance (Hong et al., 2018). Consequently, social media has been used for various supply chain tasks, such as supplier selection and in-vehicle routing (Albuquerque et al., 2016; Lin et al., 2018). Additionally, social media can be further utilized in supply chain management for different purposes, including social media mining to forecast demand (Cui et al., 2018; Sodero & Rabinovich, 2017; Yuan et al., 2018) and inventory management (Choi, 2018; Hofmann, 2017; Wood et al., 2017). In this sense, businesses have significantly benefited from using social media for supply chain management initiatives. However, it is unclear if Sri Lankan SMEs have been using social media to gain from the advantages offered regarding sustainable performance. Accordingly, SMEs in Sri Lanka could use social media to attain sustainable performance.

Sustainability Communication

Social media can improve communication, increasing SMEs' sustainable performance (Qalati et al., 2022). SMEs must build relationships with agencies, dealers, clients and other societal groups. Social media techniques can facilitate these communications. Due to their quick transmission speed, social media tools provide real-time communication with one or more people (Wang et al., 2016). Through marketing, innovation and teamwork, SMEs can improve business performance and communication in a business-to-business setting. Additionally, social media platforms can enhance communication security. SMEs are under pressure to innovate and boost their operational efficiency (Wang et al., 2016). More specifically, SMEs can learn how to leverage social media for sustainable performance by looking at bigger businesses like Walmart, which has a page dedicated to green products and services. Mars communicates its sustainable cocoa activities through cartoon characters. Social media platforms enable a two-way connection between a business and its clients, unlike traditional media channels like print media and adverts that do not permit this engagement (Fissi et al., 2022). Sharing pictures and videos on social media simplifies receiving feedback on goods and services. As a result, SMEs can use social media as an instrument for long-term communication, which can enhance output.

Waste Reduction

It is widely acknowledged that educating people about environmental issues is the cornerstone of promoting ecologically beneficial behaviour (Nguyen et al., 2016). Individuals' widespread use of social media offers efficient avenues for disseminating information in the present era (Andersson & Öhman, 2017; Fong et al., 2020). Hence, social media is widely used to share knowledge with individuals (Ho & So, 2017). In light of this, social media can serve as a tool to inform clients about waste reduction practices. Additionally, social media can help businesses reduce waste by saving money on resources essential to running their operations. SMEs can use these possibilities to leverage social media for waste reduction, which could ultimately result in sustainable performance of the business.

Building Sustainable Relationships: Social Media–Driven CRM

The findings indicate that social media can effectively enhance the sustainability practices of SMEs through improved customer relationship management (CRM; Amoah et al., 2023; Bruce et al., 2023; Hassan et al., 2019; Pellegrino & Abe, 2023). Social media allows SMEs to foster positive relationships with sustainability-conscious consumers (Bruce et al., 2023). By providing content promoting sustainable methods and products, SMEs can attract and build a community of individuals who share similar values, strengthening relationships and enhancing brand image (Amoah et al., 2023). Moreover, social media facilitates personalized customer interactions (Maecker et al., 2016; Odoom et al., 2017), addressing significant challenges faced by SMEs regarding personalized customer engagement

(Pellegrino & Abe, 2023) and fostering sustainable relationships. Additionally, social media allows SMEs to offer real-time assistance and resolve customer issues and concerns (Guha et al., 2018), resulting in effective customer service crucial for building strong and sustainable client connections (Salam et al., 2019). Therefore, SMEs in Sri Lanka can utilize social media for effective customer relationship management, leading to sustainability practices of firms.

Crowdsourcing Ideas and Solutions

Crowdsourcing is an open innovation (OI) that gives organizations access to external knowledge and experience via online platforms (Cricelli et al., 2022; Nasution et al., 2023). Crowdsourcing, as described by Howe (2006), is outsourcing a job formerly handled by an authorized agent (typically an employee) to an indeterminate, generally significant number of individuals via an open call.

SMEs encounter more significant challenges than larger companies due to limited resources. (Guha et al., 2018), making it difficult for SMEs to discover and implement alternative solutions. Conversely, crowdsourcing allows SMEs to use existing networks and identify untapped resources, overcoming their limits (Nasution et al., 2023; Qin et al., 2016). Firms can benefit substantially from utilizing crowdsourcing tools and their specialized resources. These advantages include generating innovative, rapid and cost-effective solutions (Wilson et al., 2018). Crowdsourcing allows firms to scale their operations dynamically through internal processes (Qin et al., 2016), maintaining flexibility to adjust workforce size as needed (Maiolini, 2011). Additionally, it fosters direct customer interaction and enhances geographical coverage, which is crucial in constantly evolving markets (Maiolini, 2011). Crowdsourcing can help SMEs broaden their manufacturing and design capabilities beyond a limited workforce. This can lead to a significant transformation in the new product development (NPD) process (Nasution et al., 2023) and the integration of advanced technologies (Maiolini, 2011). As a result, SMEs can achieve notable improvements in design performance and quality (Maiolini, 2011; Nasution et al., 2023; Qin et al., 2016). Ultimately, these benefits contribute to the sustainability of the SMEs. By leveraging crowdsourcing, SMEs in Sri Lanka can access diverse ideas and expertise, supporting continuous innovation and adaptation. This approach helps reduce costs and time-to-market and promotes sustainable practices by optimizing resource use and minimizing waste (Jayarathne et al., 2021). Ultimately, these benefits contribute to the sustainability of SMEs in Sri Lanka.

Marketing and Brand Building

Empirical studies have evidenced that adopting social media positively impacts SMEs' performance, particularly in sales and marketing (Ainin et al., 2015; Amoah et al., 2023). SMEs can benefit from this in several ways. Firstly, social media platforms assist SMEs in accessing a more extensive audience beyond their geographical boundaries (Bruce et al., 2023). By creating and sharing engaging content, SMEs can expand their market base, which is crucial for sustaining growth. Secondly, adopting social media allows SMEs to enhance the efficiency and cost-effectiveness of promoting their products and services (He et al., 2017) in local markets and globally (Jones et al., 2015). Thirdly, consistent connection with customers via social media helps improve brand awareness (Dwivedi et al., 2023; Marolt et al., 2022). SMEs leverage social media to craft their brand narrative, showcase core values and personally engage with their audience. Such interactions contribute to more robust brand recognition (Guha et al., 2018) and foster customer loyalty (Guha et al., 2018), which are crucial for long-term business success. Furthermore, social media sites increasingly incorporate e-commerce attributes, allowing SMEs to increase sales by selling directly to consumers (Amoah et al., 2023; Marolt et al., 2022; Noviaristanti et al., 2023). Social media analytics offer insightful consumer behaviour, preferences and demographic information. SMEs can use this information to adjust their product offerings and marketing plans to meet consumer preferences better (Amoah & Jibril, 2021). Targeted advertising on social media can significantly improve conversion rates and sales performance by reaching the right audience with the right message, thereby enhancing the sustainability of SMEs. Therefore, social media, proficiently harnessed, can be a potent tool for Sri Lankan SMEs to enhance their market visibility and facilitate sustainable business growth.

Enhancing Operations Performance

Social media is a potential enhancer of manufacturing or operational performance within SMEs through various avenues. Bruce et al. (2023) suggest that it can augment productivity and efficiency within organizations by providing efficient communication channels (Rahman et al., 2020) through real-time messaging, group chats and collaborative tools. This streamlined communication fosters teamwork and enhances overall operational efficiency. Moreover, by enhancing information-processing capacity, social media enables SMEs to manage environmental uncertainties and improve their decision-making procedures effectively (Bruce et al., 2023). This capability is essential for SMEs to react to evolving market conditions and sustain their competitive advantage. Social media also improves the quality of SME products and services (Pellegrino & Abe, 2023). By gathering customer feedback and engaging in direct interactions, SMEs can better understand customer needs and refine their offerings, leading to higher satisfaction and loyalty of customers (Rahman et al., 2020). Amoah et al. (2023) also emphasize the role of social media in enhancing cost efficiency. By reducing marketing and communication costs, SMEs can allocate resources more effectively and improve their financial performance and stability (Rahman et al., 2020). Furthermore, Pellegrino and Abe (2023) emphasize the impact of social media on transaction expansion, resulting in faster business processes and improved SME operations.

Accordingly, by adopting social media, Sri Lankan SMEs can enhance their overall performance by improving communication and collaboration, enabling better decision-making, enhancing product and service quality, increasing cost efficiency and accelerating transaction processes. These improvements collectively contribute to the sustainability and competitiveness of SMEs.

Conclusion

In conclusion, this SLR significantly contributes to understanding how social media can enhance sustainable practices in SMEs. It effectively bridges the knowledge gap at the intersection of social media and sustainability within SMEs. The primary findings from the study offer substantial insights for SMEs, policymakers, scholars and practitioners, facilitating informed decision-making regarding the adoption of social media to promote sustainable outcomes.

This chapter focused on the Sri Lankan context, organizing its findings around seven core themes: sustainable supply chain management, sustainability communication, waste reduction, building sustainable relationships through social media-driven CRM, crowdsourcing ideas and solutions, marketing and brand building, and enhancing operational performance. These themes underscore the potential strategies that Sri Lankan SMEs can employ to leverage social media to enhance sustainability practices within their operations. However, this review is not without limitations. The articles analyzed were predominantly from publications available in only four databases, which may not encompass all high-quality publications relevant to this topic. Notwithstanding these drawbacks, the study provides a solid direction for future research on social media, sustainable practices and SMEs.

Acknowledgements

We would like to express our sincere gratitude to the editors and the anonymous reviewers for their invaluable contributions in developing this chapter.

References

Abed, S. S. (2020). Social commerce adoption using TOE framework: An empirical investigation of Saudi Arabian SMEs. *International Journal of Information Management*, *53*, 102118. https://doi.org/10.1016/j.ijinfomgt.2020.102118

Abed, S. S., Dwivedi, Y. K., & Williams, M. D. (2015). Social media as a bridge to e-commerce adoption in SMEs: A systematic literature review. *The Marketing Review*, *15*(1), 39–57. https://doi.org/10.1362/146934715x14267608178686

Ahmad, S. Z., Bakar, A. R. A., & Ahmad, N. (2019). Social media adoption and its impact on firm performance: The case of the UAE. *International Journal of Entrepreneurial Behaviour and Research*, *25*, 84–111. https://doi.org/10.1108/IJEBR-08-2017-0299

Ainin, S., Parveen, F., Moghavvemi, S., Jaafar, N. I., & Shuib, N. L. M. (2015). Factors influencing the use of social media by SMEs and its performance outcomes. *Industrial Management and Data Systems*, *115*(3), 570–588. https://doi.org/10.1108/IMDS-07-2014-0205

Albuquerque, F. C., Casanova, M. A., Lopes, H., Redlich, L. R., De Macedo, J. A. F., Lemos, M., De Carvalho, M. T. M., & Renso, C. (2016). A methodology for traffic-related Twitter messages interpretation. *Computers in Industry*, *78*, 57–69.

Ali Abbasi, G., Rahim, N. F. A., Wu, H., Iranmanesh, M., & Keong, B. N. C. (2022). Determinants of SME's social media marketing adoption: Competitive industry as a moderator. *SAGE Open*, *12*(1). https://doi.org/10.1177/21582440211067220

Amoah, J., Belás, J., Khan, K. A., & Metzker, Z. (2021). Antecedents of sustainable SMEs in the social media space: A partial least square-structural equation modelling (PLS-SEM) approach. *Management and Marketing*, *16*(1), 26–46. https://doi.org/10.2478/mmcks-2021-0003

Amoah, J., Bruce, E., Shurong, Z., Bankuoru Egala, S., & Kwarteng, K. (2023). Social media adoption in SMEs sustainability: Evidence from an emerging economy. *Cogent Business and Management*, *10*(1). https://doi.org/10.1080/23311975.2023.2183573

Amoah, J., & Jibril, A. B. (2021). Social media as a promotional tool towards SME's development: Evidence from the financial industry in a developing economy. *Cogent Business and Management*, *8*(1). https://doi.org/10.1080/23311975.2021.1923357

Andersson, E., & Öhman, J. (2017). Young people's conversations about environmental and sustainability issues in social media. *Environmental Education Research*, *23*(4), 465–485. https://doi.org/10.1080/13504622.2016.1149551

Arshad, M. Z., Tang, M., Javed, M., Ali, M., Arshad, M. H., & Maneerat, C. (2020). The importance of learning orientation and entrepreneurial orientation on SMEs performance sustainable development view project strategic management view project. *International Journal of Disaster Recovery and Business Continuity*, *11*(1), 1220–1228.

Beske, P., Land, A., & Seuring, S. (2014). Sustainable supply chain management practices and dynamic capabilities in the food industry: A critical literature analysis. *International Journal of Production Economics*, *152*, 131–143. https://doi.org/10.1016/j.ijpe.2013.12.026

Brink, T. (2017). B2B SME management of antecedents to the application of social media. *Industrial Marketing Management*, *64*, 57–65.

Bruce, E., Keelson, S., Amoah, J., & Bankuoru Egala, S. (2023). Social media integration: An opportunity for SMEs sustainability. *Cogent Business and Management*, *10*(1), 1–20. https://doi.org/10.1080/23311975.2023.2173859

Chatterjee, S., & Kar, A. K. (2020). Why do small and medium enterprises use social media marketing and what is the impact: Empirical insights from India. *International Journal of Information Management*, *53*, 102103. https://doi.org/10.1016/j.ijinfomgt.2020.102103

Chen, Y., Li, J., & Zhang, J. (2022). Digitalisation, data-driven dynamic capabilities, and responsible innovation: An empirical study of SMEs in China. *Asia Pacific Journal of Management*, 1–41.

Choi, T. M. (2018). Incorporating social media observations and bounded rationality into fashion quick response supply chains in the big data era. *Transportation Research Part E: Logistics and Transportation Review*, *114*, 386–397. https://doi.org/10.1016/j.tre.2016.11.006

Cricelli, L., Grimaldi, M., & Vermicelli, S. (2022). Crowdsourcing and open innovation: A systematic literature review, an integrated framework, and a research agenda. *Review of Managerial Science*, *16*, 1269–1310. https://doi.org/10.1007/s11846-021-00482-9

Cui, R., Gallino, S., Moreno, A., & Zhang, D. J. (2018). The operational value of social media information. *Production and Operations Management*, *27*(10), 1749–1769. https://doi.org/10.1111/ijlh.12426

Dewasiri, N. J., Baker, H. K., Banda, Y. K. W., & Rathnasiri, M. S. H. (2022). The dividend decision model: A possible solution for the dividend puzzle. In S. Rana, Sakshi, & J. Singh (Eds.), *Exploring the latest trends in management literature, Review of Management Literature* (Vol. 1, pp. 249–267). Emerald Publishing Limited. https://doi.org/10.1108/S2754-586520220000001013

Dewasiri, N. J., Karunarathne, K. S. S. N., Menon, S., Jayarathne, P. G. S. A., & Rathnasiri, M. S. H. (2023). Fusion of artificial intelligence and blockchain in the banking industry: Current application, adoption, and future challenges. In A. Saini & V. Garg (Eds.), *Transformation for sustainable business and management practices: Exploring the spectrum of Industry 5.0* (pp. 293–307). Emerald Publishing Limited. https://doi.org/10.1108/978-1-80262-277-520231021

Dwivedi, Y. K., Ismagilova, E., Rana, N. P., & Raman, R. (2023). Social media adoption, usage and impact in business-to-business (B2B) context: A state-of-the-art literature review. *Information Systems Frontiers*, *25*(3), 971–993. https://doi.org/10.1007/s10796-021-10106-y

Fang, G. G., Qalati, S. A., Ostic, D., Shah, S. M. M., & Mirani, M. A. (2021). Effects of entrepreneurial orientation, social media, and innovation capabilities on SME performance in emerging countries: A mediated–moderated model. *Technology Analysis and Strategic Management*, *34*(11), 1326–1338. https://doi.org/10.1080/09537325.2021.1957816

Fissi, S., Gori, E., Marchi, V., & Romolini, A. (2022). Social media, brand communication, and customer engagement in Michelin-starred restaurants during a crisis. *British Food Journal*, *125*(13), 16–33. https://doi.org/10.1108/BFJ-04-2022-0363

Fong, K. C. H., Au, C. H., Lam, E. T. H., & Chiu, D. K. W. (2020). Social network services for academic libraries: A study based on social capital and social proof. *Journal of Academic Librarianship*, *46*(1), 102091. https://doi.org/10.1016/j.acalib.2019.102091

Gherghina, S. C., Botezatu, M. A., Hosszu, A., & Simionescu, L. N. (2020). Small and medium-sized enterprises (SMEs): The engine of economic growth through investments and innovation. *Sustainability (Switzerland)*, *12*(1), 347. https://doi.org/10.3390/SU12010347

Guha, S., Harrigan, P., & Soutar, G. (2018). Linking social media to customer relationship management (CRM): A qualitative study on SMEs. *Journal of Small Business and Entrepreneurship*, *30*(3), 193–214. https://doi.org/10.1080/08276331.2017.1399628

Hassan, S. H., Mohamed Haniba, N. M., & Ahmad, N. H. (2019). Social customer relationship management (s-CRM) among small- and medium-sized enterprises (SMEs) in Malaysia. *International Journal of Ethics and Systems*, *35*(2), 284–302. https://doi.org/10.1108/IJOES-11-2017-0192

He, W., Wang, F. K., Chen, Y., & Zha, S. (2017). An exploratory investigation of social media adoption by small businesses. *Information Technology and Management*, *18*(2), 149–160. https://doi.org/10.1007/s10799-015-0243-3

Ho, K. K. W., & So, S. (2017). Towards a smart city through household recycling and waste management: A study on the factors affecting environmental friendliness lifestyle of Guamanian. *International Journal of Sustainable Real Estate and Construction Economics*, *1*(1), 89–108. https://doi.org/10.1504/ijsrece.2017.084385

Hofmann, E. (2017). Big data and supply chain decisions: The impact of volume, variety and velocity properties on the bullwhip effect. *International Journal of Production Research*, *55*(17), 5108–5126.

Hong, J., Zhang, Y., & Ding, M. (2018). Sustainable supply chain management practices, supply chain dynamic capabilities, and enterprise performance. *Journal of Cleaner Production*, *172*, 3508–3519. https://doi.org/10.1016/j.jclepro.2017.06.093

Horváth, D., & Szabó, R. Z. (2019). Driving forces and barriers of Industry 4.0: Do multinational and small and medium-sized companies have equal opportunities? *Technological Forecasting and Social Change*, *146*, 119–132. https://doi.org/10.1016/j.techfore.2019.05.021

Howe, J. (2006, June 14). The conflicts of the faculty. *Wired Magazine*, 1–5. https://doi.org/10.2307/25599409

Jayarathne, P. G. S. A., Sachithra, V., & Dewasiri, N. J. (2021). Sustainable practices through competitive capabilities in the apparel industry: Sri Lankan experience. *FIIB Business Review*. https://doi.org/10.1177/23197145211060398

Jayawardena, N. S., & Dewasiri, N. J. (2023). Food acquisition and consumption issues of South Asian countries: A systematic literature review and future research agenda. *FIIB Business Review*. https://doi.org/10.1177/23197145231194113

Jibril, A. B., Kwarteng, M. A., Chovancova, M., & Pilik, M. (2019). The impact of social media on consumer-brand loyalty: A mediating role of online based-brand community. *Cogent Business and Management*, *6*(1), 1673640. https://doi.org/10.1080/23311975.2019.1673640

Jiménez, E., de la Cuesta-González, M., & Boronat-Navarro, M. (2021). How small and medium-sized enterprises can uptake the sustainable development goals through a cluster management organisation: A case study. *Sustainability (Switzerland)*, *13*(11), 5939. https://doi.org/10.3390/su13115939

Jin, H., & Hurd, F. (2018). Exploring the impact of digital platforms on SME internationalisation: New Zealand SMEs use the Alibaba platform for Chinese market entry. *Journal of Asia-Pacific Business*, *19*(2), 72–95. https://doi.org/10.1080/10599231.2018.1453743

Jones, N., Borgman, R., & Ulusoy, E. (2015). Impact of social media on small businesses. *Journal of Small Business and Enterprise Development*, *22*(4), 611–632. https://doi.org/10.1108/JSBED-09-2013-0133

Kang, M. Y., & Park, B. (2018). Sustainable corporate social media marketing based on message structural features: Firm size plays a significant role as a moderator. *Sustainability*, *10*(4), 1167. https://doi.org/10.3390/su10041167

Kaplan, A. M., & Haenlein, M. (2010). Users of the world, unite! The challenges and opportunities of social media. *Business Horizons*, *53*(1), 59–68. https://doi.org/10.1016/j.bushor.2009.09.003

Lin, K. P., Hung, K. C., Lin, Y. T., & Hsieh, Y. H. (2018). Green supplier's performance evaluation in belt and road using fuzzy weighted average with social media information. *Sustainability (Switzerland)*, *10*(1), 5. https://doi.org/10.3390/su10010005

Linder, C. (2019). Customer orientation and operations: The role of manufacturing capabilities in small- and medium-sized enterprises. *International Journal of Production Economics*, *216*, 105–117. https://doi.org/10.1016/j.ijpe.2019.04.030

Maecker, O., Barrot, C., & Becker, J. U. (2016). The effect of social media interactions on customer relationship management. *Business Research*, *9*(1), 133–155. https://doi.org/10.1007/s40685-016-0027-6

Maiolini, R. (2011, April). Information technology and innovation trends in organisations. *Information Technology and Innovation Trends in Organisations*. https://doi.org/10.1007/978-3-7908-2632-6

Marolt, M., Zimmermann, H. D., & Pucihar, A. (2022). Social media use and business performance in SMEs: The mediating roles of relational social commerce capability and competitive advantage. *Sustainability (Switzerland)*, *14*(22). https://doi.org/10.3390/su142215029

Mohamed Shaffril, H. A., Samsuddin, S. F., & Abu Samah, A. (2021). The ABC of systematic literature review: The basic methodological guidance for beginners. *Quality and Quantity*, *55*(4), 1319–1346. https://doi.org/10.1007/s11135-020-01059-6

Nasution, M. D. T. P., Sari, P. B., Aspan, H., Rossanty, Y., Irawan, & Hernawaty (2023). How do social media-facilitated crowdsourcing and knowledge integration affect new product development? SME agile initiatives. *Cogent Business and Management*, *10*(3). https://doi.org/10.1080/23311975.2023.2265093

Nguyen, T. N., Lobo, A., & Greenland, S. (2016). Pro-environmental purchase behaviour: The role of consumers' biospheric values. *Journal of Retailing and Consumer Services*, *33*, 98–108. https://doi.org/10.1016/j.jretconser.2016.08.010

Noviaristanti, S., Yunita, S. C., & Triono, S. P. H. (2023). Social media usage impacts SME's performance: Evidence from West Java, Indonesia. *Indonesian Journal of Business and Entrepreneurship*, *9*(2), 285–294. https://doi.org/10.17358/ijbe.9.2.285

Odoom, R., Anning-Dorson, T., & Acheampong, G. (2017). Antecedents of social media usage and performance benefits in small- and medium-sized enterprises (SMEs). *Journal of Enterprise Information Management*, *30*(3), 383–399.

Pellegrino, A., & Abe, M. (2023). Leveraging social media for SMEs: Findings from a bibliometric review. *Sustainability (Switzerland)*, *15*(8), 1–15. https://doi.org/10.3390/su15087007

Qalati, S. A., Ostic, D., Sulaiman, M. A. B. A., Gopang, A. A., & Khan, A. (2022). Social media and SMEs' performance in developing countries: Effects of technological-organisational-environmental factors on the adoption of social media. *SAGE Open*, *12*(2), 1–13. https://doi.org/10.1177/21582440221094594

Qin, S., Van Der Velde, D., Chatzakis, E., McStea, T., & Smith, N. (2016). Exploring barriers and opportunities in adopting crowdsourcing-based new product development in manufacturing SMEs. *Chinese Journal of Mechanical Engineering (English Edition)*, *29*(6), 1052–1066. https://doi.org/10.3901/CJME.2016.0808.089

Rahman, R. U., Shah, S. M. A., El-Gohary, H., Abbas, M., Khalil, S. H., Al Altheeb, S., & Sultan, F. (2020). Social media adoption and financial sustainability: Learned lessons from developing countries. *Sustainability (Switzerland)*, *12*(24), 1–26. https://doi.org/10.3390/su122410616

Salam, S., Shams, A., & Hoque, M. M. (2019). The role of social media and effect of relationship marketing on SME performance in Bangladesh: Multi-group Cfa. *Asian People Journal (APJ)*, *2*(1), 12–31.

Sodero, A. C., & Rabinovich, E. (2017). Demand and revenue management of deteriorating inventory on the internet: An empirical study of flash sales markets. *Journal of Business Logistics*, *38*(3), 170–183. https://doi.org/10.1111/jbl.12157

Solomon, O. H., Allen, T., & Wangombe, W. (2023). Analysing the factors that influence social media adoption among SMEs in developing countries. *Journal of International Entrepreneurship*. https://doi.org/10.1007/s10843-023-00330-9

Tian, H., Iqbal, S., Anwar, F., Akhtar, S., Khan, M. A. S., & Wang, W. (2021). Network embeddedness and innovation performance: A mediation moderation analysis using PLS-SEM. *Business Process Management Journal*, *27*(5), 1590–1609.

Wang, W. Y. C., Pauleen, D. J., & Zhang, T. (2016). How social media applications affect B2B communication and improve business performance in SMEs. *Industrial Marketing Management*, *54*, 4–14. https://doi.org/10.1016/j.indmarman.2015.12.004

Wilson, K. B., Bhakoo, V., & Samson, D. (2018). Crowdsourcing: A contemporary form of project management with linkages to open innovation and novel operations. *International Journal of Operations and Production Management*, *38*(6), 1467–1494. https://doi.org/10.1108/IJOPM-12-2016-0753

Wood, L. C., Reiners, T., & Srivastava, H. S. (2017). Think exogenous to excel: Alternative supply chain data to improve transparency and decisions. *International Journal of Logistics Research and Applications*, *20*(5), 426–443. https://doi.org/10.1080/13675567.2016.1267126

World Bank. (2018). *World development report 2019: The changing nature of work*. https://documents1.worldbank.org/curated/en/816281518818814423/pdf/Main-Report.pdf

Yuan, H., Xu, W., Li, Q., & Lau, R. (2018). Topic sentiment mining for sales performance prediction in e-commerce. *Annals of Operations Research*, *270*(1–2), 553–576. https://doi.org/10.1007/s10479-017-2421-7

Chapter 14

Factors Affecting the Green Purchase Behaviour for SMEs in Sri Lanka

Keragala Rallage Hemendra Lal Gunasekara

Sabaragamuwa University of Sri Lanka, Sri Lanka

Abstract

This study focuses on identifying the factors affecting the green purchasing (GP) behaviour of small and medium enterprises (SMEs) in Sri Lanka. It was conducted as a survey using a sample of 510 SMEs. An email questionnaire was employed for data collection. MS Excel was used to analyze the quantitative data. *Regulations* are a significant factor in adopting GP practices, followed by *environmental awareness* and *competition*. Further, the results indicate that perceptions of product quality, customer pressure, corporate social responsibility and cost considerations influence the adoption of GP practices among SMEs. Even though this study used previously identified factors (untested in the context of Sri Lankan SMEs) affecting the GP behaviour of SMEs, it discovered another factor, i.e. peer influence and social norms, and indeed, this finding opens a future research direction. The findings enable policymakers and practitioners to understand SMEs' awareness of environmental conservation and will help them make accurate future decisions to achieve sustainable development goals. This study contributes to knowledge by providing new literature on factors affecting GP behaviour with particular reference to an emerging economy.

Keywords: Green purchasing behaviour; small- and medium-scale enterprises; survey study; email questionnaire; Sri Lanka

Introduction

Due to the Industrial Revolution, humanity was able to shift into the 21st century. Technology and science have improved. Consequently, the production era was born. However, these advancements brought another problem to the world:

Shaping Entrepreneurial Marketing, Volume 1, 209–226

Published under exclusive licence by Emerald Publishing Limited
doi:10.1108/978-1-83708-852-220251015

industrial pollution. Since factories were small, smoke was the primary pollution source. Before the Industrial Revolution, factories were large, and operating hours were limited; hence, pollution levels did not rise considerably. The situation changed after the advent of the Industrial Revolution. Factories transformed into more giant, highly equipped industrial and manufacturing enterprises, and as a consequence, the problem of industrial pollution became more severe.

Companies concentrating on profit maximization adversely affect the environmental and social dimensions (Paulraj et al., 2017). Profit maximization is one of the essential tasks that managers must strategically handle. Those mentioned environmental and social problems occur when managers try to maximize profit by violating the rules and regulations regarding the environment, labour and human ethics. Several controversial cases reported in Sri Lanka can be taken as examples of the manufacturing sector's neglect of environmental and social obligations.

Researchers and experts in the field have introduced environmentally friendly business practices, mainly to prevent or minimize the harmful practices followed by both manufacturing and service sectors. Green purchasing (GP) behaviour is a significant green practice that enterprises and consumers in any country follow. Academics, researchers, practitioners and many others worldwide are involved in extensive discussions on the go-green concept. Hence, their significant effort encourages entrepreneurs and consumers to embrace green concepts in their business activities. The primary purpose of this study is to explore the factors affecting GP behaviour in small and medium enterprises (SMEs) in Sri Lanka. GP enables SMEs to obtain various benefits, which will be explained later in this chapter. The focus is on the importance of GP practices for SMEs in Sri Lanka. The nature of SMEs in Sri Lanka will be explained first.

SMEs in Sri Lanka

SMEs in Sri Lanka account for more than 75% of the total business entities provide 45% of the country's employment and contribute 52% to the gross domestic product (GDP). Therefore, the Sri Lankan government treats SMEs as the backbone of the economy. SMEs enable the resolution of the country's burning unemployment problem, especially among the youth and women, and provide equitable opportunities to participate in economic development. Since the world faces severe environmental problems, especially climate change, operating SMEs that contribute a considerable part of the country's GDP with environmentally friendly or greenery is vital. Hence, researching environmental cleanliness, particularly concerning SMEs in Sri Lanka, was deemed necessary for developing and greening this sector.

According to the definition given by the World Bank based on the number of employees, organizations with less than 49 employees are categorized as small-scale, medium-scale enterprises consisting of 50–99 employees, and enterprises with more than 99 employees are considered large-scale companies. The European Union categorizes companies or organizations with up to 49 employees as small-scale enterprises and companies with 50–249 as medium-scale enterprises. Organizations that have more than 249 employees are categorized as significant. The Department of Census and Statistics (DCS) in Sri Lanka defines establishments with 1–4 employees as micro-enterprises, 5–24 employees as small enterprises, 25–199 as medium-scale and enterprises with more than 199 as large-scale enterprises. Hence, the business organizations selected for this study were based on the number of employees, i.e. from 5 to 199, as defined by the DCS in Sri Lanka.

Brief Overview of GP Behaviour

GP is one of the dimensions of green supply chain management (GSCM) practices. Eco-design, green manufacturing, supplier selection, packaging, transportation, reverse logistics and investment recovery are the other primary dimensions of GSCM practices. Manufacturing SMEs play an essential role in the industrial sector in Sri Lanka. However, their involvement in achieving a green economy is not at an accepted level (Dissanayake et al., 2019). This is confirmed by Ashoka et al. (2023), who underscore the fact that Sri Lankan SMEs do not pay sufficient attention to environmental conservation within their operations due to several reasons, such as lack of customer awareness, lack of knowledge and experience, lack of commitment from top-level management to adopting GSCM, suppliers or vendors reluctant to adopt GSCM practices, cost of implementation of GSCM and lack of support and guidance from regulatory authorities. Usually, their purchasing habits depend on the cost (Dissanayake et al., 2019). There is a trend for foreign-based companies to concentrate more on GP adaptation than local companies (ElTayeb et al., 2009).

GP behaviour refers to consumers' choices and decisions to buy products and services that demonstrate environmental responsibility and sustainability. In recent years, there has been a notable global shift towards environmentally conscious consumption, with consumers increasingly considering the environmental impact of their purchases. This trend is prevalent among consumers and is gaining significance within the business sector, particularly among SMEs. Therefore, GP is defined as 'the idea of purchasing which is oriented to environmental awareness, purchasing raw materials that prioritise environmental sustainability, such as reducing sources of waste, promoting recycling and reuse, reducing resources, and using environmentally friendly materials' (Min & Galle, 2001; Sugandini et al., 2020; Zsidisin & Siferd, 2001).

Research suggests various factors influence GP behaviour, including environmental awareness, ethical considerations, and product quality and efficacy perceptions. The Theory of Planned Behaviour (Ajzen, 1991) and the Value-Belief-Norm theory (Stern et al., 1999) are commonly applied frameworks to understand the psychological factors shaping green consumer choices. Consumers are becoming more environmentally aware, which often translates into a preference for products and services that align with their values of sustainability and eco-friendliness. The rise of social and environmental concerns has led to an increased demand for products with a reduced ecological footprint and ethical production practices. Moreover, the power of social media influence and peer recommendations cannot be understated. Consumers are now more interconnected than ever, and information about the environmental impact of a product can spread rapidly, shaping the purchasing decisions of others. This social influence plays a crucial role in driving GP behaviour. Businesses, including SMEs, recognize the importance of incorporating green practices into their operations to meet the evolving expectations of environmentally conscious consumers. Adopting eco-friendly practices enhances a company's reputation and contributes to long-term sustainability and resilience in the market.

Understanding the factors that drive GP behaviour is paramount in the context of SMEs in Sri Lanka. As the global economy increasingly emphasizes sustainable practices, SMEs in Sri Lanka must navigate the challenges and opportunities associated with meeting consumer expectations for environmentally responsible products and services. This brief overview sets the stage for a deeper exploration of the specific factors influencing the GP behaviour of SMEs in Sri Lanka, providing a foundation for understanding the dynamics at play in this critical intersection of consumer behaviour and environmental consciousness.

Importance of GP Practices for SMEs in Sri Lanka

GP practices, also known as sustainable or environmentally responsible procurement, can benefit SMEs in Sri Lanka for various reasons discussed below.

Environmental Conservation

The adoption of GP practices contributes to environmental conservation by promoting the use of eco-friendly products and services. This helps SMEs play a role in reducing their environmental footprint. Given that research findings have highlighted the substantial contribution of SMEs to attaining a green economy, implementation of GP practices empowers small and medium enterprise (SME) management to rectify this unfavourable circumstance. Furthermore, the competition extends beyond individual organizations and encompasses entire supply chains in the contemporary business landscape. Embracing GP practices signifies that specific companies are integrating environmentally sustainable approaches into their supply chain operations. This strategic shift enhances their competitive prowess in the market.

Compliance With Regulations

Many countries, including Sri Lanka, are increasingly implementing environmental regulations. Adhering to GP practices ensures that SMEs comply with these regulations, avoiding potential legal issues and penalties. Violations of the law are a common issue in the country. This unfavourable situation creates a bad image for the country, directly influencing trade and diplomatic relationships.

When organizations are aligned with green practices, at least violations of environmental laws can be prevented or minimized.

Cost Savings

GP often involves energy-efficient products and materials, which can affect cost savings in the long run. Energy-efficient equipment, for example, can reduce utility bills, making operations more sustainable and economically viable.

Market Access and Reputation

Consumers are becoming more environmentally conscious, and businesses that adopt green practices may gain a competitive edge. Green practices can add significant value to a company, which, in turn, enhances its reputation and attracts environmentally conscious customers. This leads to increased market access and an improved brand image.

Supply Chain Resilience

Embracing sustainable procurement practices can contribute to a more resilient supply chain. SMEs prioritizing environmentally responsible suppliers are better positioned to navigate potential disruptions and build long-term relationships with reliable partners.

Innovation and Differentiation

GP encourages innovation and the development of eco-friendly products and services. This can give SMEs a unique selling proposition, differentiating them from competitors and attracting customers prioritizing sustainability.

Employee Engagement

Implementing green practices can boost employee morale and engagement. Many employees today value working for companies that demonstrate a commitment to sustainability, contributing to a positive workplace culture.

Risk Management

Embracing GP practices can help SMEs manage the risks associated with environmental issues. This includes potential disruptions to the supply chain due to climate-related events or increased costs associated with non-compliance with future environmental regulations.

Access to Funding

Some financial institutions and investors are increasingly interested in supporting environmentally responsible businesses. SMEs with GP practices may find it easier to access funding or attract investment from entities prioritizing sustainability.

Long-Term Viability

Adopting green practices is aligned with the global trend towards sustainability. SMEs that integrate environmental considerations into their operations are more likely to be resilient and viable in the long term as the business landscape evolves. Overall, GP practices offer Sri Lankan SMEs various benefits, including environmental stewardship, cost savings, market access and enhanced reputation, positioning them for long-term success in a rapidly changing business environment.

Literature Review

The existing literature provides various factors influencing business organizations to adopt GP practices. Government regulations (Forman & Jorgensen, 2004; Min & Galle, 2001; Ramakrishnan et al., 2015), environmental awareness (Chen et al., 2006), customer pressure (Doonan et al., 2005; ElTayeb & Zailani, 2010; Forman & Jorgensen, 2004), top management support (Ramakrishnan et al., 2015), product quality (Jabbour et al., 2014), supplier relationship (Bowen et al., 2001; Ramakrishnan et al., 2015), corporate social responsibility (CSR; Forman & Jorgensen, 2004; Ramakrishnan et al., 2015) and competition (Lozano et al., 2009) are some of the major factors or drivers identified by previous researchers.

Factors Affecting GP Behaviour

Although numerous research studies were conducted to examine the factors affecting GP behaviour, most of these investigated the GP behaviour of consumers. Therefore, this study focused on exploring the factors influencing SMEs' GP practices with particular reference to Sri Lanka. Researchers investigated eight commonly used factors identified through a literature review, which are presented next.

Environmental Awareness and Concerns

Environmental awareness and concerns significantly influence GP behaviour among SMEs in any country. As environmental issues such as climate change, pollution and resource depletion increase, SMEs become more conscious of their ecological footprint and the impact of their purchasing decisions: concerns about environmental sustainability drive SMEs to seek out green products and services that minimize adverse environmental effects. Heightened consumer environmental awareness leads to increased demand for eco-friendly products and services. SMEs respond to this demand by adopting GP practices that align with consumer preferences (Chen et al., 2006). Environmental awareness prompts SMEs to seek ways to reduce resource consumption and minimize waste generation. Adopting GP practices, such as energy-efficient technologies or waste reduction strategies, helps SMEs achieve cost savings and operational efficiencies (Horbach & Rammer, 2019). Environmental awareness extends beyond consumers to stakeholders such as investors, suppliers and employees. Pressure from these stakeholders, driven by environmental concerns, encourages SMEs to adopt GP practices to enhance their reputation and relationships (Lund-Thomsen et al., 2012). SMEs recognize that environmental issues risk their business operations, including reputational damage and supply chain disruptions. Environmental awareness prompts SMEs to adopt GP practices as a risk mitigation strategy to address these concerns (Ararat et al., 2015). SMEs understand that demonstrating environmental responsibility can provide a competitive advantage in the marketplace. Adopting GP practices helps SMEs differentiate themselves from competitors and attract environmentally conscious customers (Prajogo & Olhager, 2012).

Government Policies and Regulations

ElTayeb et al. (2009) mention that Malaysian business institutes adopt GP practices mainly in line with the country's environmental regulations. The findings from many research studies emphasize that government regulations play a significant role as the most decisive influence on manufacturing organizations and establish a significant relationship with GP (Ghobadian et al., 2001; Logamuthu & Zailani, 2010; Preuss, 2001; Zhu & Geng, 2001). Holt and Ghobadian (2009) state that the United Kingdom's existing green regulations strongly pressure companies to adopt GP initiatives. In Sri Lanka, government regulations may include waste management, pollution control, renewable energy usage and sustainable resource management laws. Compliance with these regulations often requires SMEs to adopt GP practices by sourcing environmentally friendly products and services. Additionally, governments may provide incentives such as tax breaks, subsidies or grants to encourage SMEs to invest in green procurement. These incentives catalyze businesses to prioritize sustainability in their purchasing decisions. Overall, government regulations significantly shape the GP behaviour of SMEs in Sri Lanka by setting standards, providing incentives and creating a regulatory framework that promotes environmental sustainability.

Corporate Social Responsibility

CSR plays a significant role in influencing GP behaviour within any business organization. The existing literature confirms that many studies have explored CSR as an exogenous variable towards GP adoption, and they identified a momentous relationship between CSR and GP (Forman & Jorgensen, 2004; Murphy & Poist, 2003; Preuss, 2001). As part of CSR initiatives, SMEs recognize their responsibility to minimize environmental impact and contribute to sustainable development. By incorporating GP practices into their operations, SMEs demonstrate their commitment to environmental stewardship and social responsibility. This may involve sourcing eco-friendly products and services, supporting suppliers with sustainable practices and implementing environmentally conscious policies throughout their supply chains. Engaging in GP aligns with the broader goals of CSR, including fostering positive relationships with stakeholders, enhancing brand reputation and contributing to the well-being of the community and environment. Additionally, adopting sustainable procurement practices can lead to cost savings, operational efficiency improvements and competitive advantages for SMEs.

Customer Pressure

Customers are the most critical stakeholders among other parties involved in a business organization. Hence, their pressure on business organizations to embrace environmental practices cannot be underestimated. In other words, customers constantly pressure business companies to adopt green or environmentally friendly practices within their business activities (Doonan et al., 2005; ElTayeb & Zailani, 2010; Lin, 2007; Peng & Lin, 2008). Customer pressure plays a significant role in influencing SMEs to adopt GP practices. As customers become more aware of environmental issues, the demand for eco-friendly products and services increases. This heightened awareness pressures businesses to adopt green practices (Delmas & Burbano, 2011). Responding to customer pressure by implementing GP practices helps SMEs mitigate the risk of reputational damage associated with non-compliance with environmental standards and regulations (Wagner, 2010). Building long-term relationships with customers often relies on meeting their sustainability expectations. SMEs understand that aligning with customer values regarding environmental concerns fosters trust and loyalty (Liu & Huang, 2018). Access to specific markets may be contingent upon demonstrating a commitment to sustainability. SMEs recognize that meeting customer demands for eco-friendly products or services is essential for market entry and expansion (Wagner, 2010).

Supply Chain Practices

Supplier relationship enables suppliers to make environmentally friendly goods that do not include harmful or poisonous chemicals (Bowen et al., 2001). Hsu and Hu (2010) find that adopting GP and prioritizing environmental necessities when purchasing goods and services can ensure product environmental quality. SMEs rely on various suppliers and partners to fulfil their operational needs, and the sustainability practices of these entities can impact an SME's overall environmental footprint. SMEs engaging in GP often prioritize suppliers and partners demonstrating environmentally friendly practices. This encompasses sourcing materials and products from suppliers with certifications or commitments to sustainability, such as using renewable energy, reducing waste, or implementing eco-friendly production processes. Furthermore, SMEs may collaborate with suppliers to improve sustainability across the supply chain, encouraging them to adopt greener practices and offering support or incentives. By integrating environmental considerations into supplier selection and relationship management, SMEs can effectively extend their commitment to sustainability beyond their operations.

Competition

In today's business landscape, sustainability has become a competitive differentiator, with consumers increasingly favouring environmentally friendly products and services. SMEs operating in competitive markets recognize the importance of meeting consumer demand for sustainability to maintain or enhance their market share. As a result, businesses may adopt GP practices as a strategic response to competitive pressures, seeking to differentiate themselves from rivals and gain a competitive edge. Competition compels SMEs to adopt GP practices, along with other motivations. SMEs recognize that embracing GP practices can differentiate them from competitors and attract environmentally conscious consumers, thereby gaining a competitive edge (Lozano et al., 2009). Competition prompts SMEs to seek ways to reduce costs and improve efficiency. Adopting GP practices, such as energy-efficient technologies or waste reduction measures, can lead to cost savings and operational efficiencies (Jabbour et al., 2013). Competition compels SMEs to comply with environmental regulations to avoid penalties and maintain a level playing field. GP practices help SMEs align with regulatory requirements and avoid potential legal risks (Ciliberti et al., 2008). SMEs may adopt GP practices in competitive markets to access new market segments or industries prioritizing sustainability. This expansion enables SMEs to diversify their customer base and revenue streams (Lozano et al., 2009). Competition underscores the importance of maintaining a positive reputation. SMEs recognize that demonstrating environmental stewardship through GP practices enhances their reputation, trustworthiness and brand image, thereby improving competitiveness (Lozano et al., 2009).

Perceptions of Product Quality

When SMEs perceive green products as high quality, they are more likely to adopt environmentally friendly purchasing practices. Perceptions of product quality can significantly influence SMEs to adopt GP practices. SMEs perceive that adopting GP practices enhances their reputation for producing high-quality products. Green products are often associated with superior quality due to their environmentally friendly attributes, leading SMEs to prioritize green practices to maintain or improve their reputation (Jabbour et al., 2014). SMEs recognize that consumers increasingly associate green products with higher quality and performance. SMEs adopt GP practices to meet customer expectations, maintain competitiveness and ensure their products align with perceived quality standards (Geng et al., 2010). SMEs view GP practices as a strategy to differentiate themselves from competitors and position their products as premium offerings. By integrating environmental considerations into their supply chain and production processes, SMEs aim to create a unique selling proposition based on perceived quality (Jabbour et al., 2014). SMEs perceive that incorporating green practices mitigates the risks associated with product quality issues. By adopting environmentally friendly materials and processes, SMEs reduce the likelihood of defects, recalls and negative consumer perceptions, thus safeguarding their brand reputation and market position (Sarkis et al., 2010). SMEs recognize that GP practices often improve production efficiency and reduce waste. By investing in environmentally friendly technologies and processes, SMEs can enhance the quality of their products while simultaneously reducing costs, making green practices financially attractive (Sarkis et al., 2010). SMEs perceive that catering to environmentally conscious consumers opens opportunities to access niche markets where product quality is paramount. By adopting GP practices, SMEs can penetrate these markets and leverage their reputation for producing high-quality, environmentally friendly products (Jabbour et al., 2014).

Cost Considerations

Cost considerations play a pivotal role in shaping the GP practices of SMEs, influencing their decisions regarding environmentally friendly procurement. Research indicates that SMEs often face financial constraints, making them sensitive to the initial costs of adopting sustainable practices (Boso, 2013). Consequently, they may prioritize cost-saving measures over environmental concerns, especially when resources are limited (Zhu et al., 2012). However, studies also suggest that despite initial investments, embracing GP practices can lead to long-term cost reductions through efficiency gains and enhanced reputation (Rao & Holt, 2005; Zhu et al., 2012). Therefore, while cost considerations remain significant, SMEs need to recognize the potential financial benefits of sustainable procurement in the long run.

Research Methodology

This study was conducted as a quantitative survey study. Since most SMEs are located in the western province, SMEs in Colombo and Gampaha districts were selected for the study. Therefore, manufacturing and service SMEs, which have 5–199 employees (categorized by DSC), were selected to gather information for the current study. Telephone calls, email and WhatsApp were employed to collect the data. Five hundred and fifty-eight SMEs were contacted, and data were collected from 510 SMEs (324 manufacturing and 186 service firms). The remaining 48 SMEs did not know about GP due to a lack of awareness and the highly profit-minded attitude of owners and management. Regarding size, 43 of these 48 SMEs that did not respond are small-scale firms, and the remaining 5 are medium-scale firms. Moreover, 28 out of the 43 small-scale entities are service firms; the rest represent the manufacturing sector. The study focused on eight commonly accepted factors identified through the thorough literature review. Sample SMEs were asked to select the three most relevant factors that affect the adoption of GP practices. Further, respondents were requested to prioritize three particular factors: first, second and third. Data were analyzed quantitatively using simple mathematical tools.

Please refer Table 14.1 for the key factors affecting GP practices and references.

Please refer Table 14.2 for the composition of the sample and the first choice of factors affecting GP.

Please refer Table 14.3 for the factors affecting GP practices.

Findings

The findings from the study confirm that 208 SMEs indicated 'government policies and regulations' as their priority. In comparison, 146 and 104 SMEs indicated it as the second and third priority factors affecting their GP intention. Therefore, 'government policies and regulations' are the most critical factor (41%) when considering all three choices of SMEs on GP behaviour. The second most important factor is 'environmental awareness and concerns'; since customers are

Table 14.1. Key Factors Affecting GP Practices and References.

Factors	Source
Environmental awareness and concerns	Ararat et al. (2015), Chen et al. (2006)
Government policies and regulations	Ghobadian et al. (2001), Logamuthu and Zailani (2010), Preuss (2001), Zhu and Geng (2001)
Corporate social responsibility	Forman and Jorgensen (2004), Murphy and Poist (2003), Preuss (2001)
Customer pressure	Doonan et al. (2005), ElTayeb and Zailani (2010), Lin (2007), Peng and Lin (2008)
Supply chain practices	Bowen et al. (2001)
Competition	Lozano et al. (2009)
Perceptions of product quality	Geng et al. (2010), Jabbour et al. (2014)
Cost considerations	Boso (2013)

Source: Author's own.

Table 14.2. Composition of the Sample and the First Choice of Factors Affecting Green Purchasing.

Selected Factors Affecting Green Purchasing	**First Choice**	**Composition of First Choice**		**% of the Sample (510)**	**Medium Scale**		**Small Scale**	
		Mf	**Sv**		**Mf**	**Sv**	**Mf**	**Sv**
Government policies and regulations	208	129	79	41	91	43	40	34
Environmental awareness and concerns	86	62	24	17	49	11	15	11
Competition	61	38	23	12	27	13	11	10
Perceptions of product quality	44	26	18	09	24	09	02	09
Customer pressure	40	24	16	08	14	08	10	08
Corporate social responsibility	32	18	14	06	16	06	02	08
Supply chain practices	24	17	07	04	16	03	01	04
Cost considerations	15	11	04	03	10	02	01	02
Total	510	324	186	100	247	95	82	86
Total	510	510		100	342		168	

Source: Author's own.

Note: Mf, manufacturing firms; Sv, service firms.

Table 14.3. Factors Affecting Green Purchasing Practices.

Selected Factors Affecting Green Purchasing	1st Choice	2nd Choice	3rd Choice
Government policies and regulations	208	146	104
Environmental awareness and concerns	86	102	75
Competition	61	65	72
Perceptions of product quality	44	48	59
Customer pressure	40	33	42
Corporate social responsibility	32	56	67
Supply chain practices	24	31	44
Cost considerations	15	29	47
Total	510	510	510
No idea about GP		48	

Source: Author's own.

rational and educated, they concentrate on environmentally friendly goods and services. Therefore, SMEs embrace environmental practices to provide green products and services to the market.

The factor 'competition' takes third place in the first-choice category and further, only 12% of the sample (61) SMEs selected this factor as their priority. Since the country's open economy system is dominant, enormous competition exists for most goods and services. There is a tendency to select environmentally friendly products and services in a country with predominantly rational customers. In this situation, businesses embrace green practices to expand their market share and compete with parallel (competitor) companies. Further, in this competitive situation, companies that do not implement green practices cannot survive in the market. Therefore, SMEs tend to adopt GP and other environmentally friendly practices. Overall, these findings emphasize that rules and regulations, environmental awareness and competition are the dominating factors in the GP behaviour of Sri Lankan SMEs.

Discussion

It is evident from the findings of this study that 'government policies and regulations' are the significant factors affecting GP practices. This result aligns with the previous findings (ElTayeb et al., 2009; Ghobadian et al., 2001; Logamuthu & Zailani, 2010; Preuss, 2001; Zhu & Geng, 2001). The findings confirm that 'environmental awareness and concerns' are the second factor affecting SMEs embracing GP practices in Sri Lanka. Although the environmental awareness of business persons in emerging economies is generally poor, previous findings (ElTayeb & Zalani, 2010) have been challenged by the present results, which confirm Sri Lankan SMEs' higher level of environmental consciousness. El Tayeb and Zalani (2010) emphasized that GP is affected by regulations, customer pressure and expected business benefits, but they did not mention environmental awareness as an affecting factor. However, in the Sri Lankan context, this situation may be the consequence of continuous awareness programs on environmental conservation conducted by both the government and non-government organizations. Even though numerous research findings (Doonan et al., 2005; ElTayeb & Zailani, 2010; Lin, 2007; Peng & Lin, 2008) identified 'customer pressure' as a significant factor affecting GP practices, the current study shows this factor as the fourth most important. GP is also affected by 'competition', the third most important factor. In many business sectors, observing a common practice of monitoring and responding to competitors' actions within the market is typical. Since sustainable development is a topic of concern worldwide, current business organizations especially embrace green practices to protect their customer base and achieve sustainable development goals. Hence, SMEs are keen to adopt GP practices to meet the competition from their parallel companies that have implemented green practices.

Conclusion

SMEs play a vital role in the Sri Lankan economy. More than 75% of enterprises in the country are SMEs. That is why the government of Sri Lanka recognizes SMEs as the backbone of the economy. Furthermore, SMEs provide 45% of employment and contribute 52% of the GDP. Hines et al. (1987) theorized that knowledge, skills, personality and situational factors affect people's responsible environmental behaviour. This study pointed out that government policies and regulations, environmental awareness and competition are the main factors affecting the GP behaviour of SMEs operating in Sri Lanka. However, since only 17% of the sample selected environmental awareness as the primary factor (first choice) for adopting GP practices, more awareness programs should be conducted by relevant parties. Furthermore, in the present study, the first, second and third determinants influencing GP have been delineated. Therefore, government policies and regulations, environmental awareness and competition have sequentially occupied the foremost, secondary and tertiary positions among these determinants. In addition to that, the findings of the study confirmed that the 'perception of product quality', 'customer pressure' and 'corporate social responsibility' also affected GP practices. However, 'supply chain practices' and 'cost consideration' were not prioritized by the Sri Lankan SMEs. Although this study considered eight commonly identified factors affecting SMEs' GP behaviour, another factor, i.e. 'peer influence and social norms', was also identified through the preliminary discussion conducted with several top managers to validate the questionnaire. When SMEs observe other businesses in their industry or network adopting GP practices, they may feel pressure or motivation to follow suit. Peers can serve as powerful influencers by setting examples and sharing experiences related to sustainable procurement. Positive peer influence can lead SMEs to perceive GP as a socially desirable behaviour and align their practices accordingly. This influence is powerful when businesses within the same industry or community collectively prioritize sustainability. Moreover, social norms shape perceptions of acceptable and expected behaviour within a given context. As sustainability becomes increasingly valued, SMEs may feel compelled to conform to prevailing social norms by integrating GP practices into their operations.

Implications of the Study

The findings from this study make an invaluable contribution to academia and practitioners alike. These results enable relevant stakeholders to identify the response from particular organizations to the rules and regulations enacted by government regulatory bodies in the country. Moreover, the findings from this study can be considered as feedback to the government, NGOs, academics and other relevant parties about conducting environmental awareness programs, especially for the business sector in the country. Thus, these stakeholders can make the right decisions on existing environmental programs. At the same time, they can schedule future programs benchmarking the indications given by the findings from the current study. Moreover, these findings can contribute to undergraduate and postgraduate researchers reviewing the latest literature on factors affecting the GP behaviour of SMEs in the country. As a whole, policy-makers can use these findings to upgrade the country's sustainable development and environmental conservation policies.

Future Directions

Although SMEs in Sri Lanka have sufficient knowledge of green practices, they may suffer because of numerous problems in adopting GP practices, mainly due to the ongoing economic crisis. Therefore, future research can be conducted to explore the barriers to adopting GP practices with particular reference to SMEs in the country. Furthermore, researchers have another opportunity to undertake the same studies related to large-scale manufacturing and service companies in the country. However, GP is not the only green practice. Therefore, future studies can be carried out to investigate the factors affecting other green practices such as eco-design, green supplier selection, green manufacturing, green logistics and transportation, reverse logistics and other environmentally friendly practices for SMEs. Since the current study did not focus on an exact industry, future research studies have the opportunity to conduct studies aiming at particular industries such as plastic, apparel, electronics, food and beverages, etc.

Acknowledgements

We would like to express our sincere gratitude to the editors and the anonymous reviewers for their invaluable contributions in developing this chapter.

References

Ajzen, I. (1991). The theory of planned behaviour. *Organisational Behavior and Human Decision Process*, *50*(2), 179–211.

Ararat, M., Aksu, M., & Tansel Çetin, A. (2015). Impact of board diversity on boards' monitoring intensity and firm performance: Evidence from the Istanbul Stock Exchange. *Journal of Business Ethics*, *130*(1), 145–167.

Ashoka, A. N. D., Jayasooriya, S. D., & Galahitiyawe, N. W. K. (2023). Awareness of green supply chain management practices of Sri Lankan SMEs. In *6th International Conference on Business Research (ICBR 2023)* (pp. 1–15). https://doi.org/10.31705/ICBR.2023.22

Boso, N. (2013). The impact of cost management on environmental sustainability. *International Journal of Management*, *30*(1), 309–315.

Bowen, F. E., Cousins, P. D., Lamming, R. C., & Farukt, A. C. (2001). The role of supply management capabilities in green supply. *Production and Operations Management*, *10*(2), 174–189.

Chen, Y. S., Lai, S. B., & Wen, C. T. (2006). The influence of green innovation performance on corporate advantage in Taiwan. *Journal of Business Ethics*, *67*(4), 331–339.

Ciliberti, F., Pontrandolfo, P., & Scozzi, B. (2008). Investigating corporate social responsibility in supply chains: A SME perspective. *Journal of Cleaner Production*, *16*(15), 1579–1588.

Delmas, M., & Burbano, V. C. (2011). The drivers of greenwashing. *California Management Review*, *54*(1), 64–87.

Dissanayake, K., Premaratne, S. P., Ranwala, S., & Melegoda, N. (2019). Adoption of green practices in manufacturing SMEs: Some lessons from Kochi, Kerala, India. *Journal of Business Studies*, *6*(2), 1–33. https://doi.org/10.4038/jbs.v6i2.45

Doonan, J., Lanoie, P., & Laplante, B. (2005). Analysis determinants of environmental performance in the Canadian pulp and paper industry: An assessment from inside the industry. *Ecological Economics*, *55*(1), 73–84.

ElTayeb, T. K., & Zailani, S. (2010). Investigation on the drivers of green purchasing towards environmental sustainability in the Malaysian manufacturing sector. *International Journal of Procurement Management*, *3*(3), 316–337.

ElTayeb, T. K., Zailani, S., & Jayaraman, K. (2009). The examination of the drivers for green purchasing adoption among EMS 14001 certified companies in Malaysia. *Journal of Manufacturing Technology Management*, *21*(2), 206–225.

Forman, M., & Jorgensen, M. S. (2004). Organising environmental supply chain management. *Greener Management International*, *45*, 43–62.

Geng, R., Mansouri, S. A., Aktas, E., & Lohmann, G. (2010). The importance of sustainability in determining corporate performance: Evidence from a global empirical study. *Business Strategy and the Environment*, *19*(2), 84–98.

Ghobadian, A., Viney, H., & Holt, D. (2001). Seeking congruence in implementing corporate environmental strategy. *International Journal of Environmental Technology and Management*, *1*(4), 384–401.

Hines, J. M., Hungerford, H. R., & Tomera, A. N. (1987). Analysis and synthesis of research on responsible environmental behaviour: A meta-analysis. *Journal of Environmental Education*, *18*(2), 1–8. https://doi.org/10.1080/00958964.1987.9943482

Holt, D., & Ghobadian, A. (2009). An empirical study of green supply chain management practices amongst UK manufacturers. *Journal of Manufacturing Technology Management*, *20*(7), 933–956.
Horbach, J., & Rammer, C. (2019). Energy transition in Germany and regional spillovers: What triggers the diffusion of renewable energy in firms? *Ecological Economics*, *161*, 310–324.
Hsu, C. W., & Hu, A. H. (2010). Critical factors for implementing green supply chain management practice. *Management Research Review*, *33*(6), 586–608.
Jabbour, C. J., Jabbour, A. B., Govindan, K., Teixeira, A. A., & de Oliveira, J. H. (2013). Factors affecting the adoption of green supply chain management practices: Evidence from Brazil. *Resources, Conservation and Recycling*, *79*, 21–33.
Jabbour, C. J., Jabbour, A. B., Govindan, K., Teixeira, A. A., & de Oliveira, J. H. (2014). Green product development and performance of Brazilian firms: Measuring the role of human and technical aspects. *Journal of Cleaner Production*, *78*, 90–102.
Lin, C. Y. (2007). Adoption of green supply chain practices in Taiwan's logistics industry. *Journal of International Management Studies*, *2*(2), 90–98.
Liu, X., & Huang, Q. (2018). The role of customer pressure in encouraging green supply chain management among Chinese manufacturers. *Sustainability*, *10*(5), 1456.
Logamuthu, & Zailani, S. (2010). Factors influencing the implementation of green productivity practices and its effect on organisational performance: A comparison study between EMS 14001 and ISO 9000 certified companies in Malaysia. *Asian Journal of Information Technology*, *9*(2), 45–53.
Lozano, R., Blanco, M., & Rey-Merino, M. (2009). Towards a cleaner production: The role of sustainability metrics and their application at the level of the production process. *Journal of Cleaner Production*, *17*(6), 574–584.
Lund-Thomsen, P., Lindgreen, A., & Vanhamme, J. (2012). Industrial clusters and corporate social responsibility in developing countries: What we know, do not, and need to know. *Journal of Business Ethics*, *106*(1), 127–147.
Min, H., & Galle, W. (2001). Green purchasing practices of US firms. *International Journal of Operations and Production Management*, *21*(9), 1222–1238.
Murphy, P. R., & Poist, R. F. (2003). Green perspectives and practices: A 'comparative logistics' study. *Supply Chain Management: An International Journal*, *8*(2), 122–131.
Paulraj, A., Chen, I. J., & Blome, C. (2017). Motives and performance outcomes of sustainable supply chain management practices: A multi-theoretical perspective. *Journal of Business Ethics*, *145*(2), 239–258.
Peng, Y. S., & Lin, S. S. (2008). Local responsiveness pressure, subsidiary resources, green management adoption, and subsidiary's performance: Evidence from Taiwanese manufacturers. *Journal of Business Ethics*, *798*(1), 199–212.
Prajogo, D., & Olhager, J. (2012). Supply chain integration and performance: The effects of long-term relationships, information technology and sharing, and logistics integration. *International Journal of Production Economics*, *135*(1), 514–522.
Preuss, L. (2001). In dirty chains? Purchasing and greener manufacturing. *Journal of Business Ethics*, *34*(3), 345–359.
Ramakrishnan, P., Haron, H., & Goh, Y.-N. (2015). Factors influencing green purchasing adoption for small and medium enterprises (SMEs) in Malaysia Hasnah Haron. *International Journal of Business and Society*, *16*(1).

Rao, P., & Holt, D. (2005). Do green supply chains lead to competitiveness and economic performance? *International Journal of Operations & Production Management*, *25*(9), 898–916.

Sarkis, J., Zhu, Q., & Lai, K. H. (2010). An organisational theoretic review of green supply chain management literature. *International Journal of Production Economics*, *130*(1), 1–15.

Stern, P. C., Dietz, T., Abel, T., Guagnano, G. A., & Kalof, L. (1999). A value-belief-norm theory of support for social movements: The case of environmentalism. *Human Ecology Review*, *6*(2), 81–97.

Sugandini, D., Muafi, M., Susilowati, C., Siswanti, Y., & Syafri, W. (2020). Green supply chain management and green marketing strategy on green purchase intention: SMEs cases. *Journal of Industrial Engineering and Management*, *13*(1), 79–92.

Wagner, M. (2010). The role of corporate sustainability performance for economic performance: A firm-level analysis of moderation effects. *Ecological Economics*, *69*(7), 1533–1560.

Zhu, Q., & Geng, Y. (2001). Integrating environmental issues into supplier selection and management: A study of large and medium-sized state-owned enterprises in China. *Greener Management International*, *35*, 27–40.

Zhu, Q., Geng, Y., Fujita, T., & Hashimoto, S. (2012). 'Barriers to promoting eco-innovation: A case study of SMEs in Shangyu China. *International Journal of Cleaner Production*, *37*, 44–51.

Zsidisin, G. A., & Siferd, S. P. (2001). Environmental purchasing: A framework for theory development. *European Journal of Purchasing and Supply Management*, *7*(1), 61–73.

Chapter 15

Sustaining Employee Engagement During the COVID-19 Pandemic and Beyond

Narmada Gunawardhana[a], *Ranitha Sachinthana Weerarathna*[b], *Rathnayake Mudiyanselage Nilmini Malkanthi Rathnayake*[c], *Wathudura Sanduni Dumalka Somawardana*[d] *and Hewa Waduge Mano Chathurangi Weligodapola*[b]

[a]Chartered Institute of Personnel Management, Sri Lanka
[b]Sri Lanka Institute of Information Technology, Sri Lanka
[c]University of Tasmania, Australia
[d]University of Colombo, Sri Lanka

Abstract

This chapter explores the variables that influenced employee engagement in response to the challenges posed by the COVID-19 pandemic and the economic crisis in Sri Lanka. Structured interviews were conducted in this longitudinal qualitative study to gather primary data. The study focused on 20 executive-level personnel from a selected bank, who were interviewed in multiple phases. The researchers utilized word cloud analysis to qualitatively assess word frequency, facilitating a comprehensive exploration of participants' experiences and perspectives over time. The findings from the study suggest that Human Resources (HR) managers can employ various tactics to maintain employee engagement during health or economic crises, such as decentralization, flexibility, travel arrangements, IT facilities, work flexibility, disaster resilience plans, employee recognition, empathy, stress management, communication and problem-solving. Also, financial support, recreational activities, trust and transparency are essential for building employee engagement during any economic downturn.

Keywords: Banking sector; COVID-19 pandemic; employee engagement; HR practices; human resource management; workplace adoption

Shaping Entrepreneurial Marketing, Volume 1, 227–245

Published under exclusive licence by Emerald Publishing Limited
doi:10.1108/978-1-83708-852-220251016

Introduction

A World Health Organization (WHO) risk assessment indicated that the coronavirus posed a very high global risk. On 11 March 2020, the WHO proclaimed COVID-19, the disease caused by the coronavirus, as an infectious disease and a pandemic. Due to the highly contagious nature of the disease at onset without definite treatment and the rising death toll posing a severe threat, several nations imposed measures such as lockdowns, curfews and travel bans to curb its spread. Studies showed that because the pandemic was new to the world, coping mechanisms must be appropriately implemented; however, doing so was challenging because the magnitude of the adverse effects of COVID-19 had yet to be identified closely in some industries. Moreover, changes from the existing work environment to the 'new normal' were forced, and organizations/countries needed to prepare for this unexpected shift or had not undergone similar circumstances.

Hence, this study examines the banking sector in Sri Lanka, focusing on the unique context of the pandemic and post-pandemic economic crisis. Sri Lanka's distinctiveness lies in its geopolitical position, economic vulnerabilities and the social and political challenges it faces, which provide a compelling backdrop for understanding the responses and adaptations of the sector during those unprecedented times. The banking sector comprises a formal work environment that is physical and highly regulated. As such, it was one of the sectors most affected by mobility restrictions. During COVID-19, traditional banking saw a sharp decline, while a marked increase in e-banking platforms was evident (Bechlioulis & Karamanis, 2022; Maity et al., 2022; Ul Haq & Awan, 2020). Furthermore, one of the immediate effects of the health catastrophe on the real global economy was the increased credit risk of banks, including lending for corporate and retail consumers (Mishra et al., 2014; Naseer et al., 2023). This was mainly due to the collapse of businesses and loss of income due to the sudden pandemic, resulting in their inability to service debt obligations. According to studies, the COVID-19 pandemic posed the worst threat to financial institutions (Jing et al., 2022; Shabir et al., 2023; Wronka, 2021; Yu et al., 2024). The banking sector struggled to keep its distribution routes open while adhering to social isolation guidelines and supervisory and enforcement duties never intended for remote employment. Banks had to do their best to manage sales and client expectations despite low interest rates and mounting customer pressure. As the crisis developed, market factors and customer behaviour probably had to change in unexpected directions; therefore, banks had to be aware of the strategies and brand challenges that would shape their future (Cherbib, 2024; Hai et al., 2020; Salunkhe et al., 2021).

In the aftermath of the pandemic and during the post-pandemic stages in Sri Lanka, employees faced increased responsibilities as they had to balance self-care with caring for their families and managing their professional roles more than ever. This heightened demand was driven by significant changes in the banking sector, which substantially affected employee engagement. As the industry navigated economic challenges and evolving workplace dynamics, employees were required to adapt to new pressures and expectations, underscoring the critical need for effective work–life integration. Further, during the pandemic, businesses, including banks, had to change their priorities for business survival. People's mental health-related issues appeared to be frequently disregarded, primarily during the pandemic, especially when a new virus is involved, and the crisis continues (Hamouche, 2020; Zürcher et al., 2022). Additionally, this negatively impacted global corporate sustainability. Hence, changes had to be made to working methods, and Human Resources (HR) departments had to prioritize employee flexibility to achieve organizational performance. Due to the lockdowns, sustaining employee involvement during the COVID-19 pandemic became one of the most well-known objectives for HR managers and practitioners. In those challenging and uncertain times, businesses introduced and implemented innovative strategies for motivating their workforce (Chanana & Sangeeta, 2020).

The COVID-19 pandemic affected the world, and companies had to assess its influence on working habits, employee well-being and Human Resource Management (HRM) in unique circumstances. However, the long-term effectiveness of HR policies implemented during the pandemic is still being determined (Malik & Lenka, 2019). Though many scholars have proposed various coping strategies for employees to achieve organizational performance, a blanket approach can only be followed for some institutions. Further, the work environment after the pandemic differs from before; it is uncertain and volatile. As such, substantial changes in employee performance, satisfaction and mental well-being can be expected. Therefore, new HR practices have to be devised; however, the organization has to identify the impact of these practices beforehand due to the risks of having mixed results. Therefore, the organization must ensure that newly developed HR practices will enhance employee engagement by lowering or eliminating physical and mental barriers.

In addition to the challenges posed by the COVID-19 pandemic, the Sri Lankan banking sector faced a severe economic downturn beginning in March/April 2022. This economic crisis is considered the most severe since Sri Lanka's independence in 1948. The crisis was fuelled by several interrelated factors, including significant political instability, widespread loan defaults, critically low foreign exchange reserves and inadequate decision-making at the governmental level. These issues resulted in a high cost of living, shortages of essential goods and civil unrest, which disrupted daily life and business operations (George et al., 2022).

The crisis forced organizations to adopt remote work and hybrid models due to fuel shortages and power outages. Employee connectivity was particularly challenging, as inconsistent power supply meant that some staff members had access to electricity while others did not, complicating communication and collaboration (Naotunna & Adikaram, 2024). Given these circumstances, examining the human resource practices adopted and their impact on employee engagement during Sri Lanka's economic crisis is crucial. Although organizational operations must be continued during and after (especially the economic crisis in Sri Lanka) to achieve business targets, they cannot function at their total capacity. As such, ensuring appropriate HR initiatives can become a challenge; one of the best ways to achieve organizational sustainability is by enhancing employee engagement. Also, studies show different impacts of Working From Home (WFH) during periods of economic downturn. Some studies mentioned the success of WFH during economic downturns (Naithani, 2010), while some studies argued against the suitability of WFH during economic downturns (Ogbonnaya & van Klyton, 2021).

Hence, it is essential to review the impact of the existing HR practices on employee engagement. Identifying this impact is a timely requirement; organizations must investigate this matter in depth. The current study is a timely contribution to addressing issues in this regard. It aims to fill the existing research gap by exploring the factors contributing to sustaining adequate employee engagement in the banking sector during and beyond COVID-19.

Literature Review

COVID-19 and Overall Impact

According to the WHO, COVID-19 spreads through saliva droplets or nasal discharge (H. H. D. N. P. Opatha, 2020; H. H. D. P. J. Opatha, 2020; Stiti et al., 2022). A pandemic is when a communicable disease spreads widely, causing considerable global social, political and economic disruption and increased death rates (Pillai & Sivathanu, 2021; Samsudin et al., 2024). Additionally, most COVID-19 virus-infected individuals experience mild to severe respiratory infections and recover without special care. The elderly and those who suffer from conditions including cancer, diabetes, chronic respiratory disease and cardiovascular disease are more vulnerable (H. H. D. N. P. Opatha, 2020; H. H. D. P. J. Opatha, 2020).

The pandemic significantly impacted employees worldwide; they were vulnerable to COVID-19, leading to negative consequences and putting employees at risk (H. H. D. N. P. Opatha, 2020; H. H. D. P. J. Opatha, 2020). Due to the challenges present by COVID-19, businesses had to adapt rapidly and implement creative methods to continue operating effectively and efficiently (Weerarathna, Rathnayake, Perera et al., 2022; Weerarathna, Rathnayake, Yasara et al., 2022). Since job losses grew and the bulk of people reported receiving government allowances under social safety nets (as loss of employment benefits, low-income households, etc.), COVID-19 pushed organizations to become more resilient to crises and the resultant shocks (Sekhar, 2021; Weerarathna, Rathnayake, Yasara et al., 2022).

Impact of COVID-19 in Sri Lanka

A surge in cases and fatalities was seen with the emergence of COVID-19 in Sri Lanka. This scenario dramatically impacted Sri Lanka's political, economic, social, cultural, security and welfare aspects. Thus, the right approach and work were required to deal with the threats caused by COVID-19 (Jayasinghe et al., 2022). About 8.6 million people in Sri Lanka were economically active as of 2019, 64.5% being men and 35.5% women, according to a labour market report for 2019. Nearly 3.5 million persons were employed in the private sector, compared to 2.7 million own-account workers.

Further, 81.3% of the private sector employees and 57.3% of the own-account workers were employed in the non-agriculture sector. All labour market stakeholders were affected by the decelerating economic activities during the pandemic but with varying magnitudes. Many employees in informal and precarious employment suffer without social security, making them highly vulnerable to eventual income loss. However, employers in the non-agricultural sector were more vulnerable, which probably had a massive impact on their jobs (Marso, 2022; Wimalaweera, 2020).

COVID-19 hampered employment possibilities, caused income uncertainties and disrupted the nation's economic activity (Weerarathna, Rathnayake, Perera et al., 2022). It affected economic growth, employment and way of life to a significant level, especially in developing countries like Sri Lanka (Weerarathna, Rathnayake, Yasara et al., 2022). The labour market in Sri Lanka also suffered a similar destiny as other countries, fighting to contain the COVID-19 pandemic and the severe economic crisis (Samarakoon, 2024). The safety and job security of the workforce were jeopardized as the sudden loss of revenue and the social unrest challenged corporate continuity.

Impact of the Economic Downturn of 2022 in Sri Lanka

The economic downturn in Sri Lanka reached an unexpected level where people could not tolerate the extreme hyperinflation. For example, the economic downturn impacted people's eating habits as they consumed fewer certain foods, particularly meat, fish and some fruits and vegetables. Also, people experienced difficulties obtaining fuel for their vehicles, leading to difficulties in their jobs and daily activities (Nishanthi, 2022). The same author pointed out that people's disappointment with the economic crisis stemmed from their inability to fulfil their goals and desires. The economic pressures during the economic downturn significantly negatively impacted employee productivity. Employee productivity trended downward due to a negative mindset and low morality.

Employee Engagement

Employee engagement is a mindset where employees are committed to the company's mission and values and offer their utmost effort. Well-engaged employees contribute to organizational performance, which results in higher customer satisfaction and boosts the company's sales and profit (Hamouche & Chabani, 2021). Employee engagement is voluntarily thinking about, feeling good and making meaningful connections with people while at work (Jiang & Shen, 2020). It is a psychological condition due to the much-felt need for a solid psychological link between the employer's and the employee's actions. Employee engagement is a workplace approach designed to ensure that workers are committed to the goals and values of the company, empowered to contribute to organizational progress and develop their sense of well-being simultaneously. Organizations must have employees who recognize the need to invest in themselves as drivers to achieve a complete state of employee engagement (Jiang & Shen, 2020).

Prior studies found that employee engagement in diverse European countries and industries is different from each other due to work autonomy, job demands and social support (Taipale et al., 2011). While job expectations are lower in Germany and the Netherlands, they are higher in Finland, Sweden and the United Kingdom. Additionally, Hungary, Portugal and Bulgaria too have considerable job demands. The degree of employee independence and social support varies by nation. Sweden and Portugal both have significant levels of autonomy. The level of social support has mostly remained the same across all nations. Only Sweden reported a higher level of support than in other countries. Secondly, social support and autonomy affect work engagement similarly in all nations except Finland and Bulgaria. Social support correlates substantially less with participation than autonomy in Finland and Bulgaria. According to the study, social support can significantly impact a person's commitment to their profession, while the possibility of losing their job could impact them negatively. Thirdly, only four nations, Finland, Sweden, Germany and Hungary, saw a strong impact of job demands on work engagement; the other nations did not see this effect. An organization should be welcoming and help employees balance work-related responsibilities and autonomy for better employee engagement.

The overall running of a firm depends on HRM components. Because they establish an 'environment' and 'infrastructure', HRM activities that deal with people, performance, information and work affect employees, clients, stakeholders and the overall organizational performance. Undoubtedly, HR played a crucial part in dealing with the effects of COVID-19 in various pandemic phases in organizations worldwide (Shil et al., 2020; Weerarathna, Rathnayake, Perera et al., 2022). Further, during a crisis, different aspects such as location, sector and business maturity can create issues; therefore, identifying the most challenging and vital elements and implementing the right employee policies by adopting innovative approaches to remote work is essential (Pillai & Prasad, 2022).

The COVID-19 pandemic and economic crisis in Sri Lanka have made employee engagement challenging for HR departments. COVID-19 led to workplace discrimination and exclusion against various groups, such as COVID-19 victims, women with household obligations and ancillary employees (Cooke et al., 2020). Therefore, organizations started developing creative and productive ways of engaging workers. Most initiated engagement activities, such as online family engagement practices, virtual learning, development, etc., so employees stay motivated and committed, ensuring their well-being (Chanana & Sangeeta, 2020; Weerarathna, Rathnayake, Yasara et al., 2022).

One example of organizational adaptations to preserve employee engagement throughout the pandemic was flexible work arrangements. Studies provide good examples of distributing the cumulative workload of workers affected by COVID-19 among other workers and moving some workers from non-critical to critical processes. Additionally, job rotation was proposed to reassign employees to different positions within the same unit to assist with backlogged tasks (Shipman et al., 2021). Workers working from home may have found this hurried and unplanned change challenging. The basic idea of working remotely is well-established; it has sometimes been seen as a successful and practical approach to completing tasks. Additionally, it may have a lazy or unmotivated connotation (Diab-Bahman & Al-Enzi, 2020; Weerarathna, Rathnayake, Perera, Kaluarachchi et al., 2022; Weerarathna, Rathnayake, Yasara et al., 2022).

Methodology

This study employed a qualitative research approach. It can be classified as a longitudinal study. Data was collected through structured interviews, utilizing a convenience sampling method to select executive-level employees from the designated bank. Initially, 20 participants were interviewed. The interview process was deemed complete upon reaching the 18th interview, as the data began to exhibit repetitive patterns. To ensure comprehensive data saturation, two additional interviews were conducted, confirming the saturation point of the interview protocol.

In Phase II of the study, 20 executive employees were re-interviewed to fulfil the research objectives. Each interview lasted 30–45 minutes and was audio recorded with the participant's consent. These recordings were transcribed verbatim for detailed analysis. The data collected was then analyzed using a word cloud generator to visualize word frequency and patterns for insights into the thematic content of the interviews.

Findings and Discussion

The chosen bank altered its HR procedures case-by-case to address employee issues during the pandemic and economic downturn in Sri Lanka. Such alterations would have been done with foresight, concentrating on their long-term impact on employee engagement and organizational performance. The newly introduced practices by the bank can be categorized as institutional administrative arrangements, employee well-being, work arrangements and new technology adoption. Mitchell (2021) made a similar classification. The long-term impact of these practices, introduced to address employee grievances and issues during the pandemic, on employee engagement needs to be investigated. Further, management may require a minimal indication of whether these HR practices stimulate employee engagement, crisis or otherwise.

Qualitative Analysis Through Word Cloud (Phase I)

The Word Cloud application was used to analyze data under Phase I, as illustrated in Fig. 15.1.

The data reveal that the respondents were very concerned about decentralization, freedom in dress code, transportation arrangements, IT facilities and job flexibility. They also emphasized the need for a disaster resilience plan and employee recognition and appreciation. Thirdly, the participants pointed out the need for empathy, stress management, communication, problem-solving and support for customer service. Accordingly, the bank needed to consider several

Fig. 15.1. Word Cloud Generator (Phase I). *Source:* Authors' own, based on the word cloud generator (2024).

factors when developing and amending HR practices to enhance employee engagement during the pandemic (Sekhar, 2021).

Decentralization was one of the main keywords focused on; respondents expressed that decentralization was required to some extent during the pandemic, as all employees were not required to report to work regularly. Hence, delegating power to employees enabled the banks to accelerate decision-making during the pandemic.

> There is a crucial necessity of making correct decisions by improving how the bank is managed and the need for situational leadership, especially when working remotely. (2nd participant)

This included long-term decision-making and prevention of conflict between employees. Secondly, even though the dress code was formal wear before the pandemic, employees could wear intelligent casual attire during the pandemic. Respondents explained the convenience of this dress code while emphasizing its positive impact on work performance and satisfaction. Further, these employees were expected to continue being flexible in their dress code even after the pandemic.

> We feel more comfortable with the flexibilities regarding dress code during and even after the pandemic. (11th participant)

Thirdly, as the bank provided transport during the pandemic, respondents suggested continuing this practice to ensure employee safety.

> Sometimes, this pandemic was a blessing when considering flexibility and transport facilities, which was very important for me since I was using public transportation. (6th participant)
>
> Transport facility is very beneficial. (1st participant)

Fourthly, the respondents emphasized the importance of work flexibility, proposing a few practices, such as reporting to a convenient branch, making arrangements to share the accumulated workload, and temporarily holding employee transfers, promotions, job rotations, recruitments, etc.

> Though there were many flexibilities, there was a temporary holding of employee transfers, promotions, job rotations, and new recruitments adversely affected our career progress, which somewhat demotivated me during this period. (9th participant)

Finally, to perform their tasks, all the respondents emphasized the essential requirement of introducing an e-platform for banking operations and providing IT facilities such as laptops, stable internet connections and technical assistance during the pandemic (Hai et al., 2020; Weerarathna, Rathnayake, Yasara et al., 2022).

Respondents stressed the benefits of a disaster resilience plan. Since the pandemic and its consequences were new to all, the existing business continuity plans needed to be more robust to face challenges of this magnitude.

> When we faced pandemic during its first days, we were a bit excited because, at that time, the bank had no proper resilience plan to tackle issues with the sudden changes in the country.... (15th participant)
>
> Our minds were virtually blank for a few days and came to the bank physically on a rotation basis; you know why? Because we did not have a proper practice to adopt the sudden change.... (3rd participant)

Therefore, most respondents emphasized the importance of establishing a disaster resilience plan. For example, if employees were identified as COVID-19-positive, another team would run operations without disruptions. Further, banking operations are an essential service, and employees must work continually while dealing with the risks associated with the pandemic. Considering this, respondents explained that the bank was required to recognize and appreciate dedicated and hardworking employees during pandemic times; this could be developed as a good HR practice in the bank in the future (Adisa et al., 2021; Weerarathna, Rathnayake, Perera et al., 2022).

Elsafty and Ragheb (2020) also highlighted the significance of workplace policies and support for employees during a trying period. This is because employees appreciate efforts to rebuild their confidence and motivation. Consequently, employee morale improves, and job requirements are met. In addition, the authors identified that for workers to feel content and continue interacting with the management and fellow staff, updating them about the severity of the pandemic severity and brainstorming were highly practical. Since employees were critical to implementing the suggested organizational changes and successfully combating COVID-19, it was crucial to communicate these actions to employees beforehand (H. H. D. N. P. Opatha, 2020; H. H. D. P. J.Opatha, 2020; Salunkhe et al., 2021).

A proper setup of hardware, software and technical support is required for the latest technology adaptations in the workplace to be successful and efficient (Ali et al., 2020). Organizations were advised to use online or cloud platforms to facilitate remote employee work. The local banks' revised work methods (from physical to remote) were thus similar to those in many companies worldwide that permitted or encouraged employees to do so. However, this was a first-hand experience for many employees, particularly those in underdeveloped nations like Sri Lanka (H. H. D. N. P. Opatha, 2020; H. H. D. P. J. Opatha, 2020; Weerarathna, Rathnayake, Perera et al., 2022). Hence, a mixed response was likely with varied adaptability levels, partly due to employee attitudes and other related issues and the level of employer support provided.

Additionally, technical agility for technology optimization will propel organizations to look beyond just survival and move forward, especially in turbulent times. Virtual training and capacity development programs will significantly benefit from innovation. Still, many workers may have difficulty adjusting to the new normal and the vulnerability of losing their jobs. Besides, some employees are early adopters and can adapt and perform successfully in this new way of working. Payroll management, line management and data security in technology and e-management will be future HRM challenges (Shil et al., 2020).

Since the pandemic raised various issues, establishing an effective way to communicate and resolve employee grievances was among the respondents' leading suggestions. At the same time, respondents highlighted the need for communication policies and practices for employees to perform their duties more clearly and hassle-free. Further, the respondents proposed introducing stress management practices, such as emphatic listening and motivational speeches (Weerarathna, Rathnayake, Perera et al., 2022). Finally, the respondents proposed introducing good and comprehensive practices that ensure employee safety and customer convenience, such as limiting the number of customers inside the branch premises, issuing customer numbers and proceeding accordingly.

Qualitative Analysis Through Word Cloud (Phase II)

The Word Cloud application was utilized to visually represent the data analyzed in the second phase, as illustrated in Fig. 15.2.

In Phase II, the participants identified several factors influencing employee engagement. Firstly, they highlighted the importance of robust IT facilities, equipment and data services. Secondly, they emphasized the necessity of flexible work arrangements, including hybrid and remote options. Thirdly, they highlighted the significance of financial stability through fair wages, monetary and nonmonetary support, tax relief, increments and broader economic assistance. Fourthly, the respondents preferred relationship-building activities, a supportive work environment, collaboration and recreational activities. Lastly, they stressed the importance of job security, trust and transparency.

Similar to the expectations during COVID-19, most respondents anticipated enhanced IT facilities and equipment during the country's economic downturn. Employees sought improved IT infrastructure and expected secure remote access, updated software and hardware, collaboration tools such as video conferencing platforms, reliable internet services, upgraded phone and laptop equipment, and responsive IT support services. These elements are deemed essential for sustaining employee engagement.

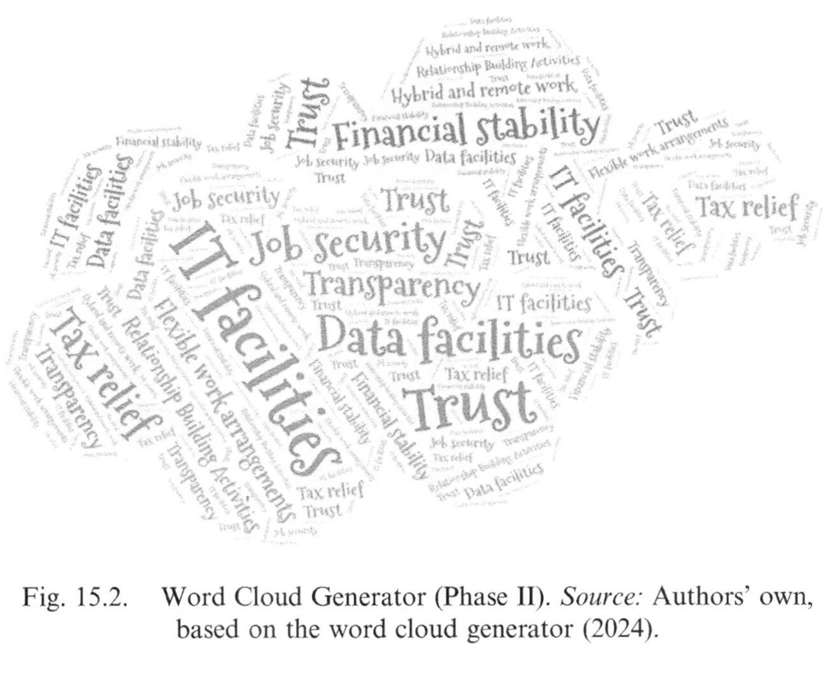

Fig. 15.2. Word Cloud Generator (Phase II). *Source:* Authors' own, based on the word cloud generator (2024).

> I do not have enough data facility, office equipment such as scanner, printer to perform the duties. Therefore, highly appreciate it if you could arrange a data facility and office equipment at my residence to continue the daily work. (12th participant)

> I expect my organisation to provide dependable IT services such as high-speed internet, secure remote access, updated software and hardware, collaboration tools such as video conferencing platforms, and strong IT support to resolve technical issues quickly. These facilities will contribute to smooth and efficient operations. (16th participant)

These findings are consistent with previous research. For instance, Carillo et al. (2021) identified that adequate telework facilities and mental health support are crucial for effective performance under the WFH model. Similarly, Naotunna and Adikaram (2024) observed that despite the availability of IT resources, individuals encountered challenges with connectivity and maintaining laptop battery life in both on-site and remote work settings. Additionally, Aroosiya (2023) highlighted concerns related to technology use, which created friction in both professional and personal environments. The same study found that connectivity issues adversely impacted employees' work–life balance.

Respondents emphasized the significance of flexible work arrangements. They preferred remote work options, allowing them to WFH on selected days of the week. The hybrid working model, which integrates both in-office and remote work, was also highlighted as a desirable alternative. Furthermore, respondents valued flexible working hours, enabling them to adjust their schedules to better balance personal and professional responsibilities. Such flexible arrangements are essential for maintaining productivity and employee engagement, particularly during challenging times.

> During Sri Lanka's post-pandemic and economic crises, I want my organisation to provide flexible work arrangements such as remote work alternatives, to maintain workplace health and safety, to offer mental health care, and to provide financial stability through fair wages and job security. Furthermore, investing in digital tools and training would help people adjust to changing work situations. (6th participant)

> We already have a hybrid model, and we expect the same in the future, with a hybrid model combining physical office work as well. (13th participant)

Many companies implemented various measures to support their employees in response to the challenges faced during Sri Lanka's post-pandemic period and economic crises. These included providing opportunities to work from nearby branches or offices, allowing alternative work locations such as cafes and establishing centres with generators to ensure uninterrupted work. Naotunna and Adikaram (2024) noted that these initiatives were crucial in sustaining employee engagement and productivity. Additionally, respondents stressed the need for flexible work arrangements, including remote work options and hybrid working models, to maintain workplace health and safety. They also highlighted the importance of mental healthcare, financial stability through fair wages and job security, and investment in digital tools and training to help employees adapt to evolving work conditions.

> I anticipate the need for monetary and non-monetary support and more tax relief support. (7th participant)

> We were not financially supported. If increment is given in the future and more economic support is given, we will be attracted to work. (15th participant)

As per previous findings, employees experienced high living costs, which led to financial stress and impacted employee productivity, motivation and engagement (Naotunna & Adikaram, 2024). The same authors noted that several companies adjusted salaries to match the high living cost. During the economic downturn, more employees expected a supportive work environment, collaborative teamwork, relationship-building and recreational activities. Below is the evidence from the participants:

> We need Zoom meetings for chat and meet each other, online events, or staff gathering for a short period. (3rd participant)

> Offer access to on-site or subsidised recreational facilities like gyms or relaxation rooms. (5th participant)

Previous research has indicated that employees seek more opportunities to connect with colleagues and friends, as the WFH model, which prevailed during the pandemic, reduced face-to-face interactions with co-workers and supervisors (Wang et al., 2021). During Sri Lanka's economic downturn, this sense of isolation was further amplified (Naotunna & Adikaram, 2024). In response to these emotional challenges, employees increasingly desired more significant interaction and collaborative workspaces.

Finally, respondents highlighted job security and transparency, especially given the recent job reductions during the economic downturn.

> There should be recognition for hard work, involvement in decision making, and transparent communication while showing empathy. (11th participant)

> I expect my supervisors and management to communicate, provide regular feedback, and offer support. Transparent decision-making

> and building a collaborative team environment are also necessary for high performance. (13th participant)

Similar research on the WFH model has highlighted that employees often experience frustration due to a lack of trust from top management, a challenge frequently observed in Asian countries (Himawan et al., 2022). These findings suggest that trust and transparency are critical for promoting employee engagement.

Conclusion and Implications of the Study

While HR practices were initially implemented as a reactive solution to the challenges that emerged during the pandemic, organizations must assess their impact on employee engagement. Understanding this impact provides a sense of preparedness for future crises. Although numerous scholars have proposed coping strategies to enhance organizational performance, institutions and industries have no one-size-fits-all solution. Each organization must evaluate the effectiveness of diverse practices. This study highlights that multiple factors influenced employee engagement during the pandemic and the economic crisis in Sri Lanka.

The findings suggest that practices tailored to the specific nature of each job, rather than a one-size-fits-all approach, are essential. For instance, remote work suits IT employees who manage IT systems. It is recommended that a comprehensive strategy for monitoring remote work be implemented, focusing on work targets such as output and quality rather than strict time-based targets. Additionally, incorporating reasonable flexibility to support employees' work–life balance is advised.

It is recommended that existing practices that contribute to employee satisfaction, such as flexibility in dress code, transportation facilities, working hours and work locations, be maintained. Additionally, measures that increase stress, such as unnecessary employee transfers and rotations, should be eliminated. HR practices like decentralization, which can expedite decision-making, should be prioritized to enhance employee engagement further. During an economic downturn, increased focus should be on providing additional financial support, organizing recreational activities, and fostering trust and transparency. These actions will be vital to maintaining high levels of employee engagement.

The practical implications of the findings from this study are that the key elements that sustain a high level of employee engagement can be identified. Management can leverage these insights to support employee engagement better and achieve business objectives. The results also provide valuable guidance for HR professionals in their organizational development efforts, emphasizing the need to adopt contemporary HR practices to ensure employees' mental and physical well-being. Incorporating feedback into a new framework can enhance employee engagement, vital for overall employee wellness. HR professionals are thus well-positioned to advocate for best practices within organizations. HR teams should collaborate with various departments to develop effective HR practices. For the academic community, this research underscores the importance of different HR practices on employee engagement during crises.

Limitations and Future Research Directions

The authors utilized a convenience sampling method to select participants for this study. Purposive sampling or other rigorous sampling techniques are recommended to enhance future research's robustness. Furthermore, this study relies exclusively on qualitative methods; integrating quantitative research approaches in future studies could provide a more comprehensive analysis and validate the findings through triangulation. Expanding the scope to include a diverse range of industries could improve the generalizability of the results, offering broader insights into employee engagement across different sectors. This approach would allow for a more nuanced understanding of how various industries respond to HR practices, thereby contributing to a more comprehensive body of knowledge on the subject.

Acknowledgements

The anonymous reviewers' insightful feedback was instrumental in refining the chapter to its current form. We also extend our heartfelt appreciation to the Team ICMR at Sabaragamuwa University of Sri Lanka for their support.

References

Adisa, T. A., Ogbonnaya, C., & Adekoya, O. D. (2021). Remote working and employee engagement: A qualitative study of British workers during the pandemic. *Information Technology & People*, *36*(5). https://doi.org/10.1108/itp-12-2020-0850

Ali, S., Choudhary, Y., Javaid, M., Haleem, A., Singh, R. P., Suman, R., & Rab, S. (2020). Makeover in the sustainable working platform during the COVID-19 pandemic. *Sustainable Operations and Computers*, *1*, 8–12. https://doi.org/10.1016/j.susoc.2020.10.001

Aroosiya, M. A. C. F. (2023). A study on work life balance during the economic crisis in Sri Lanka. *American Journal of Interdisciplinary Research and Innovation*, *1*(3), 17–23.

Bechlioulis, A. P., & Karamanis, D. (2022). Consumers' changing financial behaviour during the COVID-19 lockdown: The case of internet banking use in Greece. *Journal of Financial Services Marketing*, *28*, 526–543. https://doi.org/10.1057/s41264-022-00159-8

Carillo, K., Cachat-Rosset, G., Marsan, J., Saba, T., & Klarsfeld, A. (2021). Adjusting to epidemic-induced telework: Empirical insights from teleworkers in France. *European Journal of Information Systems*, *30*(1), 69–88.

Chanana, N., & Sangeeta (2020). Employee engagement practices during COVID-19 lockdown. *Journal of Public Affairs*, *21*(4), e2508. https://doi.org/10.1002/pa.2508

Cherbib, J. (2024). Exploring the interplay between entrepreneurial orientation, causation and effectuation under unexpected COVID-19 uncertainty: Insights from large French banks. *Technological Forecasting and Social Change*, *200*, 123090. https://doi.org/10.1016/j.techfore.2023.123090

Cooke, F. L., Dickmann, M., & Parry, E. (2020). IJHRM after 30 years: Taking stock in times of COVID-19 and looking towards the future of HR research. *International Journal of Human Resource Management*, *32*(1), 1–23. https://doi.org/10.1080/09585192.2020.1833070

Diab-Bahman, R., & Al-Enzi, A. (2020). The impact of COVID-19 pandemic on conventional work settings. *International Journal of Sociology and Social Policy*, *40*(9/10), 909–927. https://doi.org/10.1108/ijssp-07-2020-0262

Elsafty, A. S., & Ragheb, M. (2020). The role of human resource management towards employees retention during COVID-19 pandemic in medical supplies sector – Egypt. *Business and Management Studies*, *6*(2), 50–59. https://doi.org/10.11114/bms.v6i2.4899

George, A. H., George, A. S., & Baskar, T. (2022). Sri Lanka's economic crisis: A brief overview. *Partners Universal International Research Journal*, *1*(2), 9–19.

Hai, S., Wu, K., Park, I.-J., Li, Y., Chang, Q., & Tang, Y. (2020). The role of perceived high-performance HR practices and transformational leadership on employee engagement and citizenship behaviours. *Journal of Managerial Psychology*, *35*(6), 513–526. https://doi.org/10.1108/jmp-03-2019-0139

Hamouche, S. (2020). COVID-19 and employees' mental health: Stressors, moderators and agenda for organisational actions. *Emerald Open Research*, *2*, 15. https://doi.org/10.35241/emeraldopenres.13550.1

Hamouche, S., & Chabani, Z. (2021). COVID-19 and the new forms of employment relationship: Implications and insights for human resource development. *Industrial and Commercial Training*, *53*(4), 366–379. https://doi.org/10.1108/ict-11-2020-0112

Himawan, K. K., Fanggidae, J. P., & Helmi, J. (2022). The sociocultural barriers of work-from-home arrangement due to COVID-19 pandemic in Asia: Implications and future implementation. *Knowledge and Process Management*, *29*(2), 185–193. https://doi.org/10.1002/kpm.1708

Jayasinghe, N., Fernando, S., Haigh, R., Amaratunga, D., Fernando, N., Vithanage, C., Ratnayake, J., & Ranawana, C. (2022). Economic resilience in an era of "systemic risk": Insights from four key economic sectors in Sri Lanka. *Progress in Disaster Science*, *14*, 100231. https://doi.org/10.1016/j.pdisas.2022.100231

Jiang, H., & Shen, H. (2020). Toward a relational theory of employee engagement: Understanding authenticity, transparency, and employee behaviours. *International Journal of Business Communication*, *60*(3). https://doi.org/10.1177/2329488420954236

Jing, W. L., Rashid, S. B. A., & Islam, M. U. (2022). The impact of COVID-19 on financial markets & institutions: A literature review. *Science, Education, and Innovation in the Context of Modern Problems*, *5*(1), 385–413.

Maity, S., Sahu, T. N., & Biswas, D. (2022). Does COVID-19 influence in reshaping the banking habits of the individual? An empirical investigation. *International Journal of Electronic Finance*, *11*(4), 345–363.

Malik, P., & Lenka, U. (2019). Exploring the impact of perceived AMO framework on constructive and destructive deviance. *International Journal of Manpower*, *40*(5), 994–1011. https://doi.org/10.1108/ijm-05-2018-0164

Marso, A. R. F. R. N. (2022). Effects of third wave of COVID-19 in Sri Lanka: Response on unemployment and economic cost. *Journal of Human Resource and Sustainability Studies*, *10*(3), 449–463.

Mishra, K., Boynton, L., & Mishra, A. (2014). Driving employee engagement: The expanded role of internal communications. *International Journal of Business Communication*, *51*(2), 183–202. https://doi.org/10.1177/2329488414525399

Mitchell, A. (2021). Collaboration technology affordances from virtual collaboration during COVID-19 and post-pandemic strategies. *Information Technology & People*, *36*(5), 1982–2008. https://doi.org/10.1108/itp-01-2021-0003

Naithani, P. (2010). Recession and work-life balance initiatives. *Romanian Economic Journal*, *37*, 55–68.

Naotunna, N. P. G. S. I., & Adikaram, A. S. (2024). Demands and resources of working from home: From pandemic to economic crisis. *South Asian Journal of Human Resources Management*. https://doi.org/10.1177/23220937241252022

Naseer, S., Khalid, S., Parveen, S., Abbass, K., Song, H., & Achim, M. V. (2023). COVID-19 outbreak: Impact on global economy. *Frontiers in Public Health*, *10*, 1009393. https://doi.org/10.3389/fpubh.2022.1009393

Nishanthi, K. (2022). The economic crisis and its effect on life style of the people: A study in Colombo divisional secretariat division, Sri Lanka. *International Journal of Multidisciplinary Research and Growth Evaluation*, *3*(5), 455–459. https://doi.org/10.54660/anfo.2022.3.5.20

Ogbonnaya, C., & van Klyton, A. (2021, May 06). *Can remote working bring your business down during a recession?* Blog entry. LSE Business Review.

Opatha, H. H. D. N. P. (2020). The coronavirus and the employees: A study from the point of human resource management. *Sri Lankan Journal of Human Resource Management*, *10*(1). https://journals.sjp.ac.lk/index.php/sljhrm/article/view/4637

Opatha, H. H. D. P. J. (2020). COVID-19 in Sri Lanka and seven HRM-related recommendations against COVID-19. *Asian Journal of Social Sciences and Management Studies*, *7*(2), 152–157. https://doi.org/10.20448/journal.500.2020.72.152.157

Pillai, S. V., & Prasad, J. (2022). Investigating the key success metrics for WFH/remote work models. *Industrial and Commercial Training*, *55*(1). https://doi.org/10.1108/ict-07-2021-0053

Pillai, R., & Sivathanu, B. (2021). Measure what matters: Descriptive and predictive metrics of HRM-pathway toward organisational performance. *International Journal of Productivity and Performance Management*, *71*(7), 3009–3029. https://doi.org/10.1108/ijppm-10-2020-0509

Salunkhe, U., Rajan, B., & Kumar, V. (2021). Understanding firm survival in a global crisis. *International Marketing Review*. https://doi.org/10.1108/imr-05-2021-0175

Samarakoon, L. P. (2024). What broke the pearl of the Indian Ocean? The causes of the Sri Lankan economic crisis and its policy implications. *Journal of Financial Stability*, *70*, 101213. https://doi.org/10.1016/j.jfs.2023.101213

Samsudin, E. Z., Yasin, S. M., Ruslan, N. H., Abdullah, N. N., Noor, A. F. A., & Hair, A. F. A. (2024). Socioeconomic impacts of airborne and droplet-borne infectious diseases on industries: A systematic review. *BMC Infectious Diseases, 24*(1), 93.

Sekhar, C. (2021). Do high-commitment work systems engage employees? The mediating role of psychological capital. *International Journal of Organisational Analysis, 30*(4), 1000–1018. https://doi.org/10.1108/ijoa-10-2020-2466

Shabir, M., Jiang, P., Wang, W., & Işık, Ö. (2023). COVID-19 pandemic impact on banking sector: A cross-country analysis. *Journal of Multinational Financial Management, 67*, 100784. https://doi.org/10.1016/j.mulfin.2023.100784

Shil, M., Barman, R. C., Zayed, N. M., Shahi, K., & Neloy, A. H. (2020). Global transition of HR practices in COVID-19 pandemic situation: A systematic review through 5Ps model of HRM. *Asian Journal of Social Sciences and Management Studies, 7*(2), 152–157.

Shipman, K., Burrell, D. N., & Huff Mac Pherson, A. (2021). An organisational analysis of how managers must understand the mental health impact of teleworking during COVID-19 on employees. *International Journal of Organisational Analysis*. https://doi.org/10.1108/ijoa-03-2021-2685

Stiti, M., Castanet, G., Corber, A., Alden, M., & Berrocal, E. (2022). The transition from saliva droplets to solid aerosols in the context of COVID-19 spreading. *Environmental Research, 204*, 112072. https://doi.org/10.1016/j.envres.2021.112072

Taipale, S., Selander, K., Anttila, T., & Nätti, J. (2011). Work engagement in eight European countries. *International Journal of Sociology and Social Policy, 31*(7/8), 486–504. https://doi.org/10.1108/01443331111149905

Ul Haq, I., & Awan, T. M. (2020). Impact of e-banking service quality on e-loyalty in pandemic times through interplay of e-satisfaction. *Vilakshan - XIMB Journal of Management, 17*(1/2), 39–55. https://doi.org/10.1108/XJM-07-2020-0039

Wang, B., Liu, Y., Qian, J., & Parker, S. K. (2021). Achieving effective remote working during the COVID-19 pandemic: A work design perspective. *Applied Psychology, 70*(1), 16–59.

Weerarathna, R. S., Rathnayake, R. M. N. M., Perera, L. R. H. G., Kaluarachchi, K. R. M., Wickramasena, D. N., Arambawatta, L. V., & Weligodapola, H. W. M. C. (2022). The changing face of HR professionals' expectations amidst COVID-19: A comparison between Sri Lanka and foreign context. *Quality & Quantity*, 1–20. https://doi.org/10.1007/s11135-022-01533-3

Weerarathna, R. S., Rathnayake, N., Yasara, I., Jayasekara, P., Ruwanpura, D., & Nambugoda, S. (2022). Towards work-life balance or away? The impact of work-from-home factors on work-life balance among software engineers during the COVID-19 pandemic. *PLoS One, 17*(12), e0277931.

Weerarathna, R. S., Rathnayake, N., Perera, H., Wickramasena, D., Arambawatta, V., & Kaluarachchi, R. (2022). Evolving expectations of HR professionals amid the COVID-19 pandemic in Sri Lanka. *Indian Journal of Industrial Relations, 58*(1).

Wimalaweera, A. (2020). *COVID-19 & beyond – The impact on the labour market of Sri Lanka*. Department of Labour, Sri Lanka.

Wronka, C. (2021). Impact of COVID-19 on financial institutions: Navigating the global emerging patterns of financial crime. *Journal of Financial Crime, 29*(2), 476–490. https://doi.org/10.1108/jfc-03-2021-0073

Yu, W., Fei, J., Peng, G., & Bort, J. (2024). When a crisis hits: Examining the impact of the global financial crisis and the COVID-19 pandemic on financing for women entrepreneurs. *Journal of Business Venturing*, *39*(2), 106379. https://doi.org/10.1016/j.jbusvent.2024.106379

Zürcher, S. J., Banzer, C., Adamus, C., Lehmann, A. I., Richter, D., & Kerksieck, P. (2022). Post-viral mental health sequelae in infected persons associated with COVID-19 and previous epidemics and pandemics: Systematic review and meta-analysis of prevalence estimates. *Journal of Infection and Public Health*, *15*(5), 599–608. https://doi.org/10.1016/j.jiph.2022.04.005

Index

Printed and bound by CPI Group (UK) Ltd, Croydon, CR0 4YY

15/09/2026

14962490-0001